Observe—then teac

Part of Special Care Unit, Old Park School, Dudley

By kind permission of the Headteacher, Miss Mary Robinson.

Observe—then teach

An observational approach to teaching mentally handicapped children

Mildred Stevens M.Ed.

Edward Arnold

© Mildred Stevens, 1978

First published 1968
by Edward Arnold (Publishers) Ltd.,
41 Bedford Square, London WC1B 3DP

Reprinted 1971
Second Edition 1978
Previously entitled *Observing Children who are Severely Subnormal*

British Library Cataloguing in Publication Data
Stevens, Mildred
   Observe – then teach. – 2nd ed.
   1. Mentally handicapped children – Education – Great Britain
   2. Observation (Educational method)
   I. Title II. Observing children who are severely subnormal
   371.9′28   LC4636.G7

   ISBN 0–7131–4310–X

Dedicated to Children Everywhere

All Rights Reserved. No part of this publication may be reproduced, stored in a retrieval system, or transmitted in any form or by any means, electronic, mechanical, photocopying, recording or otherwise, without the prior permission of Edward Arnold (Publishers) Ltd.

Set in 10/11 pt 'Monophoto' Times and printed in Great Britain by Butler & Tanner Ltd., Frome and London

Preface to second edition

In 1966, when I began to write the first edition of this book, I made no attempt to define the term severe subnormality or to use the words 'training centre', 'assistant supervisor', or 'supervisor'. As a teacher I could not think of the group of children formally and legally (Mental Health Act, 1959) ascertained as severely subnormal in any way other than that they were children with very special learning difficulties going to school like other children. This being so I called training centres, schools; assistant supervisors, teachers; and supervisors, head-teachers, for this is how I always thought of them. I claim no originality in this. Many others thought the same long before the education of these children was administered by local education authorities in 1971.

1977   MS

Acknowledgements to second edition

In writing a book one is often presenting others with the words and the ideas that in fact they too will express sooner or later, sometimes with models of action. The brighter these 'others' are the more will they perceive the ideas as their own and then act upon them. This is the process of assimilation and adaptation. I have only experienced one author to date—Andrew Wilkinson—who in recognizing this unconscious human process deliberately apologizes to his readers in his book *The Foundations of Language*, Oxford University Press, 1971, for 'inadvertently taking ideas from others stimulating his thinking'. I wish to follow his positive example and hope that others will always do the same.

The only people involved in helping me practically with my new edition were: Miss Florence Birkinshaw, aged 70, who typed some parts of a terrible manuscript for hours on end on demand, with love and devotion. Mrs Sheila Beardmore of Poynton, Cheshire, a new friend and colleague in Special Education. She read my script in its original form and corrected it—a tedious task indeed—and worked devotedly for me in one particular week especially in order to get the manuscript to the publishers for a specified date. My husband for his continuous help and support and forbearance in times of 'creation'. My 'mums' for meeting some of my needs, for giving so much to me and to each other and thus ultimately to share with others (cf. Chapter 13). The Senior Inspector of Schools for Warwickshire, Janet Powell; the then Educational Psychologist for the school, John Presland, and the Headteacher and teachers of Chelmsley Wood Hospital School, Nr. Birmingham, for stimulating my thinking in 1974 in a variety of ways (cf. Chapter 8); Robert Wright and Sue Atherton both students in Matlock College (1977) of Education—one for suggesting a short snappy title for my book; the other for giving me an idea to write Chapter 12.

Contents

Chapter

1	Introduction	1
2	Observing and responding	23
3	Techniques of observing. When and how	32
4	Observing and teaching the young mentally handicapped child	40
5	Observing and teaching the adolescent	59
6	Observing in special situations	68
7	Observing conversations	74
8	Observing in a one-to-one teaching session	96
9	Keeping records	125
10	Role of the headteacher in encouraging record-keeping	133
11	Cumulative record cards	136
12	Observations on some historical aspects	163
13	Observing the special needs of mothers of mentally handicapped children	187
14	Concluding remarks	203

Appendices

1	Early notes on observation taken from my lecture notes (1961)	204
2	Interviewing mentally handicapped adults	206
3	Musical games to stimulate fun and language	209
	Useful reading	213

About the Author

The author has had over thirty years' practical experience teaching people with special learning difficulties. For ten years she was the Principal of a small college in Manchester, established by the National Association for Mental Health (MIND), researching new methods of training teachers of severely subnormal children. With a team of colleagues under her direction Mrs Stevens was responsible for the specialized initial training of over 300 teachers, many of whom are now well-known Headteachers of schools for the mentally handicapped or hold special posts of responsibility. From 1964 to 1974 the author was additionally a part-time Special Lecturer to the Advanced Course for Teachers of the Handicapped in the Department of Education at the University of Manchester. She introduced many qualified teachers to the field of mental subnormality, some of these teachers have now become Tutors to courses for teachers of the mentally handicapped, Heads of schools and research workers.

The author, in her capacity as a freelance lecturer from 1972 to 1975, travelled 45,000 miles in the United Kingdom organizing and lecturing on LEA/DES In-Service Courses. In 1972 she was a visiting Professor to New Brunswick University, Canada. Mrs Stevens has written a number of articles, reports and papers on the training of teachers in addition to her three previous books—*Observing Children who are Severely Subnormal*, *The Educational Needs of Severely Subnormal Children* and *The Educational and Social Needs of Children with Severe Handicap*. Currently an Honorary Lecturer of Manchester University and a lecturer in Social Education at Matlock College of Education, Derbyshire, she is also an Open University Tutor to the course 'The Handicapped in the Community'. Once a week the author works as a community volunteer with mothers of mentally handicapped children.

Mildred Stevens (née Williams) lives in Cheshire with her husband, an industrial scientist. Together they enjoy travel, TV, music, reading, cooking and talking with friends.

1 Introduction

The children, described in the Mental Health Act of 1959 as severely subnormal,* were the responsibility of Local Health Authorities and Hospital Management Committees.† They attended schools called junior training centres.The majority were taught by untrained but dedicated and committed women. Men teachers were in the minority. A few qualified Burnham teachers were also working with these children but mainly as headteachers. During the 'fifties and 'sixties highly specialized 1-, then 2-year courses of initial training developed in various parts of England and Wales.

Students seconded for training by local health authorities and Hospital Management Committees prior to 1965 came from all walks of life, some with experiences enabling them to share another's grief. Some were already qualified as nursery nurses, others as nurses. Such factors meant that these women and the few men coming for training had a great deal to offer mentally handicapped children in much the same way as present teachers of normal children taking the one-year Emergency Teacher Training Scheme just after the Second World War. If we think of the latter, some of those teachers have become the most respected and valued members of the teaching profession. The same applies to those we trained. Their teaching ability was often of a very high standard. Some of them have become outstanding headteachers. What is of even greater significance is that they knew without hesitation that they wanted to teach the mentally handicapped. They were committed too. Their pay was minimal *and* the possibility of promotion too.

Since the passing of the Education Act (Handicapped Children) 1970, any teacher qualifying from a College of Education, or University Department of Education can teach these children. This is in accordance with the English tradition that a teacher is free to apply for a post in any kind of school. Many local education authorities, however, have seen fit to organize their own specialized one-term in-service courses for teachers wishing to teach the mentally handicapped.

---

* Now as ESN(S), Educationally Subnormal (Severe).

† Hospital Management Committees organized the work in Mental Subnormality Hospitals under the aegis of the Regional Hospital Boards before 1971. From over 300 teachers of the mentally handicapped trained in Manchester (by those of us employed by the National Association for Mental Health from 1961 to 1971), less than a score were seconded for training by these hospitals. Of those 300 students, 8 were seconded by Brockhall Hospital in Lancashire. Gordon Bland, headteacher of the school, was obviously using his influence as an educator, even at this time, to have his staff trained. He tutored the first course at the Harris College, Preston, for a term whilst still being headteacher of a school. He later became a member of the Central Training Council.

2   Introduction

Teachers currently teaching in special schools for these children receive almost £400 more salary than their colleagues in schools for normal children. Many local education authorities have appointed a classroom assistant to each class. Others have appointed a special classroom assistant to 'cope' with just one very difficult or disturbed child. In nursery classes it is not uncommon to see a teacher with two classroom assistants. The classes rarely contain more than twelve children. The figure suggested by the DES some years ago was ten. All the children, however, have individual needs. They also need teaching individually in a systematic fashion in a one-to-one relationship particularly in the very early years. The teachers as part of their professional integrity, responsibility, commitment and specialism need to work in very close co-operation with the parents. This is especially so if the education they provide for the children is to be successful, supportive and effective. Teachers have shorter hours in these schools. They are 9.30 a.m. until 3.15 p.m. in many instances, although I do know of one headteacher insisting that her staff are in school by 9 a.m. in order to prepare classrooms ready for the children's activity. I know of other schools where the teachers come in to school on the same bus as the children at 9.30 a.m. or just three or four minutes before this time. However, most teachers of mentally handicapped children do make regular visits to the homes, organize week-end activities, take the children on holiday and organize play schemes during vacations to continue the children's experiences and support the family in practical ways.

During the years 1945–71 a great deal of expertise developed relating to the education of mentally handicapped children. A wide and multidisciplinary group of professionals from administration, medicine, social work and education became involved. I have written about some of this expertise elsewhere. There can be little doubt that those designing many of the present new schools took into account the collective wisdom and experience of those educators training teachers of the mentally handicapped in the 'sixties. Another offshoot of our work seems to be that more educational psychologists are now observing children in classrooms as well as in the more standardized situation of the clinic. Observing in free activity situations will certainly supplement their findings from formal tests.

One would like to think that the DES staff devising the new forms for the 'Discovery of children requiring special education' DES Circular SE I-5 (S stands for Special, and E for Education) were influenced to some extent by the experience of those in the field of mental subnormality. Certainly the new emphasis on these forms seems to be on the psychologists doing much more detailed recorded observation of a child's behaviour in a variety of situations. Ideally this observing might be taking place in environments that are familiar to the child. Some research psychologists are now clearly accepting observation as assessment.*

One cannot now envisage *any* child 'slipping through the net' by not

---

* Foxen, T. (1977) *Observation as Assessment.* Paper presented to the British Psychological Society. From Hester Adrian Research Centre.

Introduction 3

receiving the medical, psychological and educational help he requires if these forms are well used; if all teachers, without fear that their own professional competence will be questioned, are encouraged to refer and follow up any child with a problem that should be investigated by a team of specialists. If the psychologist or doctor discusses the findings on these forms with the teachers and the parents in language that is understood by all concerned* then the child cannot fail to benefit. Perhaps the professionals will also gain from each other. One day in the near future, perhaps parents will be invited to discuss some aspects of the Special Education forms. I think that they will certainly be demanding to see any material that is written about them or their child.

I called the first edition of this book *Observing Children who are Severely Subnormal*. This was quite a deliberate choice. It seemed to me as a newcomer to the world of severely subnormal children that in developing theories about their education few of those concerned had indeed observed these children in educational settings and recorded their *spontaneous* behaviour in any detailed way. To a certain extent this meant that no one really knew them as children with needs, interests and abilities—the main emphasis seemed to be on their difficulties and weaknesses. Tizard† in his research at Brooklands was perhaps alone in attempting to provide a particular kind of educational climate for these children and to evaluate the results in terms of the whole child.

As a teacher of normal, subnormal and maladjusted children doing research for my master's degree in the early 'fifties I had already become interested in devising methods of recording children's spontaneous behaviour. I felt that some of these methods of recording could be developed in this highly specialized but relatively neglected field of education. My association with Mary Lindsay in 1961 reinforced my own beliefs. A special education teacher herself and later an HMI, she became, on retirement, the Honorary Adviser to the National Association for Mental Health. She encouraged my interest in training teachers to observe, and in fact invited me to lecture on the subject on the 1962 NAMH annual refresher course for staffs in junior training centres (as the schools were then called).

Observing children who are severely subnormal through one-way mirrors, micro-teaching techniques and tape recordings, etc. and keeping records is so much a part of the everyday conversation in some of the schools and the colleges now that one tends to forget that specific methods were used by some of us‡ to draw attention to, and focus on, the

---

* Stevens, M. (1968) *Observing Children who are Severely Subnormal*, Chapter 9.

† His film *Mentally Handicapped Children Growing Up* (Concord Films) is a must for all those interested in handicapped children. It is an old film but its underlying educational philosophies are as relevant today as in the 'sixties when it was made.

‡ Stevens and Veronica Sherborne (well known in this country and abroad by physical education specialists and teachers of the mentally handicapped) used movement and creative dance as a focal point of observation training. She can be contacted at Redlands, College of Education, Bristol, for she has written many papers on Movement and produced several films.

importance of what now appears to be obvious and what everyone thinks they know about and can do—that is to say observing behaviour. It was only by watching these children carefully in specific conditions that curriculum development could in fact take place. We did not know initially what mentally handicapped children were capable of educationally or what they were spontaneously interested in.

I should like to spend a short time in this introduction describing the methods I used initially to enable my students to gain an interest in observing human behaviour and an understanding of the importance of detailed recording. Fortunately I have my notes from the 1962 refresher lecture. The strategies I and my colleagues used in the mid 'sixties are fully described elsewhere.*

The reader is asked to see these experiences against the background of a course of training lasting one year. There were lectures in the first term; a teaching practice of 6 weeks at the beginning of the second term; an examination of three 3-hour papers taken in May; and another 6 weeks' teaching practice at the end of the third term. Results and diplomas were received a few days after the end of teaching practice—truly an educational principle well carried out in terms of instant feed-back to the student.

The story book method

The students in the first term were invited to carry a small notebook in their pocket or handbag and to jot down anything that they saw any child (or any group of children) doing in the park, in the street, on the bus, in their homes, in school playgrounds, and so on. They were asked to describe quite spontaneously (without thinking too much about their English expression) exactly what they saw or heard and to try not to describe and include their own feelings, ideas, or interpretations about the situations they came across. This was a very simple way of suggesting that the act of deliberate observation with all one's attention was important. It was also intended to suggest that to be useful the observation should be carried out with some degree of detachment. It is difficult for those who were not involved in this field of education at that time to realize the importance of this particular approach. Perhaps it was important because there was an over-all impression (and here I *too* am inferring rather than relying on collected facts) of sentimentality towards these children without much thought about their possible educational progress. Love was a word too frequently used (though now it seems we have perhaps swung too far away from the concept in this field I think) with little evidence to me at any rate as a newcomer that much was done about the 'love' in a way that could be described as professional.

The number and quality of the recorded items in these observation notebooks at the end of a term seemed to indicate varying amounts of interest

---

* Stevens, M. (1976) *The Educational and Social Needs of Children with Severe Handicap*, E. Arnold, London.

in such an exercise and individual levels of development in skilful observing and recording on the part of the student group. The way in which some of the observations were recorded indicated that many of the students needed encouragement to become more detached, more objective in their approach to recording their observations. Some students included words such as thrilled, love, amazed, irresistible; still others had to describe their own part in the situation (though on reflection this would appear to be a further stage in developing observational skills, i.e. where one is involved in activity with a child and one is not only watching the child's response but also oneself in terms of movement and language). Other students showed by their records that they had observed in a variety of places and had observed children from a very wide age range and from very different kinds of homes. Some records indicated that a student was not afraid to record observed 'obscenities'. A great many situations were recorded. Amongst them—children scribbling in the dust, reflections in windows, mothers answering children and mothers not answering children's questions, mother's comments, children's superstitions, adolescent girls and boys, children's ideas, temper tantrums, adult standards and values, children taking things from the shelf in a shop ($2\frac{1}{2}$-year-old), curiosity, rude words, practising skills, repetition of actions, and protectiveness in children.

You will see from such observations that there was a starting point for all kinds of discussion in terms of child development and activities. During the act of deliberate observing and in the choice of material that was recorded the observation often triggered off the early childhood memories of the observer. From this experience it was envisaged that the adult would gain more facility to get 'into a child's skin' as it were and therefore be more likely to cater for a child's needs.

Some of the stories indicated that the observers had seen the way in which children used simple unsophisticated materials and materials costing no money—bricks, boxes, stones, sticks, puddles, old planks of wood. Perhaps these experiences would remind them that an adult's standard of what constituted an educational aid differed from that of a child. Perhaps they would be reminded that children (and I now observe that I wrote 'we' instead of the word 'children' in my description ... identity with the child!) were satisfied with things for which the adult often saw no use. It was not a novel discovery but a useful one for future teachers of severely subnormal children. Severely subnormal children had been denied their rights to play for too long. Little money was available for buying materials and equipment for the junior training centres. It seemed essential therefore that their future teachers saw from children themselves what use could in fact be made of waste/scrap/basic materials in the learning situation.

Some of the entries in the notebooks showed that the children had often been seen representing various objects of their imagination in their play with other objects: a trolley was a train, a stick was a gun, a chair was a car, a mother's skirt was the reins (the mother was the horse), a piece of card flung into the air accompanied by noises was an aeroplane. The value of such observations from the play of normal children seemed to be that in many cases the ages of the children were noted. This information could form the basis for comparing the play of severely subnormal children with that of normal children as provision for play was indeed made more available in the centres. I was reminded as I lectured about representation in play of a severely subnormal boy aged 12 who had represented a light bulb with a ball of clay.

Some students had made records about children from a variety of social backgrounds. It was felt that they could perhaps have more guidance in collecting information about the different home backgrounds from a trained sociologist.* Accordingly time was always given on some of the subsequent courses for students to carry out a 3-day sociological study of an area 'of which they had had no life experience'— some chose the slums, others chose highly residential areas.†

The value of such an approach in view of the fact that mentally handicapped children are born into all classes of society was perhaps in enabling them to understand a phrase still bandied about in this field of education 'to make him more acceptable in society'. It seemed to me that it was the particular group in society that HE came from not that to which the teacher belonged that it was important to help him to be acceptable in. Perhaps the experience of a variety of home backgrounds might help the teacher to have realistic expectations for a child's behaviour—expectations that were linked to the child's way of life in the home to which he belonged.

This research with a story observation book method, simple though it seemed, was certainly a useful one in training teachers. Not only did it enable them to become more aware of the spontaneous behaviour of normal children, but it helped some of them to use their eyes and ears in a systematic and deliberate fashion perhaps for the first time in their lives.

Nursery school observation week

Tizard‡ writing in the early 'sixties stated that 'The contribution of child psychologists to the nursery school has been to emphasize the importance of being guided by the child's level of maturation as it manifests itself in its interests in the planning of an educational programme. Informed observation is the basis for action. In the junior training centre for mentally handicapped children the training derives little from observational studies of what the child can or cannot do. Most of the day is spent on

---

*We managed to gain the interest of Dr Ronald Frankenburg, now Professor of Sociology, University, Keele.

†The material collected during this experience in terms of photographs and notes was exhibited at the end of a specified time. It was examined by the group, commented upon, and discussed with R. F. above.

‡Tizard, J. (1964) *Community Services for the Mentally Handicapped*, Oxford University Press, London.

Introduction   7

an endless round of routines and habit training.' Acquaintance with his work soon tells us that he had been influenced by the work of Dorothy Gardener. She had been a 'disciple' of Susan Isaacs—both of them keen observers of children's spontaneous behaviour. The former, with Joan Cass, was to become keenly interested later on in her career in observing the spontaneous behaviour of teachers in the classroom.* I had seen Tizard's film of Brooklands in December 1960, given for the first time at the education section of the British Psychological Society in London. I knew from my own research in the late 'forties in the primary school that an observational approach in an active environment enabled a teacher to get to know the children in her class.† Such an approach was perhaps a sound strategy to use in helping students to understand the theoretical concepts underlying child development. The most fruitful area for such an experience was the nursery school and 'good' day nurseries for young children administered by the local health authority.

Accordingly, students spent a whole week of the one-year course with very young children. They had a detailed guide for this exercise. There seemed little point in sending students out into schools or indeed into any place to observe if their attention was not brought specifically by an informed observer to some of the aspects of their study and to the way in which they might carry out the observing part of their experience. The brief for observing was as follows:

(1) Choose a child to observe for 1 hour on each of 3 days of the 5 days spent in the nursery.
(2) Choose a group of children to observe over $\frac{1}{2}$ hour on each of 3 days. Sit well away from the children. Do not become involved with them. If they ask you what you are doing tell them that you are writing a story about them. The teacher will help you in this I know. Write down everything you can over the periods specified for the individual child and the group. Mark off your observations with the time every 5 minutes (time sampling technique).

In addition to presenting an observation notebook, and the children's work (art, collage) for an exhibition at the end of the experience, the students had to present their observations of the individual child in a particular way.‡ A circle 2–3 feet in diameter was divided into twelve segments. Each segment represented the 5-minute periods of timed observation. Observations from the notes were then transferred in tele-

---

* Gardener, D. E. M. and Cass, J. E. (1965) *The Role of the Teacher in the Infant and Nursery School*, Pergamon Press, Oxford.
† Stevens, M. (1954) *Some Aspects of an Active Approach in the Junior School*, unpublished M.Ed. Thesis, University of Manchester.
‡ Dorothy Gardener had used this method in training her advanced child development students to observe. Joan Unsworth, one of her students in the 'fifties (now a lecturer in Fielden Park College, Manchester, and one of the few teachers I ever observed as a teacher really providing for the play needs of maladjusted young children), shared this idea with me.

8   *Introduction*

grammatic form into each segment (usually coloured in different colours for easy reference). Careful study of the complete circle would enable the students to track the movements, activities, and interaction with other children or with adults over the hour made by the individual child. When all the 'circular diagrams' were displayed the students were able to compare the behaviour of their particular child with that of another. These charts clearly provided a useful starting point for discussion.

Values of the nursery school observation period
One needs to understand these early notions about the specific value of this particular guided experience I gave to students against a background of severe deprivation of experiences for the children in Junior Training Centres caused by ignorance, lack of money, and lack of expectation; also against a background of attitudes where preoccupation with masturbation in the children and the importance of toileting initially took precedence in discussion over the student's ability in the main to see the necessity to provide appropriate and essential learning experiences. Students had to be encouraged to let the children take risks.

In these 'new' observation exercises of young normal children the students observed:

(1) children's need for space and all kinds of materials and equipment with which to experiment;
(2) their need for companionship;
(3) their need for a warm personal relationship with an adult who is not afraid to show this warmth, sometimes by physical handling;
(4) their need to form relationships in their own way—sometimes their immaturity meant that they hit out at another child in order to form a relationship with him (adolescent horse play seems to be an extension of this with qualitative differences, particularly with regard to their behaviour towards the opposite sex). An understanding adult will know when to interfere. She will never expect the child to 'say you're sorry' (an adult abstract notion with little meaning for the child at this stage);
(5) the child's need to do 'naughty' things (as judged by the adult) as part of his normal development;
(6) the child's need to wander about his immediate environment;
(7) the kind and the number of activities chosen by small children during an hour's period from a choice of well-provided materials.

Some people* state that nursery school methods were the mainstay of our approach to the mentally handicapped in the 'sixties. Whilst to a certain extent active, child-centred methods were focused upon in the early

---

*Cunningham, C. C. (1974) The relevance of normal educational theory and practice for the mentally retarded. In: *Mental Retardation: Concepts of Education and Research*, Tizard, J. (ed.), Butterworths, London.

Introduction 9

'sixties because these were the only appropriate educational models on which to build our curricula, it did not take very long for those of us who were professionally involved with these students to introduce a more diagnostic individualized* approach to these children within the lively educational settings we believed were the children's right. We even studied behavioural programmes in 1961. These are described by Gunzburg† and included those of Hafmeister (1951) and Rosenwieg (1954) for toilet training, washing, bathing, and personal safety. In the light of our own educational approaches and experience with the children we decided that it was difficult to be rigid with them and that flexibility and a more natural approach based upon informed sensitive observation was likely to help the children develop emotionally and socially. With intensive individual teaching we were sure they would develop intellectually too. We also took motivation into account. If the children were getting ready to go for a walk or to dance in bare feet they were more likely to want to dress/undress themselves than if they were just practising a skill. Teachers need to be sure that the children are still getting time to practise these skills. To some extent the new classroom assistants are very often 'doing the job' for the children in order to be in the 'hall' on time.

Observation of children (1970)

Before leaving this topic of training teachers to observe in a more detached manner I should like to draw your attention to an interesting little booklet published by the National Association for Mental Health 2 years after the publishing of my own book on observation. It was written by Dr K. S. Holt, a consultant to the Wolfson Clinic in London, and Dr Joan Reynell a well-known language specialist also working in the Wolfson Clinic. Whilst this booklet is now out of print, MIND might be persuaded to do a reprint if enough people enquire about its availability.

The booklet consists of seven sections—the nature of observation and its importance, looking and seeing, the difference between observation and inference, methods of study and recording, the use of observation methods in assessment, case studies, and training in the use of observations. Each section is valuable but in particular their emphasis on the value of observational skills in all walks of professional life is particularly useful.

Recent observationally based studies

C. C. Cunningham and D. Jeffrees, two research workers from the teaching profession, organized and carried out a number of workshops with

---

* I have tape recordings from 1963 in which students were being encouraged to 'test' the mentally handicapped children visiting our college and think out interesting programmes of experiences for them. This seemed a common-sense approach to children with severe learning difficulties and delayed maturation and to students training to teach them. This was particularly so as I had been practising profiling and evaluating children's progress for a very long time as a remedial teacher.

† Gunzburg, H. C. (1958) Educational problems in mental deficiency. In: *Mental Deficiency: The Changing Outlook, 1st Edition*, Clarke, A. M. and Clarke, A. D. B. (eds.), Methuen, London.

10 Introduction

parents of severely subnormal children and their colleagues from the Hester Adrian Research Centre, University of Manchester in 1970. Their work is fully documented in *Working with Parents: Developing a Workshop Course for Parents of Young Mentally Handicapped Children.** The parents were given lectures by specialists in the field of mental handicap, including two of my colleagues. They also had the advantage of small group seminars over a period of 8 weeks with the other research workers concerned. During the seminars the parents were invited to discuss their problems. They were also shown how to observe the behaviour of their child. The aim of training their observation skills was in order to establish a firm base upon which to decide whether to produce certain wanted behaviours or to eliminate undesirable behaviours.

A summary of the stages in a programme of behaviour improvement

	Observation	Training	Follow up
Producing behaviour	During observation decide on training objective and discover suitable rewards.	Starting with some response the child can already do, reward for progress in small steps towards desired goal.	Has the period of training produced long-lasting results?
Eliminating behaviour	What at present is rewarding the child for the maladaptive behaviour?	Break the present reward pattern. Reward child for appropriate behaviour. Ignore otherwise.	If the maladaptive behaviour has returned use stronger time out methods.

This work perhaps represents the first attempt in this country to involve groups of parents in the systematic direct observation of their own children. It was certainly the first time in the North West that the modification of children's behaviour was examined in any depth from the point of view of strict operant behavioural principles. In addition to a description of the work that was specifically carried out with the parents, two useful developmental charts were introduced, compiled by the organizers of the parents' workshops. The first was about normal child development. The second was designed to focus the parents' attention on language development. All goal-based (Kushlick, A., Open University material, Unit 9, 1974) enterprises concern themselves with evaluation of the results. Accordingly the goal-based parent workshop experiment contains an in-

---

* Published by The National Society for Mentally Handicapped Children, North West Region, Manchester.

teresting description of the parents' evaluation of the experience. A questionnaire was provided and an analysis of the answers was made. Reference to this analysis indicates some of the conclusions available to the research workers about the needs of these parents in a workshop situation, e.g. in answering Question 8, 'Have you any advice on how to improve the approach?'

'Need to group parents differently'.
'Avoid covering the same ground too often'.
'Need smaller groups so that we get more individual attention'.
'Need a coffee break'.
'Need more visual aids, film, diagrams, etc.'
'More workshop work (small group sessions and discussions)'.
'Need longer time to get to know people—a bit shy at first'.

I know that many more workshops have been developed in the UK and abroad because of this early work of the 'seventies. They are of such great importance and few schools relatively speaking are running their own workshops in spite of its known value to the parents, that I had to mention it to you.

Meeting special educational needs through teacher's observations
(A. E. Tansley, Staff Inspector in Special Education, Birmingham, 1975)
This* is a résumé of a talk that Mr Tansley delivered at the Conference organized by the National Council for Special Education and held in Bradford University in 1975. In his introductory remarks he pointed out the fact that psychological testing procedures often end up with numerical scores rather than prescriptive programmes. To counteract this he decided to equip his teachers with the necessary tools and skills to make a 'differential diagnosis for themselves, however crudely, in order to devise methods and circumstances for meeting the needs of the children more adequately'.

Through in-service teacher training the Birmingham screening procedures were devised, resulting in the observation that 1 in 4 or 1 in 3 of infant age children were in fact at educational risk. He describes how 300 teachers were in fact trained to observe more accurately and specifically by the use of these screening devices and as he says 'Schools which have been doing the programme now for some 4 years are getting so good at this improved observation-based treatment that they realize that the screening test is no longer necessary', and 'It seems to me that it should be possible for well-trained teachers, by using improved methods and standards of observation, to arrive at a sufficiently good differential diagnosis of the needs of the children upon which prescriptive education can be used'.

---

* Conference proceedings obtainable from Happy Printers and Carriers Ltd., Oakworth, West Yorkshire.

12 *Introduction*

The characteristics of 120 children in day care centres in Glasgow (Olwen Gregory, Tutor to the Glasgow Course for Instructresses in Occupation and Day Centres, 1976)
I have dealt in more detail with this work in another book but Mrs Gregory's research is the first attempt in this country to observe the reactions and responses of profoundly handicapped children to a specific Piagetian-based assessment scale devised by two American psychologists, Uzgiris and Hunt in 1966. The scale, which I modified* in 1974, describes in detail all those behaviours that one might expect/encourage in a severely subnormal child in the very early years of his life.

Observing children and parents at play (Kay Mogford)
Kay Mogford works in the Child Development Centre of Research in Nottingham University. This is directed by John and Elizabeth Newsome. The Centre contains a toy library used by parents from all over the East Midlands. There are also technological resources for the detailed observation of mothers playing with their handicapped children. One of the useful outcomes of this work for adults working with handicapped children is the way Miss Mogford, observing her video recordings, has produced lists of all the play behaviours that can be expected encouraged when a child plays with a specific toy. There is no doubt in my mind that when these lists are published the quality of children's play opportunities will be increased, as well as the quality of the adults' understanding of play.

An initial survey of the language of ESN(S) children in Manchester (The results of a teachers' workshop, Brenda Kellett)
The work that is described in Chapter 4 of *Language and Communication in the Mentally Handicapped*, edited by Paul Berry, is an observational study of the language of all the children in schools for the mentally handicapped in Manchester and two assessment units containing non-mentally handicapped children. As a member of the first workshop on language, I originally suggested (1971/72) that such a survey should be planned. The group and I worked out a preliminary observation check list. Ultimately, however (because I left the group), the real work was done over a period of 18 months by Brenda Kellett and Paul Berry with those teachers still attending the workshop. The survey was in the nature of a pilot study and it formed the basis for the much larger study of the language of the mentally handicapped in the North West carried out by the Schools Council under the direction of Ken Leeming.
   A useful short questionnaire was compiled—its appeal to me as a teacher is its brevity. Developmental in essence it contains items concern-

---

*I started work on this in 1973 for an in-service course of a week's duration in a mental subnormality hospital. The handout has been distributed all over the UK through workshop sessions at The Spastics Society, Castle Priory College, Wallingford, Berkshire, and through other LEA in-service courses.

Introduction 13

ing gesture, articulation, and the productive and receptive aspects of language. There were twelve items concerned with production. Item 1, 'Does the child cry, shriek, scream, grunt?' Item 11, 'Does the child use adequate (if ungrammatical) speech, e.g. "me go your room", "want go back now".' Eleven items were included in order to help the teacher focus on the receptive aspects of language, e.g. 'show me your hands' (my *reflection* on this instruction is that in saying this the teacher would have to be very careful not to look at the child's hands and give a visual cue), 'Put one of your hands on the table', 'Touch the back of your chair with the hand that is not on the table'.

Three hundred and fifty-two children took part in this survey and some very useful facts emerged. Results were assembled by the author. You need to read the whole chapter to gain a really informed impression but one or two of these results are perhaps interesting to note here.

Reception. 14 per cent of the children did not respond to sounds at all; 25 per cent responded to an instruction containing six 'ideas'; and 10 per cent responded to Item 11.

Production. 10 per cent of the sample cried, shrieked, grunted only; 40 per cent used adequate speech as at Item 11; 28 per cent (probably some of this result included the children from the assessment units where there were non-mentally handicapped children) used spoken language above the level of Item 11.

Unfortunately the chapter did not inform its readers about the numbers of children in each age group in this general survey, but it does go on to analyse the language of all the children in one particular school in the city. With such a survey instrument now available, each school could in fact systematically carry out its own survey annually, compile prescriptive programmes, provide the necessary real life experiences to motivate language, and monitor each child's progress in language.

Patterns of interaction in the mentally handicapped (Michael Beveridge, in the same publication as the above)
This chapter describes an attempt to observe mentally handicapped children in a naturalistic classroom situation and in particular the ways in which the children interacted as a form of communication. I have already commented elsewhere that the play environment in which the video observations took place was a rather limited one (jigsaw puzzles, painting, and sewing) (p. 32‡) that of itself was not very stimulating to encourage the children to communicate. However, some interesting results accrued which I would like to share with you and comment upon (Table 1.1). Beveridge expresses some surprise at his results, but when we learn that the children in Senior 1 were 10 years of age and over, our own recorded observations of these children (over a number of years in stimulating classroom environments where no effort was spared by students initially providing these social climates) are indeed more precisely substantiated. They

14   *Introduction*

Table 1.1 Number of interactions initiated by children in six classes during four 1-hour observations sessions.

Infant	3
Special care	0
Junior 1	10
Junior 2	6
Senior 1	100+
Senior 2	100+

Table 1.2 Frequency of child behaviour when initiating an interaction

Avoidance	3
Interference	23
Assistance	11
Pushing person away	1
Greets	3
Commands	3
Requests object	11
Giving information/comments	142
Shows affection	4
Expresses attitude	7
Contradicts	2
Asks for information	68

follow well the expected play development level for the age and stage of the children. In other words more parallel play will be found in mentally handicapped children under 10 and will still occur in many of the children over 10 years of age (cf. Appendix 3; Stevens, 1976), i.e. the play is individual but he gets along with other children (Edgar Doll*). Beveridge observed that there were twice as many occurrences of the children giving information as asking for it. This order of behaviour is the reverse order found in the initiation of interaction of normal children. Assuming that many of the children would in fact have mental ages of between 3 and 4 years, and that they would mostly therefore be in the preoperational stage of development in which it would be normal not to see things from the other's point of view, again I would say that it is reinforcing to see stated that so many observations concerned themselves with the giving of information by the children. Perhaps we should be asking ourselves whether in fact the statements made by the children might have been

---

* Doll, E. A. (1947) *Vineland Social Maturity Scale*, American Guidance Service, Minnesota, USA.

Introduction   15

interpreted as questions. What I am attempting to say here is perhaps the children did not have the question words or syntax in their language at the particular stage of development they were at. Examples of the precise language behaviours to illustrate the generalizations would have been useful to the reader. They would also have helped to provide the link between theory and practice. It would appear to me that we always need specific concrete examples to allow our minds to operate on in our own way instead of reading generalizations and trying to work out what the writer has experienced to enable him to generalize.

Observing the social life of severely and profoundly handicapped children in Poland
The following extract is taken in toto from a book I received from the author* some few years ago. It seems to be one of the few examples we have in the literature on the mentally handicapped of a sociometric approach to their social life. With her permission I am including the whole chapter.

Graphic presentation of the social life at the centre by *Hannah Olechnowicz*

To help our teachers to better understand the place occupied by each pupil in relation to the others, we have used a very simple graphical method to present the data relevant to socialization.

Three parameters were taken into account: mental age, personal–social development, and social links between pupils.

Mental age was assessed by the Psyche Catell and Terman–Merrill tests standardized for a Polish population.

Personal–social development was assessed by an inventory which included items related to this aspect of development.†

Social links were drawn on the diagram on the basis of estimates arrived at by

---

*Dr Hannah Olechnowicz. If you write to her you are likely to receive a copy of a book published in Warsaw entitled *Studies in the Socialization of the Severely and Profoundly Retarded*. Address: The Day Centre of Psychoneurological Institute, Warsaw, Poland. Send her a book in exchange for hers. It is free. This book is now translated into Serbo Croatian (Yugoslavia).

† The inventory consists of 42 items related to behaviours typical of the personal and social development of the child, up to the level of the normal 4-year-old (cf. H. Olechnowicz, paper read at the IASS Congress held in Warsaw, 1970). The impact of particular psychomotor skills, including active speech, is reduced as far as possible. To illustrate, Item 11 ('Does the things he is asked to do') enables a positive score irrespective of the degree of difficulty of the task involved.

Some items concern behaviour in the social communicative context manifested in an objective manner as for example in Item 6 ('Offers objects to other persons on his own initiative').

Other items concern manifestations of internalized parental behaviour and attitudes, as in Item 28 ('Teaches or disciplines dolls or younger children').

The arrangement of items in to odd/even sets permits assessment of two major aspects of child behaviour. Odd numbered items refer to behaviour patterns with prevailing elements of emotional dependence, as in Item 15 ('Misses an absent parent and shows longing for him'). Even numbered items describe behaviours involving emotional autonomy, as in Item 20 ('Wants to do things for himself'). The child can obtain a score of 1 or 2 for each item. The total score is the sum of scores obtained, the maximum being 85 points.

16 Introduction

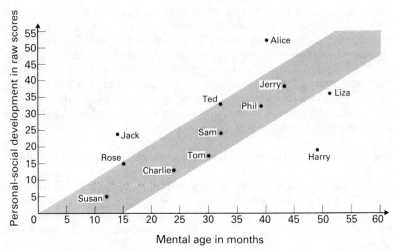

Fig. 1.1 Location of 12 pupils in terms of score on Personal–Social Development Inventory and Mental Age.

a consensus of staff opinion. Social links refer to interchild contacts displaying some stability over the last school year. Pupils included in Fig. 1.1 are the twelve who were tested in May and June, 1972. Assessment of personal–social development was made at the same time. For some of the pupils MA scores could not be obtained due to deafness or lack of co-operation during testing, or because attendance at the day centre was interrupted or discontinued. The latter group is included in Fig. 1.2 only, where their names are distinguishable from those of the others by circles instead of dots.

Figure 1.1 shows the Mental Age (MA) scores of the twelve pupils tested, which can be read along the bottom horizontal scale, and their personal–social development

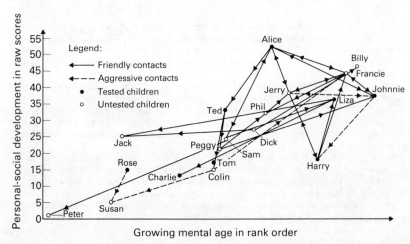

Fig. 1.2 Social contacts among day centre pupils during school year 1971/72 (see text for explanation).

Introduction 17

raw scores, which can be read up the vertical scale. As this diagram clearly demonstrates, the higher the MA of a pupil, the higher his personal–social development score tends to be. Thus, nearly all the names can be found located on the shaded diagonal band running from lower left to upper right. There are, however, some exceptions. Harry's score on personal–social development is lower than could be predicted from his MA; Alice and Jack, on the contrary, scored higher on personal–social development than we would expect from their MAs. This result seems not to be accidental in view of the characteristics of these three pupils presented in the previous section.

Figure 1.2 is drawn on the same pattern as Fig. 1.1. The second figure differs from the first by the fact that it includes all the pupils attending the center in 1971/72, i.e., also those pupils who could not be tested for intelligence and are assessed only for personal–social development. Therefore, no numerical values are marked on the horizontal axis of this figure. The place of the added group of pupils along the left–right dimension (corresponding to MA in Fig. 1.1) was arbitrarily estimated on the basis of a common staff judgment of overall performance level as compared to that of the tested children. To illustrate, Francie's performance was judged to be a little better than that of Liza; Billy's performance was better than Francie's, but both were inferior to Johnnie's.

Once all the children were located on this figure in the manner described above, lines linking their names were drawn, continuous lines to represent positive (friendly or nurturing) contacts, and broken lines to represent aggressive contacts. In each case the arrow points in a direction from the active to the passive partner. In many cases, where contacts were reciprocal, double-headed arrows are used.

Figure 1.2 shows, firstly, that occurrence of aggressive contacts tends to diminish with growing mental age and personal–social development, and, secondly, that the profoundly retarded are often the passive social partners or objects of nurturance on the part of the less retarded and in this way are not excluded from the social life of the group. *This we consider to be one of the main achievements of our educational work*. The total number of positive connections mounts as we look toward the upper right of the diagram, i.e., toward the rising MA–PS scores. Two of the moderately retarded deaf children formed a focus of the group's social life.

It should be stressed that the graphic representations contained in Figures 1.1 and 1.2 do not meet the requirements of a psychomatic tool, and ought not to be used as such. Their purpose has been mainly to aid the staff to gain a better understanding of each individual pupil by seeing him within the context of the group's social norm. They are included here to illustrate the group pattern of social behaviour.

Observation and music therapy for severely subnormal boys (Juliette Alvin, British Society for Music Therapy, 48 Lanchester Road, London)
Alvin, a well-known musician in therapy circles, describes in some detail her observations of the ways in which three groups of very severely subnormal boys living in Binfield Park Hospital responded to music. The research sets out to observe and report upon each individual boy's reactions to sound and rhythm in highly structured (groups 1 and 2) and some free choice of instrument situations (group 3)—the cello, a selection of instruments including the melodica and the autoharp, records without a compulsive beat.

Nineteen boys took part in the experience with Juliette Alvin and her assistant. Fifteen of them had no speech, thirteen were over 12 years of age. The other six were 7, 11, 11, 12, $12\frac{1}{2}$, and $12\frac{1}{3}$. Many of them had never attended a training centre and three of them had been excluded. Note the date, 1968–9. The sample of nineteen was divided into three

18   *Introduction*

small groups according to levels of ability. Each boy taking part in the experience is carefully described. Three separate evaluation/observation of results scales were devised for the boys in each of the three groups.

One of these specimen scales is quoted in detail to encourage you to send off for the full document. It will certainly repay attention. This scale was devised for the group with the highest abilities, age range 15–19. None of them were epileptic, 4 were mongols, 1 had fluent speech, 3 had no speech, the others a little; 5 had never attended a training centre.

Reaction to sounds. Soft; loud; percussive; attention; watching.

Awareness. Of the instrument (in the other scales); of the therapist; of others; pitching voice to cello.

Instruments. Own volition; manipulation; deliberate movements; cello; bow.

Response to rhythm. Sitting (hands, feet); standing (moving about, following beat); communication (with therapist, with others).

The evaluation scales (if all three are used) clearly give those adults working with these children another positive experiential area in which to observe these children and see their development in awareness, perception, body rhythm and body image, emotional motivation (curiosity and interest, a desire to move), pleasure in sound, happiness. As Alvin states in summing up 'Even in the most regressed or seemingly hopeless cases one may discover some unsuspected channel of communication'.

A few months after this action research was written up, the hospital decided to continue employing a music therapist and an assistant on five weekly sessions. The sessions were arranged as follows:

(1) one session for five boys;
(2) one session for seven boys;
(3) one session for individual boys who might benefit;
(4) one large group session for all the boys in school—musical games and exercises, country dancing, vocal training, listening to music;
(5) one instrumental session for six of the most gifted boys with melodica, drums, and cello.

Dr D. W. Winnicott in his book *The Child, The Family and the Outside World* rightly condemns some of the attitudes still existing in the general teaching profession. He writes, 'Diagnosis on a scientific basis is the most precious part of our medical heritage and distinguishes the medical profession from the faith-healers, the osteopaths, and all the people we consult when we want a quick cure.

'The question is, what do we do when we look at the teaching profession that corresponds with this business of diagnosis? It is quite possible that I am wrong, but I feel bound to say that I can see but little in teaching that is truly equivalent to the deliberate diagnosis of doctors. In my dealings with the teaching profession I am frequently disturbed in mind by the way in which the general mass of children are educated without first being diagnosed.'

How much more would many of the practices existing today in some of our schools for the severely subnormal child be condemned by similar writers if they saw that even more of a hit-and-miss method of dealing with the most challenging of children still prevails?

I have rewritten this book in order to continue to help these interesting children. I have made some very simple, necessary, practical suggestions. My aim is to help all those coming into contact with them understand more deeply that by watching carefully and keeping systematic records of their behaviour they will discover the children's many needs and interests; they will in fact begin to make a deliberate study of each child.

Records kept about these children prior to 1963 were often based upon subjective opinions without relating these opinions to continuous written records. They were general rather than specific. It seems obvious too that because of inadequate, unskilled, and unrecorded observation there was a lack of continuity and purposefulness in the programmes.

One of the impressions I have recently gained is that still too few teachers, even in 1976/7, are really looking at CHILDREN and developing some part of the programme at least from each child's *spontaneous* behaviour. I do not think that this is a more difficult teaching technique than employing methods using commercial teaching aids and having learning packages to work from. Teachers are perhaps not having sufficient time during initial and in-service training to learn how to observe skilfully and utilize their findings in the interest and well being of the child.

I am restating what might seem obvious at some length because I consider the points I am trying to make still to be of the utmost importance in the education of children who are mentally handicapped. I know also that skilful recorded observation of these children still needs to be practised by educators so that it becomes incorporated into their work behaviour. These records also need to be examined on a regular basis by the headteacher.*

Peter Cummings in his Book *Education and the Severely Handicapped Child*, published by the National Society for Mentally Handicapped Children, describes his findings regarding record keeping (amongst other aspects) in 25 hospitals and 24 schools. Some had efficient systems and some just carried out meaningless ritual.

---

* I am reminded as I write of one headteacher trained by my observational methods some years ago saying that the way in which some of her present teachers recorded their observations indicated the lack of specific training in objectivity. Too many of them were in fact inferring the nature of the child's behaviour (action, response) observed instead of describing the behaviour itself (cf. Holt and Reynell, 1970; and Chapter 9). Observing precisely is a difficult skill without technological help, i.e. audio video aids. Although I have tried to develop this skill over a lifetime you will discover countless examples in this book showing that I too unfortunately draw inferences.

Introduction

	No records	Gunzburg P.A.C. forms*	Weekly	Monthly	Annual
Hospital	4	7	11	11	0
Schools	All kept records	12	4	2	6

These findings, even on such a small sample, reinforce my belief that this book still has its uses and particularly now that all schools whether in a hospital or in the community have a specialist educational adviser visiting on a regular systematic basis. Surely we have not arrived at the stage in educational development (and particularly in a field of special education only recently recognized) where an adviser feels he cannot ask for teachers' record books. Another survey in the next 5 years might indicate areas where successful and varied record keeping is in fact taking place.†

Cummings reporting on a teacher's statement writes 'We have to write daily and monthly reports but as we are not briefed about what to look for, the reports make negative reading'. All I want to ask is 'Has that teacher not heard of child development scales?' Why is she/he in special education without such a concept? I am curious to know what Cummings replied. Again, quoting a nurse 'Not too fussy about the records as nobody ever reads them', Cummings is certainly right when he asks 'For whom do writers write?' Such remarks clearly indicate that some teachers and nurses, once qualified, never read; and that many professionals, in spite of training, do not see record keeping as part of their professional responsibility.

One of the reasons for this direct observational/recording approach as I see it is that the individual differences existing between these children in any one class are always wide. Whichever developmental scales are used one will observe behaviour that is not described in a scale but which nevertheless one can use as a useful starting point for teaching if one is a sensitive observer and a spontaneous thinker.

Teachers need the opportunity of seeing these differences in some detail. To do this they must learn how to observe. Then they will begin to understand quite simply that different methods, other than those formal ones current today (1975/6) in many of the schools for the severely subnormal, are desirable and that children with different kinds of handicap require teaching methods adapted to their very special individual needs

---

* Gunzburg, H. C. (1963) *Progress Assessment Charts*. Obtainable: MIND, 22 Harley Street, London.

† I have recently interviewed twenty-one teachers in the New Fosseway School, Bristol. One of my students is its headteacher. The many varied ways used by these teachers to record and measure progress are well worth examining.

Introduction   21

(O'Connor, N. Marshall, A.).* One authority I know appointed a classroom assistant to 'look after' one disturbed little girl who was scratching the other children. One year after this intensive individual care the little girl seems to be 'fitting into' the class much more easily. Perhaps the root of the problem has been solved, perhaps she has matured, perhaps the teacher is using different methods. Whatever the reason the approach seemed positive and worthwhile.

If the adults learn to observe skilfully they will also begin to understand that punitive responses OF ANY KIND† on their part (somehow still today accepted and condoned by some in this field of education) are not necessary. Indeed such responses are to be judged unethical because of the child's lack of intention and inability to report to his parents the behaviour he receives from others. They will also begin to understand why they as teachers need to be special.

Another reason for the points I am trying to make in this book is that teachers always need to check the progress and development of each child so that wherever it does not happen the reasons are fully examined. Enabling severely subnormal children to learn is a most difficult and challenging task. The teachers have to remind themselves continuously that progress is recognizably slow. Progress is so slow that unless systematic observational records are kept and referred to they will not be able to see the results of their work—surely the mark of highly skilled professionals in wanting to assess themselves. They will also not be able to decide when more specialist help should be called in to solve the many learning difficulties encountered.

Teachers need to spend time in order to understand the needs of each child. Continuous handling by the same teacher is therefore a very necessary feature of this work even if a withdrawal system is also in vogue in a school. Such continuous handling will ensure that at least one person knows the child really well and can 'pull all the threads' about him together whenever this may become necessary.

Perhaps the time will arrive when this concept is understood or its value refuted. Then teachers will be allowed to work with each child for a couple of years at least and for an even longer period if visible progress that can be described precisely is the result. In terms of job satisfaction it would appear that most teachers wish to see the progress which they themselves have brought about by their skill and efforts. Such progress will be made

---

*O'Connor, N. and Hermelin, B. (1963) *Speech and Thought in Severe Subnormality*. Marshall, A. (1967) *The Abilities and Achievements of Children Leaving Junior Training Centres*, National Association for Mental Health, London.

† Smacking (however gently), putting a child in the corner, sending a child to stand outside the room—these were the mainstays of normal education years ago and these children need *special* education and consideration without sentiment. Gumbra, I. (*Nursing Mirror Review*, 1976) stated that my other book was marred by constant references to 'bad teaching'. Because the children cannot complain I will always do so on their behalf. I know that most of my colleagues will support me in this.

22   Introduction

all the more certain if the activities they provide are appropriate,* at the child's level of development in ALL areas of growth and take into account as well his future life.

Although educational research about mentally handicapped children has grown in quantity in the decade since the first edition of this book, the implications of some of this research in practical terms are still not being disseminated quickly enough. Many researchers, however, are now beginning to write in much simpler terms. Perhaps teachers, therefore, by referring to their own objective observational findings will discover an evaluative and self-support system enabling them to work more successfully and with a large measure of satisfaction.

---

* Dr Gunzburg writing in *Mental Deficiency, The Changing Outlook* (edited by Clarke, A. M. and Clarke, A. D. B., 3rd Edition (1973)) on educational planning for the mentally handicapped complains that few educationists 'seem as yet to have paid attention to the fact that ALL definitions of mental subnormality contain an explicit statement regarding the social incompetence of the defective'. He continues 'nearly all educational work concentrates on how to overcome his *academic* [the italics are mine] weaknesses even though these weaknesses can be tolerated by the community quite well and have comparatively little impact on the main problem. It is surely a disservice to the subnormal adult if his childhood education represents a prolonged imitation of an academic even if "normal" school life whilst the preparations for his adult life are disregarded. The lower down the IQ ladder the child is placed the less justification there is for giving a normal education, even if less of it, and the greater necessity for providing special education preparing him for HIS way of life at a later stage.' The tragic fact as it appears to me is that there is more of this 'academic' education since the children became the responsibility of the local education authorities. More precise observation might substantiate the impression I have gained. More in-service courses organized by the Inspectors of Special Education in each authority might enable many more teachers to understand the needs of the mentally handicapped child more fully, and to concentrate on those features of life likely to be responsible for his ultimate well being.

2 Observing and responding

There were many major problems confronting those training teachers of mentally handicapped children during 1960–70. One of these was inevitably the lack of practical suggestions to indicate the form such training should take, though the Scott Report outlined in some detail the nature of the syllabus that was considered appropriate. The experts in learning theory and those who had scientifically observed the mentally handicapped recorded their findings mainly for other experts, often doing this only against the background of their own medical, clinical, or psychological training. Relatively few practising educationists had concerned themselves seriously with the education of these children or with the training of their teachers. Some of the experts tried to relate their findings to what might be described as the 'classroom situation' but they did not always explain them in simple enough terms and consequently their works were not read widely or with understanding by the majority of the practical workers dealing day to day with the children.

One educationist in England who, in fact, set forth in print useful ideas about teacher training, as it applied to helping severely subnormal children to learn, was Mary Lindsay. In a paper* given to the International Congress on the Education and Social Integration of the Mentally Handicapped, she described some broad, general principles for those training teachers for this highly specialized job. Two ideas in this paper that reassured me and stimulated my thinking at that time are contained in the following remarks: 'Nothing in my experience as a teacher of the mentally handicapped children, nor what I have seen so widely of other people's work, leads me to believe that the fundamental needs of mentally handicapped children are different from those of normal children', and 'We need in this field the stimulus of new ideas, not only of ways of teaching but ways of training teachers'.

The ideas of Mary Lindsay coupled with my own research† experience as a primary school and remedial teacher stimulated my thinking about methods of helping teachers to know the children for themselves. Observation of teachers, admittedly in a subjective manner, suggested that too few were able to do this well. The initial problem of training teachers of mentally handicapped children was to devise methods which would bring their attention to the many educational needs of the children in a

---

* *The Training of Teachers of Mentally Handicapped Children*, Mary Lindsay (1963). International League of Societies for the Mentally Handicapped, Brussels, Belgium.
    † Unpublished M.Ed. thesis, Manchester University, 1954.

24   *Observing and responding*

non-theoretical manner. I preferred this approach to one suggesting specific and untried teaching methods or to approaches demanding too rigidly and dogmatically the content of what had to be taught. It seemed more important to encourage flexibility, initiative, and experiment in a profession where it was obvious (because of the kind of training they received prior to 1960) that teachers would follow the rigid schemes of work provided by the headteachers and at the same time fail to look at the individual children involved. This is no less true in 1976 than it was in the early 'sixties.

What follows will show how this problem was tackled in training students to teach severely subnormal children. The emphasis was always on skilful observation and recording, and responding purposefully and whenever possible, immediately, to the children in a variety of situations.

We take it for granted that observation is an obvious part of everyday behaviour needing no particular practice to achieve. We look around, we listen, and we gain impressions. Teachers and other professionals too often fail to understand that they need to spend time developing and increasing their own powers of deliberate attention to the spontaneous behaviour of children.* Important as this is for all concerned with children, it is even more important for those working with severely subnormal children to cultivate the habit of conscious attention to the child's behaviour at all times for they can then learn to form judgements about the child's needs and respond immediately and purposefully to what they see and hear. If they do this consistently, the children will make an effort, will become active, and so will learn within the limit of their handicap.

This often means doing what countless intelligent mothers are doing instinctively day by day with their own children when they talk to them, play with them, answer their questions, and let them do things in the home. Teachers must respond to children with learning difficulties more systematically and consistently than mothers generally do and they must always relate the children's response to normal learning development.

Many teachers are indeed now responding purposefully and *immediately* to the children in a variety of interesting ways. This is largely because of the positive use they are making of their own skilled observations in the learning situation. The following examples illustrate not only how teachers responded to ideas the children gave but also how they used these ideas to plan their daily curriculum.

John (10 years old) had little speech beyond a few words. He was unable to join in with other children whilst his teacher was reading a story. One day he wiggled his fingers in some water and listened to the splashing sound they made. He was intent upon watching the air bubbles made by the quick movement of his fingers, and he bent his head forward until his face almost touched the surface of the water, then lapped it with his tongue. He concentrated on this activity for ten minutes.

---

* It is interesting to note that many more psychologists and research workers are observing these children in the natural surroundings of a free play situation. Fortunately they now have money and technological resources (audio–video tape recorders) to help them in their work.

Observing and responding   25

While he was busy his teacher quietly tipped a piece of foam rubber into the water tray and left him to discover it for himself. When he found it, he pressed on it and watched it carefully. He lifted it to his mouth and bit into it with his teeth, making the water trickle out of the foam. He continued experimenting and concentrated for a further ten minutes. What was he learning? He was learning to listen to soft sounds, to watch dripping water; he was learning that foam rubber can be squeezed. He was also learning how to play by himself. When his teacher saw his interest in the water, she gave him another learning experience, knowing that his play with water would be valuable in helping him to wash himself later on in his development.

Here we can see how the teacher provided new material in order to respond to John's concentration and interest in the water. She was extending his sensory experience. She was *not* forcing him into a group situation for which she knew he was not yet ready.

One of the ways in which adults should be almost continuously responding to severely subnormal children is in language. Opportunities will present themselves daily as the simple, everyday examples quoted below will illustrate.

The examples have been deliberately chosen for they show that the chance to respond to the children's comments and behaviour by reciprocal comments, explanations, or questions is there to be extended in almost every sound, word, or sentence uttered, and in most situations. Developing language is one of the most important aims and one that can easily be neglected because of the energy and thought it demands not only in constant talking with the children about their activities but in providing the situations and the equipment to motivate the children to talk with us and with each other.

Mobiles placed in front of an open window caused a little boy to comment. His teacher immediately asked, 'What is making it do that?'
'The wind,' he replied.
'It bubbled,' Tommy shouted.
'What bubbled?' asked his teacher.
'The clock,' Tommy replied.
In his desire to wash paint from the face of the clock, he had placed it in a bowl. This caused him to use the descriptive word 'bubbled'. The incident was handled in a positive way by his teacher for she responded in a way that encouraged his language.
Child: 'Can I play out tomorrow?'
Teacher: 'If it's nice.'
Child: 'Can I bake tomorrow?'
Teacher: 'What will you bake?'
Child: 'Buns.'
Teacher: 'What do you make buns out of?'
Child: 'I'm looking at this sand-pie.'
Teacher: 'Are you? Make another one then.'
'Is there any school tomorrow?'
'No.'
'Why is there no school?'
'It's Saturday tomorrow.'
'What's the next day?' asked the teacher.
'Let me see who can lie flat on his tummy. Now show me how you can go across the floor.'

26   *Observing and responding*

'Like a crocodile,' called Brian (13 years).
'Yes, that's right: like a crocodile,' encouraged his teacher.

In the movement lesson the busy, anxious or unobservant teacher might very well expect the children simply to listen to instructions to move and yet to remain silent. Creative movement work, however, not only enables the children to express themselves imaginatively in movement itself, but often encourages them to use their language.

Frank was kneeling on the floor with a toy car in front of him, chattering his teeth together for quite some time. When his teacher finally noticed him she imitated the movement and the sound he was making. He stopped and listened intently, then the sound ba—ba—ba— came from his lips. His teacher later recorded these sounds in her notebooks, for they were important ones in his language development. As she made a quick response to him she knew that he would continue to make more sounds.

The next day Frank was really stimulated when she brought her tape recorder, taped the sounds he made and played them back to him. His attention was truly caught.

The following taped conversations between a child and an adult show how each lead given by the child was extended, how new words were taught, and how, through conversation, the child's ideas and knowledge were developed.

JANET'S CONVERSATION

Teacher: 'What is that you are drawing, Janet?'
J: 'House.'
Teacher: 'Oh, it's very nice, Janet. Can you tell me about that house? Can you tell me anything about that house?'
J: 'Yes.'
Teacher: 'Go on, then.'
J: 'Windows.'
Teacher: 'Yes. Anything else, dear?'
J: 'And a roof.'
Teacher: 'Anything else? What else have you done? You are drawing something very nice.'
J: (something inaudible) 'Where my Mum lives.'
Teacher: 'There's a man in the house.'
J: 'No, where my Mum lives. I got Uncle Charles.'
Teacher: 'Uncle Charles lives in your house. Have you got a Dad, Janet?'
J: 'Yes: John.'
Teacher: 'You are clever knowing your Dad's name.'
Teacher: 'My Mum was called Lily. What is your Mum called?'
J: 'Edna Mills.'
Teacher: 'Now draw a man in a house.'
J: 'He has no family?'
Teacher: 'He has no family?'
J: 'No.'
Teacher: 'Is it another man?'
J: 'Yes.'
Teacher: 'Who's Pete?'
J: 'Pete? That's my uncle.'
Teacher: 'And have you got some aunties as well?'
J: 'My auntie's died.'
Teacher: 'When?'

Observing and responding 27

J: 'In April.'
Teacher: 'And where is she now?'
J: 'In heaven.'
Teacher: 'She's gone to heaven? Was she a good lady?'
J: 'Yes. I sit on Grandma's knee. I sit on my grandma's knee.'
Teacher: 'I see. When? When do you sit on your Grandma's knee?'
J: 'About eight.'
Teacher: 'Eight o'clock at night you mean?'
J: 'No, I was eight.'
Teacher: 'Is your Grandma dead as well? She died as well?'
J: 'Yes.'
Teacher: 'Where has she gone?'
J: 'She's gone to heaven.'
Teacher: 'What happened to her when she died?'
J: 'She got burying.'
Teacher: 'Yes, she got buried.'
Teacher: 'What did they put her in before they buried her, do you know?'
J: 'Soil.'
Teacher: 'Yes, they put her in the soil.'
Teacher: 'They put her in something else before, Janet.'
J: 'The box.'
Teacher: 'Do you know the name of that box?'
Teacher: 'It's called a coffin.'
    'It's as long as the person.' (gesturing)
Teacher: 'Did you see this box? It is not usual for little girls to see the coffin. Where
    is the box now?'
J: 'The box is in the soil.'
Teacher: 'Where is the soil? Where is that earth?'
J: 'In the sky.'
Teacher: 'No dear. It is in a place called a cemetery. Have you been to the cemetery?'
J: 'Flowers.'
Teacher: 'What sort of flowers do you take to the cemetery?'
J: 'My Grandmother's birthday.'
Teacher: 'On your Grandma's birthday? You put them on the ——, what, Janet?'
J: 'The grave.'
Teacher: 'On the grave: that's right. Do you go to church with your family?'
J: 'I got my friends.'
Teacher: 'Your friends go to church but not you?'
J: 'I've got Kathleen and Pauline.'
Teacher: 'They are your friends, are they? I see.'
J: 'They take me to church every day.'
Teacher: 'They don't take you every day. Every Sunday perhaps. Do you go to
    Sunday School?' (Pause)
J: 'Just church.'
Teacher: 'Do you go to what's called Sunday School?'
J: 'Yes.'
Teacher: 'In the morning or at night?'
J: 'Morning.'
Teacher: 'And what time is it when you go to church?'
J: 'Nine o'clock.'
Teacher: 'Nine o'clock in the morning. It was lovely—really lovely to talk to you.
    Would you like to hear your voice on there now?' [the tape recorder].
J: 'Yes.' (with enthusiasm).

If we examine this conversation we shall see that the following facts
emerge:

(1) the teacher uses 365 words to the child's 109 words;

28   *Observing and responding*

(2) thirty questions are asked;
(3) questions are asked by the intonation of the speaker's voice;
(4) seven explanations are given;
(5) six repetitions of the child's phrases/statements are used;
(6) specific encouragement is given on two occasions;
(7) one instruction is given.

All schools for the mentally handicapped have some disturbed children of one kind or another. What to do about such children often poses a serious problem to their teachers, since the teacher with a very large group of children cannot always work with individual children as those in the first two examples were able to do. What is apparent, in observing a great many teachers over the years, is that wherever they have been fully understanding the idea of working from the child's spontaneous* behaviour on some occasions and have given opportunities for constructive and purposeful development of apparently aimless and sometimes even negative activities, the outcome has generally been a positive one in terms of increased ease in the management and handling of the child.

Linda destroyed and maltreated all the dolls in the house corner. Her teacher decided to respond to this by helping her to make her own doll. Through the creative enjoyment of making the body, the head, and the clothes which she herself had sewn with the help of her teacher, her behaviour, which was usually loud and attention seeking, became more controlled. From sewing the doll and its clothes her teacher helped her to colour pictures of dolls, to talk about the pictures, and finally to match the words they had used in connection with making the doll and its clothes. A positive response to what the adult considered to be negative behaviour helped Linda to co-operate and to become more accepted in the group.

Leonard was an habitual twirler of string: twirling it into small balls and then throwing them into the air was the activity he preferred. He also liked sorting out tea cards carried around in his pocket. It occurred to the teacher that if she made him a large ring-board and rings to throw, perhaps his attention could be deflected from the apparently aimless action of throwing string into the air. His tea card collection

---

    * A useful observational piece of research on patterns of spontaneous reactions in the mentally handicapped is that by Michael Beveridge (cf. p. 13).

    If we examine the stages of play and social development (cf. Stevens, 1976; Appendices 3 and 4) we shall see that this substantiates the necessity for an emphasis to be put on the teacher always 'working out' the mental level of each child year by year (for this increases, however slowly, according to the degree of handicap), and comparing it with the expectations (to some extent at any rate when we first begin to teach the mentally handicapped) for normal social interaction development.

    Too many teachers working with very young handicapped children (with mental levels below 18 months to 2 years) are still saying 'Say you're sorry' to a child who has hit out at another child in his experimentation with an 'object' (the child) outside himself. One of the most useful books I discovered helping me with this concept in the early 'sixties was *Infants without Families*. The abstract adult concept of 'sorrow' seems ludicrous. What the adult needs to do is to remove the 'offending' child to another part of the room with something positive to do (positive distraction technique) unless the 'hit' child is able to respond. In this situation the children will teach each other. Clearly we have also to take into account (if the child is at the imitation stage of learning) the fact that he might have seen an adult smacking—in which case the child is only duplicating a gesture he has seen without intention to hurt.

Observing and responding 29

was mostly of trains. The suggestion that he might paste them on to the wall so that he could look at them and then perhaps make a train with his teacher was well accepted: his interest had been captured. The making of the train, singing a song with the group about trains, and finally visiting the railway station was a natural way of responding to him and helping him to become more aware of his environment and more acceptable in it.

Jean had played imaginatively and continuously in the sand for many months whenever she had the chance to choose her own activity. One day she was seen using a rolling pin which her teacher had put on the sand table as part of its equipment. She was rolling out the damp sand as though it were pastry. Her teacher had been waiting for many weeks to encourage Jean (who at 16 was considered too old to be using sand) to use pastry, first in her play and later on in a cooking session at a more acceptable and grown-up level. She hurriedly made some pastry and began to roll it out in front of Jean. Her efforts were ignored and Jean continued to make 'cakes' with the sand and the pastry tins. Her teacher rolled out the pastry, cut it into circles and placed them in the tart tins. Without a word she left Jean to her own devices. Some time later Jean was seen using the pastry and the rolling pin in the same way as she had observed her teacher using it. She seemed ready now for more directed activity.

Jimmy, a most difficult, disturbed and noisy adolescent boy, told the teacher that he had been to Blackpool. When she took him for his individual session she suggested that together they made a model of Blackpool Tower. It was difficult for him to concentrate for long on this activity, but with quiet determination on the part of the teacher the tower was built bit by bit in papier mâché. Jimmy was proud of what he had made. Different behaviour, which other teachers noticed and commented upon at the time, was no doubt due in some small measure to the immediate response his teacher had made when he told her about his visit. Had no response been there, the chance of helping Jimmy to become better adjusted through a personal and individual approach to his interest might have been lost for ever.

The children were visiting a near-by museum with their teacher, and the boys in the group were fascinated by the pottery and asked many questions about it. The following morning they found a large lump of pottery clay on one of the tables. They were invited by their teacher to make some pottery with it. 'I saw a rat in the yard,' Keith called out. 'You make a rat, then!' was the teacher's response. The painted and glazed rat that emerged from this experience was a source of great satisfaction to Keith and encouraged other boys in the group to make something for the interesting display of creative work in their classroom.

Barry and John (13 years old) had chosen the large box of wooden bricks to play with. These were all shapes and sizes. First they built towers and knocked them down again. Then one day their teacher noticed that together they had built a ramp-like structure which led up to a 'house'. She saw them running small cars up the ramp and into the 'house'. She encouraged the boys to tell her about their play and from their conversation concluded that they might like to make a garage and cars and lorries of their own with the various boxes and materials that she kept in her 'bit' box.* The next week or two was spent making these. It involved much experimenting with creative materials, discussion with each other and the teacher, comparison of size and shape of the boxes, painting, pasting and cutting, and a great many other learning experiences.

---

*A large 'bit' box suitably covered in bright paper or plastic should be a part of every teacher's classroom equipment. It might contain boxes of varying sizes and textures, ribbons, cotton reels, printing objects, silver paper and coloured paper, cartons, string, and so on. In fact it should have everything to encourage the children to be creative and to use their own imagination. Needless to say, it will need constant replenishing.

30 Observing and responding

From this last example it can be seen how the teacher had a very definite part to play in talking to the boys about their activities. Because of her guidance she was helping them to widen their interests and their ideas. She also encouraged them to bring some boxes from home to add to those she had in the bit box. In this way she was encouraging them to talk about their school activities at home and was thus bringing home and school closer together.

Joyce and Anne (15 years old) dressed themselves up in hats, high-heeled shoes, and summer dresses from the dressing-up box. They wandered arm in arm around the classroom. 'Are you going to the shops?' they were asked. 'No,' was their reply. 'Where are you going?' continued their teacher. 'To Blackpool,' was their answer. 'Have you your tickets?' 'No.' 'You must have tickets before you get on the train. Who will help me to make the ticket office so that Joyce and Anne can buy their tickets?' Several children placed tables to represent the counter. Some went to the headteacher to ask her if she had any tickets. The teacher composed a notice, 'TICKET OFFICE'. Other children were encouraged to place chairs in rows facing each other to form the 'train'. From dressing-up activities the teacher helped the children to enact the whole drama of buying tickets, giving them up at the barrier, getting on the train, talking on the journey, arriving at the destination, handing in the tickets. This dramatic play was continued spontaneously for many days by the same children. The teacher kept the interest of the children alive by making a more realistic ticket booth, cardboard tickets, and obtaining railway posters. She also arranged for the children to go on a real train journey, as part of their learning programme.

In this way the teacher made language an important part of the play by her questions about the children's activity and in the imaginative follow-up responses she gave to their answers. It is essential that the teacher seizes every opportunity she can to give the operative words of the activity to the child *at the time* it is taking place. She can sometimes do this by joining in with the child's dramatic play and using the 'play' language: at other times she can provide extra play materials and talk about them as they are being used.

Graham (12 years old) went to the dressing-up clothes-hooks, took one or two dresses off the hangers and then told his teacher that he 'wanted to do his packing to go on his holidays'. She provided him with a small case so that he could carry out his own suggestion and so develop his own activity in creative play.

Rosie (12 years old), when she came into the playroom, noticed the very large rag doll, almost four feet tall. Her attention had been caught because it was so big. She needed it for her hospital play. She found two long sticks, wrapped a blanket around them to make a stretcher and with the help of her teacher carried the doll over to the 'operating table'. The doll was carefully lifted from the stretcher to the table. She discovered that the legs dangled over the side, and looked puzzled. The length of the doll posed a problem. 'What do you need?' she was asked by an observant teacher. 'Another,' was her reply, indicating a table at the other side of the room.

Not only was Rosie using her imagination to play out a variety of roles in connection with her hospital play—she was also gaining ideas of longer, shorter, too long, too short. She was also informing her teacher that she had the idea of 'another one'.

Judy (10 years old) wanted to play in the water corner. The other children in the group were all busy painting, pasting, cutting, talking to their teacher, and playing

Observing and responding 31

in the house, but Judy remained on her own. She began to fill a small pan with water and sand and, taking a spoon (provided among the play materials by the teacher), she stirred vigorously. 'Are you making something nice?' asked her teacher. 'Soup,' answered Judy. 'Are you going to cook it?' 'Yes,' Judy said. 'Where is your stove?' asked her interested teacher. Judy looked amongst the play-equipment in a box and found a tin, stood it on the table and placed the pan on top: this was her stove. She continued to stir the 'warming soup'. Later, when it was 'ready', everyone was invited to 'taste'.

A pan, a spoon, and a tin helped Judy to use her imagination and to show her teacher, through play, that she had watched her mother stirring the food at the stove. The teacher's spontaneous response helped the child to extend the meaning of her play activity. It is not difficult for us to see that a teacher with less understanding of Judy's level of development might have forced Judy into the activities of the group and in so doing deprived her of the opportunities to experiment and use her own imagination.

These stories, chosen carefully to illustrate specific teaching points, are intended to show some of the ways in which the teacher played her part as a result of observation: by providing extra materials, by seeing where the activity could be led into acceptable channels, by responding with meaningful language, by learning about a child's stage of development, and by using immediately what the child gave spontaneously. At all times the teacher was called upon to use imagination, to think quickly, and to be spontaneous too.

Making an immediate response of one kind or another to a child *because of what has been observed* seems to be a necessary teaching technique that the teacher of the handicapped needs to develop to an extreme degree. I sometimes refer to it as the 'immediate response technique' of teaching. Its link with present popularized behaviour modification methods is the immediacy of the response, for because of the teacher's response the child's activity will be positively reinforced. He will begin to learn that *something* will happen as a result of *his* activity. When he learns that his teacher notices when he tries to do something or when he shows interest in the world around him, he will be spurred on to further self-action and increased learning. Perhaps one of the major differences between this approach and behaviour modification techniques is that the teacher and others are more likely to concentrate on the child and his needs rather than on specific adult-centred goals, as is so often the case.

Observing and using a momentary interest, even if this interest seems unimportant and meaningless to us as adults, and helping the child to sustain and to develop an interest is, therefore, an extension of what the teacher should be able to do with confidence as the habit of becoming a skilful observer becomes established with disciplined practice.

3 Techniques of observing. When and how

Ideally teachers will see that they need to give conscious attention to the behaviour and activities of the children whenever they are with them and whatever the activities happen to be. However, this is a difficult skill—it demands practice. A useful approach to understanding this concept is to examine some of the most fruitful situations in which to carry out methodical observation of children.* One of the observed needs of this group of children (and it is certainly not being met in all schools) is to have at least one, possibly two, unbroken sessions daily, $1\frac{1}{4}$–$1\frac{1}{2}$ hours in length, in order to become self-directed and learn how to plan and solve their own problems. For this to happen they need *time* to become organized. A sensitive observer can also begin to see needs. Such sessions are, of course, only possible when the children are provided with a really wide variety of activities and experiences† and where on most occasions the adult plays a participating and responsive part.‡ It is during this time, indeed, that we will see the children as they really are and so will learn about them.

It is important, however, that on several occasions during the week all those concerned with the children should try to become a non-participating observer for $\frac{1}{4}$–$\frac{1}{2}$ hour without actually becoming involved with the children. This is sometimes difficult, particularly with severely subnormal children, because some child in the group nearly always needs his teacher's attention and, because of his handicap, cannot always be expected to wait for it.

---

* Since the late 'sixties and early 'seventies research workers and those training the teachers in the colleges have had the advantage of using audio-visual aids and closed circuit television to observe these children. This has often meant that they could repeat the observation of the behaviours over and over again in a truly scientific way. Kay Mogford in Nottingham University has been carefully observing all the possibilities for play with specific toys. Members of staff from the Hester Adrian Centre in the University of Manchester have also been using these technological aids with some obvious success if we examine the materials they have produced.

† The School Experience Record Card Sections 5, 6, and 7 suggest some of the activities schools are now attempting in curricula developed by educators since the late 'fifties and early 'sixties. Ideas relating to the provision of materials and equipment in Chapters 4 and 5 suggest others.

‡ I was dismayed in 1976 (10 years after writing the first edition of this book) to note that children were being observed by research workers in environments that still could not really afford the children adequate opportunity for choice, though their ultimate findings were the same but stated more precisely, viz. 'the observations took place during a free play situation in which the children were *sitting* doing such things as jigsaws, painting, and sewing' (cf. Stevens, 1968; Chapters 4 and 5).

Several possibilities based upon my observations of the organization and administration of schools I have visited are open to those wishing to become skilled observers, in order to get over this difficulty. These do not make impossible demands on staff, but they do, admittedly, demand different attitudes on their part. They also require a change of emphasis in the teacher's mind, from an 'I work in my own classroom with my group of children' approach, to a 'team' approach which involves the co-operation of the whole school.

Headteachers of schools will, no doubt, make their own arrangements for the observing sessions suggested once they become aware that their staff need some special sessions for looking at the children more closely. They should not be afraid to experiment and to take note of the results both in the reactions of the children when two adults are working with them and in their teachers' ability to use their observation skills. Some might possibly like to adopt some of the suggestions made here and then adapt them according to their own needs and circumstances.

It is worth remembering that there will be some schools where recently trained staff will have had little methodical practice in observing children skilfully. The increasing academic approach to training teachers (B.Ed.) leaves little time for adequate practical work with the children. So it is even more important that others concerned with the teachers take over a 'training role' when normal training is completed. Perhaps this needs to be quite specific in terms of those wishing to teach the mentally handicapped. Many teachers with no special education training at all are now entering this sphere of education. I was interested to note that since 1971 Tansley has been using special techniques on In-service courses in Birmingham to encourage teachers to observe and assess special educational needs. He reported this experiment to the Conference of the National Council for Special Education in Bradford, 1975.* He found that his teachers (300 of them from 70 infant schools in the city) became so 'good at observing; they were able to observe so much more thoroughly and scientifically that they were better able to discover and deal with the special needs of the children'.

(1) The headteacher might arrange to spend some of her time with each class in turn during the week, supervising the activities planned by the class teacher whilst the teacher herself becomes the recording observer.

(2) A large room of the school could, perhaps, be turned into a 'choice of activities room' for certain periods during the week. Two classes could join together and their teachers could arrange for one of them to become the non-participating observer, whilst the other was responsible for attending to the immediate learning-needs of the children.

(3) Responsible voluntary workers attached to a class for certain periods could be involved, under the guidance of the teacher, in attending to

---

* Conference report obtainable from Bradford and District Branch, National Council for Special Education.

34 Techniques of observing. When and how

the children's immediate needs, whilst the teacher became the recording observer during the short period of time suggested, i.e. $\frac{1}{4}-\frac{1}{2}$ hour.

(4) It is now common practice for the teacher to have nursery helpers working with them, particularly in classes for the young ESN child. Most local authorities have also appointed a 'helper' to each group of children. Such members of staff can be directly useful to the teacher whenever she wishes to spend time observing the children in an active classroom environment as well as in more formal ways (in dining, toileting, individual feeding, and dressing sessions, and in testing sessions).

(5) Teachers might also use students on teaching practice, for they could be busy with the children and their activities whilst the class teacher observes them.

I am not suggesting that the above techniques should be continued indefinitely, particularly when the staff become skilled in observing and recording but it seems to be an essential as well as a possible measure to take for varied amounts of time. Especially is this the case when staff have had no training in direct observation techniques or are even not familiar with the idea that deliberate observing of the children's behaviour is perhaps the most important part of their work.

One of the most difficult things for any teacher to do is to stand aside and watch without teaching. The phrase 'without involvement with the children' means exactly what it says. The teacher needs to sit away from the children in a corner of the room, the playground, or the garden, preferably in a small low chair, so as to be as inconspicuous as possible.* She should have a notebook and be sitting in such a position that all the children are well within her view. This is often difficult, for the children often demand attention from a seemingly passive and sitting adult, especially when she is familiar to them. They can also be curious about a 'visiting' adult and come to investigate, though my own impression when I was observing students on teaching practice was that the more involved the children were with interesting activities the less attention they paid to a seated adult. Co-operation between members of staff can overcome this obstacle, the participating teacher/helper encouraging the children to become interested in the activities provided. The children would also become accustomed with the situation as they did in our early research into the special training of teachers of the mentally handicapped in 1963.†

---

*Since writing the first edition of this book, many new schools for the child with severe learning handicap have been built by local education authorities. Some of them have included a special observation room with a one-way mirror for research and individual teaching purposes.

† I have an old film showing the ten children concerned (p. 35) being observed by students on the 1964 course. I am indebted to the National Association for Mental Health (now MIND, 22 Harley Street, London) for providing us with a small amount of money for this film. Professor R. A. C. Oliver, Manchester University, 'loaned' us his staff from the Educational Technology Department to take the film.

Techniques of observing. When and how   35

The observing teacher may decide to record all the activities of all the children in the group, or she may decide to devote each session to observe an individual child. At all times she needs to remember that these particular sessions are intended to increase her skill as an observer. She has to remember that she has to record exactly what she sees (and hears, if possible, although this is much more difficult) in as minute detail as possible. Some of her recordings might then be transferred to her own class record books or to the school record cards. When, at the end of the special session, she becomes once more the participating observer of the children in her class (that is to say, she responds spontaneously to the children in some of the ways suggested in previous pages as a result of her observations), she should find herself becoming gradually more easily aware of all the children, with their many needs and difficulties. I do not want to suggest that the teacher records every single incident about every child each day when she is fully in the teaching situation. This is clearly an impossible and unnecessary task, but by placing herself in a self-imposed and disciplined routine from time to time, the teacher can provide herself with the opportunity of developing a skill which then can be used profitably in the teaching and testing situation.

In order to demonstrate more fully this principle of non-involvement in developing observational skills, detailed jottings made by a student about a particular girl who was severely subnormal are reproduced on the following pages. The jottings are long because they describe, in some detail, activities which took place on three separate occasions, each lasting an hour. They are not edited because edited notes would not have had the precision of detail which was the aim of practising the skill. The notes are taken directly from the student's records on this particular child and show how the student drew no conclusions about the child's behaviour at the time she was recording. Only during later discussion were the child's needs, her behaviour, and her purposes examined and commented upon and these on the basis of what had been observed and recorded during the special observation sessions. But first let me explain how these sessions came about.

Ten children who were severely subnormal visited our college on one afternoon a week. They came to be observed by the students and staff and were allowed to choose their own activities for an hour. They could paint or make things with waste materials, dress up in hats and costumes provided, experiment in the music corner and at the water, sand, and pastry tables. They could play with the dolls' house and furniture, or make things with real tools at the full-sized woodwork bench. Whilst the children were working, three of the students were with them to see that they came to no harm, to make suggestions, and to provide materials which the children could not obtain themselves.

The activities took place in a large hall, the observing students sitting at one end. Each student observed and recorded the activities of one child. A row of tables separated the student group from the children. The observing students were instructed that, as far as possible, they were not to

36 *Techniques of observing. When and how*

respond to any child's advances but to encourage him to return to his activity.*

The observations recorded here refer to a girl we shall call Sylvia, almost 13 years old. She was grossly overweight and had reached puberty. She found difficulty in buttoning up her coat. We had little information about her home, no knowledge about her medical history and no psychological information. Indeed, the conditions under which we came to know her were like the practical teaching situation for the teachers at that time. In spite of this, however, we were able to reach some useful conclusions about her personality and her needs after four sessions of intensive observation.

First Week. Straight to the sand. She filled beaker to top with sand, patting it with her hand. Screamed 'Be quiet' to hammering group. Used a spoon to put more sand in beaker. Did it carefully, screamed to friend 'Be quiet'. Playing alongside Gerald. Using the whole bowl of sand. Showing teacher how she could use the scales. Pushed another boy out of the way so that she could get at the dry sand. Showed annoyance when the boy used the scales. Wanted him to put sand on the scales from her bowl. Emptied beaker and began to fill again. Put dry sand and wet sand in the beaker. Emptied it on the scales. Filled beaker with wet sand. When half full she poked the spoon in the sand, making hole. Continued to fill beaker with dry sand on top. Emptied sand on scales. Beaker held close to her face. Told teacher she was making a pie. Filled another beaker with wet and dry sand and put it on scales. Lifted all sand off scales and emptied it into her own bowl scraping bits off side. Told teacher she was making custard pie. Watched K. painting. Took someone else's paper and began to paint using bright red and black paint. Used orange, blue, and yellow paint. Paints were on her left side. She changed brush from right to left each time she painted. Watched children playing. Sylvia painting a pattern on another piece of paper. Watching teacher mixing paint. Shouted 'Shut up'. Painted all over the paper in different colours. Shouted 'Be quiet you. Shut up'.

Second Week. To sand. Spooned sand into scales then emptied some on top. Covered sand with dried peas. Put more sand on top of peas. Patted sand with spoon. Left the sand and asked R. where paper was. Looked round for a chair. Found herself one. Sat at painting table. Shouted to teacher that she wanted to paint. Began talking to the teacher and began to paint. Told her that she was painting a dog. Talked to R. Painting and talking to R. Smacked R. Shook paper up and down to see what happened. Asked for more paper. She did potato cuts. Woodwork bench and hammered nail down centre of bobbin for funnel on boat. Smacked J. and tried to take hammer from her. Took hold of screwdriver and tried screwing it into piece of wood. She asked J. for hammer. J. gave it to her. Using the hammer wrong way round. She could not hold nail by herself. Miss J. persevered and Sylvia tried to hold her own nail. Said she was making a table for her mother. Hammered the nail

---

* An analysis of the students' recordings was carried out and the findings were presented in a paper to The International Association for the Scientific Study of Mental Deficiency in 1964 in Copenhagen. I have described this research more fully in *The Educational and Social Needs of Children with Severe Handicap*. As a result of the interest of Asher Cashdan (a lecturer in the University of Manchester) in my approach in training teachers to observe directly the behaviour of mentally handicapped children I became a Special Lecturer (part-time) on his Advanced Course for teachers of the handicapped. This post enabled me to encourage about seventy qualified teachers to practise and adopt positive attitudes towards observing and recording detail in the behaviour of mentally handicapped children. Many of these teachers did their dissertations and M.Ed.s in the sphere of mental handicap. Later they became Heads in hospitals and schools for the mentally handicapped. One became a well-known research worker and two of them Tutors to Courses for teachers of the mentally handicapped. One became a Tutor to an Advanced Course for teachers of the handicapped.

Techniques of observing. When and how   37

vigorously. Used the hammer the wrong way round when Miss J. left. Tried to fix vice. Was unable to. Went to paint table. Painted an egg box with red paint. 'You guess', she said when Miss J. asked her what she was making. Then said, 'Plant pots of course'. Used paint brush first in one hand then in the other. Paints outside the box then inside. Tried to cut some corrugated paper. Tells Miss J. that the cardboard is 'flowers'. Pulling the paper rather than cutting it. Persevered. Tried to cut another piece of paper and manages it. Had painted it first. Sylvia cut small irregular shapes and these were flowers. She pastes large pieces on top. Presses a piece of paper full of paste on to table then folds up one edge of it. Got annoyed with P. because he was blowing a balloon in her neck. G. got off chair and got paper. Folded paper in three and started to cut it. Painted paper piece of grey paper. Put paste along edge. Went to ball box. Bounces red ball. Asked to go to toilet. Complained of a pain.

Third Week. Came into room and went to the shop. Wanted to know what went into empty rhubarb tin. Gathered chairs from around the room. Arranged them round the room. Argued with Miss J. about Pauline's chair. Arranged them in rows and counted them. Went to shop and found Xmas cards. She arranged them and said she was selling them. Tells Mrs R. to leave her alone. Picks up box from floor and puts it on the table pulling all Xmas cards out. Says to Miss H., 'Move it' referring to 'pie' on table. Stares at L. throwing rings on the board. Taking an interest in the 'pie'. Touches the 'Jam' (red paint) with her fingers. Stands all Xmas cards upright. Puts big ones at back small ones at front. Pulls glasses down on nose. Looks at the observers. Walks all round the table. Moves blackboard to one side. Tells Alan to go away when he approaches her and asks how much are the cards. 'A dollar'. Pointing at cards as though counting. Miss H. asks for three. She received one. She takes glasses off and refuses to put them on. Plays with cards. At same table as J. picks up a spoon. Green spoon she says. Plays with red paint. Tells Mrs R. and Mrs M. to go away. Stirs paint and shows Mrs T. When asked what she is doing she is making patterns. Alan approaches with a balloon on a stick. Sylvia shouts, 'Get away, get away', putting glasses on and off. Watches J. and Pauline playing with a balloon. 'Get off you little pig', to Miss T. splashing paint on to paper. Scraping as much paint out of the tin that there is. Resists suggestions from Miss K. to print with the printing materials. Miss H. shows her how to paint one of the printers. Sylvia paints over it. Later she paints the printing apparatus and begins to make a pattern. Makes patterns with end of spoon by herself.

During the first week we discovered from her behaviour that she needed glasses, for we had noted *'beaker held close to her face'*. Inquiry not only confirmed our suspicions but brought to light that she owned a pair of glasses but had not yet formed the habit of wearing them. Here, then, was one of her many needs. An understanding teacher, with immense determination, was now needed to ensure that over a long period of time Sylvia was encouraged to wear her glasses each day until she herself found that she benefited. In co-operation with the home it was now necessary for a busy teacher to carry out an irksome but necessary task. In helping Sylvia it would be vital to keep a pair of glasses in school, so that the excuse *'they are at home'* might not upset the teacher's plan to help her establish the habit of wearing them. Perhaps a special reward system might need to be devised too. We also discovered in the first week that Sylvia did not get on very well with other children and that she tended to push, to threaten both adults and children with her body as well as in words. Another of her needs, therefore, was for us to discover the reasons for the behaviour and to help her to be kinder to the other children and to share with them the materials and attention from adults.

38   *Techniques of observing. When and how*

The general preliminary picture of this child seemed to suggest that some home visits might be useful. Such visits might ascertain what sort of difficulties existed which tended to make Sylvia so aggressive in our free situation. It is probable that she was imitating the behaviour of her parents.*

The records tell us that Sylvia needed to have experience of, and to experiment with, many of the materials that she found available in the playroom. She needed to be able to touch and manipulate some of them; she needed to be shown how to create something with others. The way in which she held her paint brush and constantly changed hands to use it informed us that she had not yet established hand-preference and that she might, in fact, need specific guidance in this matter from her teacher. On the other hand, hand-preference is part of normal child development and it was reasonable, therefore, to expect that this would occur without special help unless the eye defect caused this particular aspect of development. Teachers might be interested to observe when hand-preference is stabilized in the children in their groups. It might be one of the readiness signals for them to spend time on more academic learning with those children achieving it.†

Words used in her conversation show that she had some idea that an action was going to take place in the future, that she associated the word 'dollar' with money values. She had obviously arrived at the stage in play when adult activities were enacted with some enthusiasm; the notes show that she concentrated on 'shop activity' with the Xmas cards for forty minutes. The activities we observed and recorded infer that she enjoyed using her imagination, not only in the sand when she represented a 'custard pie' in sand, but creatively when painted egg-box sections became 'plant pots' and when she cut 'flowers' from the cardboard.

One can see from these records that Sylvia became absorbed in the painting activities. Later records show that, although this was her main interest, she became, in fact, more interested in the activities of other children as well as more affable towards them, in spite of occasional lapses into aggressive and difficult behaviour. One would hope that attention to the factor involving the wearing of her glasses, to her weight, and the provision of experiences which were satisfying her, would help her to integrate more successfully with the group.

If the teacher perseveres with these rather special observing sessions, it may be found that the habit of conscious attention to all aspects of the children's behaviour becomes an established part of her relationship with them, i.e. whenever she is with them she is noticing not only obviously interesting but also apparently trivial aspects of their behaviour and, whenever possible, is responding purposefully to them.

The importance of observing and attending to the apparently trivial came to mind particularly when I was with children in Special Care Units.

---

* Inference added 1976 after meeting her parents.
† Two years after these notes were written, Sylvia had established hand-preference (i.e. at 15 years).

Techniques of observing. When and how   39

They were all matters of communication. One of my intentional personal habits as a teacher has been to wear something which attracted the children's attention and often caused them to communicate in some way or other with me about it. (A doctor known to me, working in the homes of the severely subnormal and the maladjusted, found similar responses to her fur.) Sometimes this was a piece of costume jewellery.

I recall how one small young girl, with no speech and unable to walk, apparently having no interest in anything around her, slowly moved her eyes in the direction of my brooch, looked into my face and then to the brooch again. The observed movement of her eyes communicated to me that she wished to be picked up and put into such a position that she could touch and look more clearly at the object which had, apparently, caught her attention. When this was done, I spent some time with the child, talking about the brooch, taking it off, showing her the pin, fastening it on again and letting her touch it.

A speechless mongol boy pointed to my woollen hat and then to his teacher's head. I asked her to look at what he was trying to say. 'Do you want me to put on Mrs S.'s hat?' she asked. In quick response, he nodded.

Peter, a blind spastic boy who had lain on a mattress for years in a Special Care Unit,* was observed making some slight controlled banging movement of his right leg. 'That's where we might begin,' his teacher commented, 'with the movement in that leg.' She responded by making him a specially improvised instrument from wood and a toy concertina, the sound from which could only be brought forth by Peter if he used the controlled banging movement in his leg against the instrument. She also made him a 'frieze' which was placed on the wall against which his mattress had been pushed.† The frieze contained many textures which he could feel with his feet. An egg carton fixed to the frieze could, because of its three dimensional quality, also be pushed off with his strong foot with obvious enjoyment.

---

* 'Special Care Unit' was the name given to a class within the schools for mentally handicapped children with very profound degrees of handicap either in terms of multiple severe sensory defects or gross motor defects; highly disturbed hyperactive behaviour or withdrawn behaviour patterns. The Salford Mental Health Department was an early pioneer in this field. It provided an educational approach with parental involvement in research as early as 1960. The Medical Officer's Reports of that time will give interested readers the details of this work as will specific reference to those individuals working in Salford at that time, e.g. A. Kushlick, M. Susser, R. McKay (now Consultant Paediatrician at the Agnew Unit, Manchester Royal Children's Hospital), E. Lunzer (currently Professor of Education, University of Nottingham), Pamela Harding (currently a senior psychologist in Warwickshire), Anwys Riley (currently psychologist at the Agnew Unit), and Dr A. Wiseman (sometime Assistant Medical Officer of Health, Salford). Many schools have experimented (since the late 'sixties) with the practice of integrating these children amongst the more competent children in the school. To my knowledge no comparative research has yet been done to examine the pros and cons of such an approach in the field of mental handicap. Perhaps the 'individualness' of each child would militate against useful findings in such an exercise.

† In my more recent visits to hospitals and schools I have seen a wide variety of 'feely friezes'. The imagination of the students and the teachers making such friezes has known no bounds. To date I have not heard of them being made by educational supply companies.

4 Observing and teaching the young mentally handicapped child

When he is playing with an adult: 1st stage

One of the games I like to play with adults attending my play workshops is to present them with the sight of a large, closed holdall. I then suggest that they get into small groups for 3 to 5 minutes and tell each other what they think is in the bag, suitable for young children to play with. In using this involvement strategy, members of a course are being encouraged to project and share their own experience of what they provide for young children, or to use their imagination and knowledge of the question of what they would provide if they had to. At the end of such a 'buzz' session each member of the group chooses one toy to tell the whole group (including me) about and how it is/might be used with a particular child. Then I open my bag and show the actual contents. They are the materials I have used when playing with and observing pre-school young mentally handicapped children at home, usually in front of their mothers.

Strings of different textures, colours, lengths; transparent/non-transparent squeezy bottles—some left as they are sold (of course emptied of their contents and well cleaned out), some with the tops cut off to make a larger opening for the child to stuff things into, put his hand into or to rake things out that the adult has put in. The cut-off part becomes in fact a funnel for play in another way. 'Crisp 'n Dry' triangular-shaped bottles and light-weight plastic lemonade bottles used as toys give the handicapped child in the early stages of intellectual and play development plenty of opportunity for experimenting in throwing, banging them together, feeling them. They give the involved adult (and the adult *must* be involved at this sensori-motor stage) an opportunity to observe and record (preferably on a tape recorder because the responses are so quick and so varied) whether, what, and *how* the child plays with them. Because they are real objects, although being used as play objects, they can in fact be given names quite easily as the child is playing with them. Slow and very, very fast movements can be made by the adult playing with the child, for example, with the string—putting it into any of the openings of the plastic bottles and pulling it out in front of the child ... s ... l ... o ... w ... l ... y, or quickly. When the child has had sufficient experience of this kind, and if he has no physical handicap, he will do it for himself in his own way for the adult.

My holdall also contains a collection of varied coloured nylon and woollen scarves and a lot of leather belts and purses in a handbag. The handbag also has a spectacles case, a ring case with rings in it, a pair of

Observing and teaching the young mentally handicapped child   41

furry gloves, a comb, and a brush. The scarves are particularly useful for hiding one's own and the child's face under. A large teddy bear extends the hiding and 'dressing' up play, for he can have his face hidden. He can have scarves put round his neck by the adult or the child. Playing with a child straddled between one's legs (trousers are needed) in front of a mirror is a useful teaching position technique and one that I can thoroughly recommend.

Thick paper, thin paper, moulded biscuit/chocolate box paper, cardboard pieces, thick card, corrugated cardboard, tin foil, tracing paper, tissue paper, paper hankies, in other words all kinds of paper—can give a handicapped child many learning experiences in the realms of listening and touching. This learning aid also costs no money but it does take thought and time to collect. These materials were all in my holdall. The aids for learning are so very often right under our noses but we fail to become aware of them and their uses because we are always in the habit of looking for commercial aids and toys. We do not always live in the kind of creative climate that encourages us to innovate, to use our imagination—especially with regards to waste materials. The other important thing to remember with all these 'costing no money materials' is that they are clean, and can be destroyed without our worrying about the cost (or requisition 'checks'). They are safe when being used by a child, with an adult alongside him, playing with these 'toys' too.

Perhaps my favourite toys are those that move. The children learn to focus, to pay attention to these in particular, and whilst they are looking at the toys being activated by the adult they are 'thinking' about what makes them move. I call them causality toys.* I know they are useful in the learning process but of course you as the adult have to enjoy playing with them too. I have a little walking policeman, a moving upright mouse, a mouse that moves along when you move him backwards and forwards on a surface, a butterfly that moves his wings up and down when wound up, some winding up, jumping frogs, and some flapping dolphins (moving their fins when wound up and flapping them in water). I look for these moving toys not only in toy shops but in newsagents shops too. They are relatively inexpensive but invaluable when playing with the very young mentally handicapped child. I also have a monkey who climbs a string when pulled and two wooden jointed dolls from Africa whose arms and legs 'dance' when the strings are pulled. A retractable sewing tape measure, involving pulling and pressing, is a great source of fun and a serious anticipation activity.

In collecting such toys I have slow- and fast-moving, as well as soft- and loud-sounding, ones in view. The jumping frogs make a terrible din. A slow-moving wind-up crocodile, and a very fast red car complete my moving toys collection. Toys that do not move but do make interesting sounds or even no sound, depending upon the surface thrown on when

---

* Cf. Gregory, 1972 in Stevens, M. (1976) *The Educational and Social Needs of Children with Severe Handicap, 2nd Edition,* pp. 47–52.

42   *Observing and teaching the young mentally handicapped child*

banged or thrown by the child or the adult, are among my collection here—several velvet mice, and a large velvet frog shape (stuffed with hard but small items—lentils or rice, not polystyrene). In referring back to the moving toys I ought to say that generally speaking these are not toys that the child can manipulate himself (although older mentally handicapped children under 5 do have the physical strength to do so). Such toys not only catch and keep the children's attention. Their movement characteristics give him something to assimilate perceptually.

Plastic bowls varying in diameter and size are clearly very useful learning toys. My particular set cost well under a pound and I have had them for at least 5 years. They are childproof. Objects can be hidden under them (moving objects that make a noise are especially exciting for the child in the teaching programme). Very tiny children can be put inside the bowls and moved around the floor or round on the spot by the adult.

But what else does my holdall contain—many small musical instruments. As I have explained in *The Educational and Social Needs of Children with Severe Handicap* (p. 64), adults working with little handicapped children need to know the joy of relaxing with them through music. An old tin tray, tin lids and tins containing a variety of substances (stones, rice), toothbrush holders containing grains of rice, silver cake balls, a musical toothbrush* (from Boots the chemist), a pull-out string toy (as the string returns into the small box a nursery rhyme is played), a plastic hammer (Woolworth's) containing tiny beads, two wooden pop guns, two kazoos, two small tambourines, rattles of varying sounds and sizes, several bells with different qualities of sounds, a plastic hand puppet that rattles, a whistle, pan pipes, and bells.

There is also a small collection of children's records so that sometimes we could accompany the record with the instruments. I would like to see all teachers of the young mentally handicapped child, and nurses and parents too, with such a collection of toys, for ideally speaking the children should have had all these play experiences before they come to school. Most local education authorities are not yet making provision for the under-5s so it is possible that they will not have had such learning experiences with these 'opportunist' materials—materials where the teacher, nurse, or parent can seize an opportunity for learning. Clearly there is no limit to the kind of plaything an adult can provide, at no great cost, if he collects items of all kinds over the years and 'treasures' what he collects, even if it is only a specially shaped bottle. The concept needs to be gained that *all* objects are toys to a child. Objects often have names. Some

---

*It was interesting when I attempted to encourage David (2 years and very physically handicapped) to hold the tinkly toothbrush in his right hand. He dropped it every time. I put it into his left hand and he held it for at least a minute. We must always examine our own concepts when working with a handicapped child. If we do it that way he will not do it—if we present it in a different way he might. R. I. McKay† suggests that we stroke the back of a child's hand in order to enable him to open it and thus enable us to put some object into it.

† McKay, R. I. (1976) *Mental Handicap in Child Health Practice*, Butterworths, London.

Observing and teaching the young mentally handicapped child 43

toys do not. I have found my particular collection of objects extremely useful in my own play experience with handicapped children having a mental age under 3 years. It has also enabled me to understand more clearly the underlying structures inherent in the sensori-motor stage of development.*

So many mentally handicapped children suffer severe perceptual deprivation. This has often happened not always because of the child's own difficulties, but because the adults he knows do not always know the kind of toy to provide in his early stages of development. Then they are surprised when later he is unable to play. Sometimes these toys are not placed in a wide enough variety of positions so that the child can 'do things' to (operate upon) them. Piaget, in playing with his own babies, provided so many object experiences for them that those of us who are interested in the importance of play in learning cannot afford to ignore his actual provision.

Once more I have studied his observations rather than his theories and 'taken out' the toys he gave his children to stimulate their thinking processes before they were 2 years old.† After reading about these experiences you will surely realize how deprived some of our young and profoundly handicapped children are. Especially will this be so when you compare what they are often given, with what Piaget gave his children, e.g. a stick,‡ a chain, spools attached with elastic, celluloid parrots (they would be plastic now), a sponge, a paper knife, a rubber monkey, an unfolded newspaper, a big box, knick-knacks (he does not specify what these were but we all have them in our homes), a pipe, a toy lamb and a bear, a bird shape mounted on a plank of wood with wheels on it, an indiarubber, a hanging puppet, a slide rule, a plastic protractor, a strap, a stick of sealing wax, a watch, different dolls, a wallet, a tin box, a cushion, a beret, spectacles, a big piece of paper, a cigarette case, a plastic duck and doll and parrot all on the same string,§ a matchbox, playing with all objects along with a cushion (think of the various sizes and textures and colours here), a thimble, a piece of wood, a ball, a red balloon, a ball of wool (somewhere else I have suggested a bandage; this must have been my

---

* Cf. The Uzgiris and Hunt Scale and my own list of structured activities in *The Educational and Social Needs of Children with Severe Handicap, 2nd Edition,* pp. 47–55 and p. 85 onwards.

† Cf. pp. 176–356 in *The Origins of Intelligence.*

‡ Nathan, a normal child (14 months), saw a plant on his mother's kitchen surface. It had been brought by a guest that morning. Among his play things was a long cardboard tube from tin foil. He began to use this as an extended arm to reach the plant. The action was an interesting one developmentally. Socially it was not a useful skill if it meant breaking the plant. This was just removed by his mother without comment.

§ Parents of very young handicapped children need to remember to hang objects over the child's head when he is sitting in a swing chair, and also alongside the swing bars. As the swing goes backwards and forwards the child will hear interesting sounds. This will be particularly so if the toys are changed each week with some regard paid by the teacher to the quality of the sound presented. I saw this latter opportunity provided for a child in a Special Care Unit class by a student (Audrey Coates) in 1965. It certainly attracted the child's attention.

44 *Observing and teaching the young mentally handicapped child*

assimilation of his ball of wool with my own adaptation to the suggestion), a straw table-mat, a notebook, a wooden elephant, a beaded bag, a big red crayon, a thermometer, a plush toy cat (this has a ribbon round his neck—mine has green bead eyes), a wooden hen with a ball and string attached to its head to actuate the movement, a necktie, an empty metal shaving-stick case, soap, a soap case, a piece of bread, a plug, a wooden horse, a postcard, a toy plush dog and rabbit, two cushions, a watch, and a box, a bottle on a handkerchief, a brush (I can think of a variety—can you?), a necklace, a shoehorn, objects attached to string, ribbons, a pail and a stick (it could be plastic), a flask, a leather donkey, a very large cork, Russian dolls, a cardboard hen, a book placed in different positions, a quilt and a lamb and a fish (shaking the quilt to make the animal/fish move from the top to the bottom), a long wooden ruler, a cup, various lengths of stick, different-sized apertures through which to push things, a shawl, an ivory plate containing two holes and a pencil, a fish, a swan, and a frog.

I have listed all the objects (toys) that Piaget introduced to his own children before they were 2 in order to stimulate your thinking about the possibilities inherent in such objects for giving a child rich play experiences. The more you experiment with and think about the characteristics of these objects the more you will discover their value for stimulating structured responses in the young mentally handicapped,* and sometimes in the older profoundly handicapped child. You will of course COMBINE your own selection of objects in order to give the child the opportunities you feel are 'right' for him at his particular stage of development. For those adults who are interested in the accurate recording of a child's behaviour when in the company of an interesting and interested adult I can do no better than to refer you to the original recordings of Piaget and in particular to those observations indicating the results of particular experiences he gave to his children over a period of hours/days.†

If you read the recorded observations of Piaget himself you will come to realize how really easy it is to 'play' with children—in a way that is concerned with the learning process. The difficult thing seems to me to be in persuading adults that play is indeed so valuable and one of the rights of all children.

When he is playing with the adult and is able to remain seated spontaneously for periods lasting between 5 and 40 minutes: 2nd stage

The length of time a child can remain seated perhaps depends on the adult's ability to use his imagination and language relevant to the child's

---

* I wanted to stimulate licking and the putting out of the tongue in a very, very handicapped baby. I used a fluted glass beer mug. The raised parts and perhaps the coldness of the glass itself clearly gained a positive response.

† In *The Origins of Intelligence in the Child* (1966), translated Margaret Cook; Routledge and Kegan Paul, London, pp. 282–7 and 290–4.

Observing and teaching the young mentally handicapped child 45

stage of development as much as upon the child's stage of development. I would like to suggest that this particular form of play will arrive after he has played in the ways suggested by the toys I have already described, i.e. when he is able to conserve objects and some events, when he is at the associative and imitative stage of play. In playing myself, and in training teachers of the mentally handicapped to understand this kind of 'reconstructive' play, I have provided the following toys structured and initially arranged in ways suggesting specific activity for child–adult participation, and in ways which encourage a give and take kind of situation.

Table play
Strong wooden dolls' table about 8 inches high and 10 to 12 inches long. Two wooden chairs to fit this particular-sized table. Two or even three dolls for this set—if one doll can be a man doll so much the better. A kitchen cupboard with easy opening doors and shelves with hooks. Sets of two cups and saucers and plates, knives and forks and spoons (in metal and plastic, and in different colours).* Salt and pepper set. Two wooden egg cups and egg shapes. (I have had pot eggs from the pet shop. Somehow they have not yet been thrown so as to hurt or to damage anything. Papier mâché eggs could be made.) Plasticine to make pretend 'food'.

I do not think that any further explanation is necessary to demonstrate how the adult should play with such a collection of toys. If you follow the child and lead him as well *without inhibition* then you will be surprised at your own ability to play with a child so young and mentally handicapped as well. Remember to tell him stories using the toys.

Cooking play
Another set of toys includes: a stove 6 to 8 inches high with knobs to turn it on and off, a battery-driven light (the reinforcement in a realistic play situation) which appears when the stove is 'on', small pans, a casserole dish with lid, and a frying pan. Plasticine 'potatoes', peas, sausages (all in miniature) can afford the child much pleasure and the adult the opportunity for using words in a meaningful situation. The child is always in this situation being given an opportunity to imitate mother in the kitchen, to become aware of mother in the kitchen.

This particular set of toys can be used separately from the next set.

---

* The idea of providing different sizes/colours/materials in terms of the cups and saucers, and knives and forks, was suggested when I was playing with Jamie (a Down's Syndrome child of 4 years). I asked him to bring me the fork and I pointed too. He failed to see the fork because of course it was made of white plastic (motorway cafés are a lovely source of play material if you keep it). His mother was frustrated because she knew he knew 'fork'. Clearly it was only the fork he used at his own table. Writing about this experience suggests that perhaps we should be using the child's own objects to play with, particularly if we are playing in the home with the child. Matching cards are a familiar activity in all schools for the mentally handicapped. How often do we see photographs of the child's own clothes, furniture, etc., with the real objects to match or a second set of pictures to match? Would the cost be so prohibitive? W. Gillham, in his book *The First Hundred Words* (in press) George Allen and Unwin, suggests the extensive use of a Polaroid camera.

46 *Observing and teaching the young mentally handicapped child*

Combining them can perhaps enable the adult to play for a longer period of time with the child. Whichever plan he decides to follow he should try to think out some of the words including nouns (names), verbs (doing words), and prepositions (spatial words like on, in, or at, etc.) he is going to use in his conversation with the child. The child's actions should help here—that is if you give your whole attention to the task in hand and become involved.

Washing-up play
(1) Small stainless-steel sink unit with taps that really turn on water, a plug to let it flow away,* complete with a drawer, and a cupboard.
(2) A rack for the tiny plates, cups and saucers, plates, jug, and teapot.
(3) Different sets of cups, saucers, plates, and cutlery that will fit into the sink.

These toys have given endless hours of pleasure to children as well as giving the adult an opportunity to structure the child's learning experiences. Some Plasticine modelled into shapes can enable the child and the adult to have a pretend meal and then 'wash up' later. A small tablet of soap and a tiny tea-towel can add to the reality of the play situation. Such experiences are surely preparing the child for the later experience of washing and drying his own hands.

Washing and getting ready for bed play
Providing the child with a plastic bowl, a dressed doll, soap, towel, nail brush, toothbrush, pyjamas, and a bed is yet another set of structured toys one might see both in the pre-school years and at school in the earliest years, e.g. up to 8, 9, or even 10 years.

Bedroom play
The items for this include a small pillow, blanket, sheet and cover, two small dolls, a chest of three drawers, and an armchair.

My play with A. when he was 3 and able to sit *spontaneously* for short periods of time with me and the little toys began with this particular set of toys. We talked about mummy and daddy, making the bed, one in the bed, one sitting on the chair, etc. At one point he placed a doll on its stomach in bed (his mother's sleeping position, I discovered from her).

Park play and the Weebles
An extremely well made and durable set of toys. The people are egg-shaped and plastic. They wobble but they never roll away. A slide, two swings, a roundabout, and a swing boat complete the set. Expensive initially (£3–5), but worthwhile in terms of the motor activity involved that will give the child spatial concepts; in terms of the language the child could hear from an adult *when he is free to choose and initiate his own activity.*

---

* Available through a mail order firm at no more than £5 for each piece of equipment.

Observing and teaching the young mentally handicapped child   47

One aspect of a discovery approach (and my own observation experience as a teacher of teachers of the mentally handicapped leads me to believe that the mentally handicapped child needs such an approach as do normal children) is that the teacher must know she has to be an excellent provider. At the risk of incurring the displeasure of my nursing and teaching colleagues, and the impatience of some reviewers, I must state that my general impression is that still (1977) not enough of the right kind of learning materials are being provided in schools and perhaps in homes too to cater adequately for the educational needs of these children. I must continue stating this fact for I know that money is not always the problem. Imagination and initial effort is needed to design and MAKE (or arrange for the making of) teaching aids especially for the mentally handicapped. Whilst some special and most interesting books have been compiled to help parents play with their young handicapped children,* there seems to be a dearth of 3-D teaching material published by educational supply firms. There seems to be a block on their part in approaching those working specifically with the mentally handicapped to use more effectively ideas that have been 'floating around' for years in this now accepted field of special education.

The kind of social climate where children are free to choose and initiate their own activities will afford the best scope for the teachers to observe. It might be the best environment anyway in which most of the children will find it easier to learn because above all it will be relaxed, and it will be stimulating because the adult has the children's needs in mind in preparing for them.

The more experience one has with young mentally handicapped children in school the less one can refer to them in terms of age or say with any certainty what each child needs to have in the classroom. Some of them will undoubtedly have developmental ages of under 1 year, others will be functioning at a $2–2\frac{1}{2}$-year-old level. One thing is certain, however, and that is the environment itself needs to be structured in such a way as to stimulate and excite the curiosity and the action of the children. It must enable them to 'operate' (think about, do something to, and think about) upon the materials provided. Because of the wide range of development that will inevitably be presented within this group, an enormous range of activities must be provided initially and added to and developed by the teacher as she sees the needs of the individuals within the group.

The results of the experiences gained by the children with the aid of genuinely interested, involved, and skilled adults will depend to some extent on their determination to experiment over a long period of time with many ideas before deciding to reject those not thought to be working. By using the phrase 'a long period of time' I am thinking in terms of about

---

* *The Barnaby Books* (1976), Jeffrees, D. and McConkey, R., published by L.D.A. Park Works, Wisbech, Cambs. PE13 2AX. *Let me Speak* (1976) and *Let me Play* (1977), published by Souvenir Press Educational and Academic Ltd., 43 Great Russell Street, London WC1B 3PA.

48   *Observing and teaching the young mentally handicapped child*

18 months to 2 years. This will apply to teachers and others who have had no specialized training in this work. Either they will have worked in more formal environments with children or they will go into schools where the methods I am advocating have not yet been implemented for one reason or another.

The experiences the adults will give to the children will not only depend upon their growing understanding from detailed observation of their behaviour followed up by some kind of recording, but also on their ability to use the many developmental scales and assessment techniques coming into their own in this field of education. Dr Robert McKay, consultant pediatrician at the well-known Manchester Royal Children's Hospital Assessment Unit, Pendlebury, Lancashire, has provided us with a comprehensive list of available scales.* He has also made useful comments about them regarding whether anyone can use them, whether they are closed tests (i.e. to be used by psychologists or doctors, etc.), and where they can be purchased.

Children coming from restrictive homes and from those which are said to be overprotective† will need special consideration; so will those children whose development is more stunted than it might be because of poor teaching and the lack of appropriate stimulation and experiences. Such children are always part of the educational community whatever school they attend and however much money is spent on educational provision.

However, there is broadly speaking a group in every school for the mentally handicapped which is young and physically small. It is with this group, whose mental levels as I have suggested previously will range from below 1 year to $2\frac{1}{2}$ years, that the following paragraphs are concerned. An essential part of the environment seems to be an open door leading to somewhere that is interesting, affording the child space in which to find himself, and still be safe. These children are at the 'in and out of everything' stage if they are allowed to be themselves and not forced to sit and be quiet. They do need maximum opportunities to explore the immediate safe environment amongst familiar, interested, and friendly people—people who are concerned about the quality of the experience the child has in his life, people who are aware at all times about the kind of

---

* *Mental Handicap in Child Health Practice* (1976), Butterworths, London.

† Whenever descriptions of the parents of mentally handicapped children are made, we need to question on what basis the description has been made and to ask ourselves if we were the parents of such and such a child would we behave in any different way. I have quite recently come across a school where those concerned have refused to take in a 6-year-old blind mongol child with a heart lesion unless the mother can have her there for the school assembly! The child does in fact not wake up until the middle of the morning and the mother has several difficulties to cope with in this situation as you might imagine with all her handicaps. Such a mother is described by the authority as being overprotective towards her child. The family has the added complication of anticipating this child's early death. Whilst one has to fight against a sentimental approach towards the mentally handicapped and their families, there do seem to me to be limits of expectancy beyond which my profession should not go. Caring and feeling for another human being in distress seems to be an element that is missing in much of our past *and* present teacher training programmes—having things 'correct' of much more significance!

Observing and teaching the young mentally handicapped child 49

emotional atmosphere that might exist in his own home. When one sees some of the present practices in schools for the mentally handicapped one can only conclude that many of the teachers somehow manage to inhibit* their thinking about the homes the children they are teaching come from. Perhaps the parents have a duty here to invite the teacher home to tea.

Mentally handicapped children, as do normal children, like to look at themselves in a mirror. A large mirror safely attached to the classroom wall is of use in helping the children learn about themselves and the movements of their bodies. I should remind you that when I first suggested this to my students in 1961 there was hardly a mirror to be seen in the schools (junior training centres), neither was photographing the children 'allowed'. Hiding the children away from themselves and from the community at large was certainly a very common feature of their lives 20 years ago. There will be times during the day when a child will leave his chosen activity and seek the personal attention of an adult. Sometimes he will wish to sit on her knee to listen to her talking to him, to hear a song, to look at pictures. A comfortable easy chair and perhaps a settee would enable a very secure relationship for both adult and child to emerge. They would also afford a skilled observer opportunity to note the child's behaviour at very close quarters.

Edith Cave, speaking at a symposium reported in *Mental Retardation, Concepts of Education and Research*,† reiterates my earlier observations of the needs of these young children, for she states, 'I was interested to observe how the whole programme was inspired less by preconceived ideas of structure or design than by the teacher's own concept of good mothering for young children, so one needs to appoint the right kind of teacher in addition to compiling a suitably structured programme.' I should like to add that we need to be much more careful in our selection of students to present initial courses for teachers of the mentally handicapped. Many of the colleges organize academic courses on mental handicap and demand high academic standards of those entering the college. We need highly intelligent students on such courses but we also need those able to use their imagination, to be spontaneous, and have practical gifts of one kind or another. Perhaps we need to attempt to assess their commitment to the mentally handicapped so that time AND public money is not wasted enabling them to find out whether they are committed or not. Perhaps a medical examination of the students before admission to college needs to be more stringent and communicated to the tutors concerned. I have recently discovered at least one student with sight in one eye only and another with some hearing loss. The disabled need to be involved with the mentally handicapped in a wide variety of ways, but as I see it teaching demands an adult without such handicaps, particularly when this involves the mentally handicapped. As this book will suggest, skilled observation in the visual and auditory fields of behaviour need to be noted and

---

* Perhaps this is a safeguard against their anxiety in this particular teaching situation.
† Tizard, J. (Ed.), (1974) Butterworths, London.

50   *Observing and teaching the young mentally handicapped child*

recorded in order to satisfy the child's needs. How can this be effectively carried out if a teacher is disabled?

Large play apparatus (climbing frames and bars, slides, and swings for both indoor and outdoor use) is absolutely essential in order to enable the children to develop gross body movements and body awareness. It is also essential that the adults recognize the child's need and right to use this at will and not only in specific planned periods. In some areas known to the writer, too much time is being spent by the teachers getting the child used to sitting down so that he will 'behave better for his parents'. As I understand it the greatest need of these children, as of all young children and those normal children in first and middle school, is to move about spontaneously without too much adult restriction. If the child has this freedom, with all due attention given to his safety, he will grow in confidence in the use of his body in space. Admittedly some children will need additional attention to their movement activities—activities such as those suggested in the individual programmes designed by R. Nicholls*—but the majority of these children will move easily and naturally if they are given the fullest opportunities to do so. Large apparatus will also stimulate the child's imagination and help his social development.

Plenty of pushing and pulling toys in a variety of shapes and sizes should be available, as well as rocking toys. Simple and very sturdily built trucks will allow the children plenty of choice in ways of playing with them. Fitting toys and form boards† of all kinds, as well as nesting cups and barrels, are also essential. However, such toys should be part of the adult's teaching apparatus and should be used in the individual teaching situation. Too often one sees teachers giving out the apparatus to sitting children accompanied by helpers, and no record of the child's response to the apparatus, or whether it is too difficult or easy, is kept. If a dated record of all the table apparatus used by each child is kept for all to see, the same old pieces of apparatus will not then be presented to the child over and over again with little extension of the activity. Jigsaw puzzles and inset boards unfortunately are so very often just filling-in activities, as are so many of the matching cards flooding our classrooms for the mentally handicapped in the 'seventies. Teachers need to sort out such pieces of apparatus and grade them according to difficulty and interest level.

Other teachers on the other hand, encouraged by their headteachers and LEA organizers, are encouraging their assistants to use toys in specific ways. Bricks of varying sizes and textures (wood, rubber, foam, plastic) will stimulate the children to play and will also give the observing teacher an indication of their levels of development in play. Trays, tins, boxes, and bags to fill and empty will widen the children's experience and give them early impressions of space and 'volume'. If varying sizes of cloth shopping bags in the same colour are made by the teacher and presented

---

*Obtainable from R. H. Nicholls, Tesdale and Bennett House Schools, Abingdon, Oxfordshire.

†I have designed a 'tea time' inset board. Those wishing information about this should write to me. I have compiled a set of games to accompany this apparatus.

Observing and teaching the young mentally handicapped child   51

to the children in the pretend shop, the children will discover that they cannot fit as many bricks into that bag as that one, providing the bricks are the same size too.

The easiest, cheapest, and most popular toy that any young child can have, whether he is handicapped or not, is a large collection of cardboard boxes. Some of these will be large enough for him to climb into. Whilst strongly made wooden and plastic boxes are now available from educational suppliers (and since 1971 the headteachers in schools for the mentally handicapped have had more to spend on equipment), the weight of even quite large cardboard boxes is generally such that the children can move them around and tumble about in them without hurting themselves.

One of my students, the Head of a Spastic Society School, cut out different-shaped holes in the side of the box and seating a child in the box with a lot of toys gave the child a 'big posting experience'. An adult outside the box retrieved and returned the toys, sometimes over the top of the box, sometimes through the same hole as the child had pushed the toy through, and sometimes through a different one. In discussion with another student needing help on her teaching practice with young mentally handicapped children I suggested that she placed a line of really large cardboard boxes along the whole length of a wall in her room. In order for a child to gain entrance to the box in different positions she was encouraged to think of different kinds of openings. One can imagine that such an idea could in fact be commercialized—in fact the boxes could be made half in perspex, half in an opaque material. The perspex sides could be in a variety of colours too. Such a toy would afford the children a wealth of motor and closure experiences.* Perhaps the cost would be prohibitive! However, imaginative teachers might discover ways and means of making such a piece of apparatus more cheaply and share their ideas with their colleagues and the parents too.

As I write another idea occurs to me. The Toy Library Association has developed its ideas in the past few years. I have not yet heard of a school, however, organizing a toy library for its own children with a special post for the teacher acting as librarian. Such a post might be comparable to that of the librarian in a comprehensive school.

Posting boxes in wood or strong card are popular at this stage. They do not always need to be bought from shops. In addition to being rather small they are generally rather expensive and they are rarely structured in their design with mentally handicapped children in mind. A variety of cardboard boxes, some cuboid, some oblong (shoe boxes), could be used as could all the plastic containers for food and ice cream. Recycling them for children would cost little and afford the children essential learning experiences. I would like to see sets of these boxes with one hole in the top, two holes, then three, etc. Each hole would be the same shape so that the child would really gain the motor experience of the shape. Perhaps

---

* For an understanding of the term 'closure' refer to the revised version of the Illinois Test of Psycholinguistic Abilities.

52   *Observing and teaching the young mentally handicapped child*

some shapes would be those of objects instead of abstract circles, squares, and triangles. The fall of the object seems to be a motivator in terms of the activity. Most commercial posting boxes have a number of holes on top of the box. Teachers designing home-made ones might consider the possibility of putting holes in different positions of the box itself, e.g. at the side. Schools could perhaps involve church and WI groups in making these simple toys for the young mentally handicapped child.

The essential point about posting toys is that young children need holes through which to push objects. Not only are they having a motor experience in playing with such toys but a visual one as well. If toys being pushed make a noise, yet another experience will be gained. The teacher needs to think out here the number of modalities she wishes to give the child experience of. A large pillar box provided in the classroom, and made by the classroom assistant in the classroom, after the children have actually posted a letter or a postcard, is another useful posting experience, particularly if some thought is given to the shape, size, and weight of the 'letters', cards and parcels being 'posted'.

One of the advantages of the old 2-year courses of training for teachers of the mentally handicapped (1964–72) was that one was afforded the opportunities of functioning in a spontaneous creative climate, particularly when one had creative colleagues alongside one—students and staff triggered the thinking of each other. Jean Fraser was teaching the other students a song, 'There was an old woman who swallowed a fly, I wonder why she swallowed a fly, I think she'll die'. As the students were singing I had an idea for a posting-box aid for this song—it was gruesome from the adults' point of view but those students making it in their own way and using it with mentally handicapped children found out how much they liked it.

Another student, Mrs Nye, made a large cardboard cut-out of an old woman in a bright apron and mob-cap. She mounted her on the side of a cardboard box and gave her a gaping hole for a mouth. A square-shaped hole covered with see-through plastic represented the stomach. A 'door' in the cardboard box enabled the posted creatures (cardboard, wood, etc.), fly, spider, bird, cat, dog, horse, to be retrieved and the song/game was done over and over. What fun it was!

A variety of interesting objects and toys for dropping and picking up, for rolling, for twirling round, and for carrying about and transferring from one place to another might also be part of the environment in which we teach these young mentally handicapped children and note their responses. Such a collection of toys will stimulate those activities expected of children in this range of development. Fortunately many excellent plastic toys are easily available. Woollen, cloth, and plastic air-flow balls should also be part of this stock, as well as very large home-made rag dolls (at the height of the children and perhaps taller too for comparisons). These could represent mother, father, sister, etc. in terms of their clothes.

Observing and teaching the young mentally handicapped child　53

There is certainly a dearth of these toys in many schools I have visited, particularly since 1971. They are expensive to buy but voluntary groups or even adult training centre students could be encouraged to make them. They do not need to be complicated. They will give the children a host of imitative and imaginative play experiences as well as early 'feelings' of height and weight. When the dolls are 'taken for a walk' by the child and the adult a sense of symmetry will be gained—you are on that side and I am on this side of the doll. In 1972 the then Inspector for Special Education for Cheshire invited me to organize a full week of in-service training in one of the special schools for untrained and inexperienced staff. We worked on various aspects of the curriculum. One of the sessions included the value of dolls in play and language. Each teacher present had been invited to make two life-sized dolls and to make an arrangement of them for the group on a particular morning of the course. The hall in which we were holding the course contained a climbing frame. In the discussion that followed on from the display that was made, the teachers showed how the dolls could be used to introduce a wide variety of verbs and spatial words to the children. The dolls had been arranged sitting, standing, propped up, lying down, upside down, upside down on their heads. Visual concepts of language were immediately available in this situation. We naturally discussed how the dolls could be used to introduce nouns to the children as well as adjectives.

In describing toys for these young mentally handicapped children it seems important that a number of them should make a noise when touched, moved, pushed, or squeezed. Children like to see the effect of their own physical strength and actions upon objects, especially large ones. Mentally handicapped children are no different in this way from normal children. They are usually physically older and 'bigger' when they separate themselves as it were from 'that' out there. Punch bags, large dolls, gonks, large and small coloured animal shapes, light balls and balloons suspended from the ceiling by elastic, and thick string or rope will give the children lots of opportunities for this experience. Such equipment will also help co-ordination of hand and eye particularly if an adult is involved in the child's play. Hoops, bells, and tyres suspended in much the same manner (perhaps out of doors) will give them other opportunities and further ideas for motor experimentation. 'To get the child to act motorically and to interact with the things and people around him is one of the primary aims of motor training programmes.' The environment I am suggesting will certainly enable the children to achieve this aim.

Basic play materials such as sand, water, and dough are familiar features of all progressive schools for the mentally handicapped these days. When I wrote the first edition of this book we had been encouraging students to provide these materials for the children for several years beforehand. They had even to provide the containers, sand, and dough in the very early 'sixties. However, new schools built under the auspices of the local

54   *Observing and teaching the young mentally handicapped child*

education authorities have their water and sand areas often excitingly named. Most of the children have the experience of baking and using dough. I would still make a plea for spontaneous use of dough for it will certainly help some of them in the eating situation. If they are allowed to use dough with the cutters and the rolling pins and the baking tins without being taken to an end result they will certainly gain very satisfying emotional experiences.

I think it important that the children are given access to these activities throughout the day rather than at set times. Young children do not have an in-built 'clock' to tell them that now it is time for water/sand/dough play. Saturation of interest is something that we need to think about in education generally but it seems of particular interest in working with mentally handicapped children. We do need to give them an opportunity for arousal of interest, for organizing themselves, and for allowing them to concentrate on something that interests them. How we use what they become involved in indicates our teaching skill and knowledge of where their communications can be led.

In addition to providing these basic materials for the children we need to be considering the kind of play materials that go along with them to stimulate the children's thinking whilst they are playing. Water needs containers of all shapes, sizes, and colours, spoons, pans, sieves and funnels of all sizes, things to squeeze, soap, squeezy liquid, dolls' baths, cloths, clothes, rubber tubing, as well as floating and sinking objects. Janet Taylor (1967) provided an interesting collection of objects for the water-bag assignment I gave the students in 1967 to encourage them to think about what the children were learning when they were playing in the water. She provided the following: red rubber gloves, a whisk with a red handle, a variety of pink and green hair curlers, transparent tubing, a green vegetable sieve with a long handle, a dish mop, a rubber plunger used when we wish to clear our sink when it is 'stopped up', and a red funnel. At the end of the day when the children had finished playing with the toys they were put away in a transparent bag and hung up on the classroom wall.

The children needed objects to blow over the water and to sail on it. I made a lovely light boat with a Fairy Liquid container. I cut out a part of one side of it. When the children took off the screw at the top and put it in the water, it sank. When I put on the screw top again it floated. An easy, quickly made, no cost toy.

Although the children in these groups will not all be at the stage when they are ready to do creative work with the teacher (gross body play is their most important need), some of them will in fact enjoy opportunities for painting, cutting, pasting, scribbling, tearing paper, and using clay (not Plasticine). Each child could have his own book (large) for scribbling in. Perhaps it is important to say here that if the adult wishes to help the young mentally handicapped child to 'keep' at the task she should have a boxful of different-coloured crayons, felt tips, and pencils available, for the moment the child has done his scribble with one pen/pencil/colour

Observing and teaching the young mentally handicapped child   55

he will probably get up and go away from the task. If the adult immediately gives him another colour he will scribble again and so on until all the colours are used. When young mentally handicapped children are painting they often put the brushes in their mouths to have a good suck at them. The adult needs to see that the brushes and the paints are clean, for the sucking seems to be a necessary positive response to the situation as the child sees it. What seems important too is that wherever the child is allowed to choose the teacher will know when she needs to provide extra equipment and where she can lead the communication of the child into purposeful pursuits.

Encouraging the children to communicate about their families is another important feature of the adult's role. A family photograph album for each child should be in the classroom to make the teacher's task much easier. Once more when using it she will be able to discover many interesting facets of the children's development in imitation, gesture, vocalization speech, and language.

Domestic play activities should always be available to the children for what goes on in the home is perhaps of the utmost importance to the child.* A well-constructed and well-filled home area will stimulate the children's thinking and enable an involved adult the opportunity of giving the children the relevant words of the situation *as it is happening*. The tendency to allow the children to play whilst attending to the 'formal' education of another child is just not relevant in the education of mentally handicapped children at this stage. The teachers must evolve techniques to train classroom assistants to become involved in the play situation. For this is what is needed most, not just minding assistants. There are some experienced mothers employed as classroom assistants. With guidance, encouragement, and explanation they could fulfil a positive role in responding to the children's behaviour in all play situations.

Dolls of varying sizes (with sets of clothes for winter, summer, a party, swimming, going to bed) will encourage the children to experiment with size and length. It will give them opportunities to see the dolls being dressed and undressed by the adult and so try for themselves. Cupboards with shelves and doors and kitchenware to fit as well as stoves with cooking equipment will give the children realistic opportunities for arranging, ordering, sorting, matching in a natural situation. Some of them will be ready for imitative play and some will indulge in imaginative play with a friend. The adult can make it all the more real for the child if she provides items to put into the pans and dishes (flour and salt sausages, cakes,

---

* One is struck by the lack of such areas in so many of the schools for the mentally handicapped. One reason that is often given is that the children have 'real' domestic science rooms or flats now. What I should like to emphasize is that the home area in the classroom enables the children to reconstruct their experiences *in their own way* after the experience at home or in the school is over. The observant teacher will know what sense he has made of the 'real' experience when he acts it out. Reconstructing one's experiences is a vital and necessary part of the learning process.

56 Observing and teaching the young mentally handicapped child

biscuits, peas, beans, etc.). One student made 'cakes' from coloured foam cut out in the shapes of sponge-cake slices. The objects alone are not sufficient in themselves at this stage to stimulate the play. The children are at the associative level of thinking and so they need items that will suggest the appropriate activity to them. Later on they will be able to put the 'imaginary sugar' in the cup and stir it with an imaginary spoon.* Give them the real experiences at this stage and it will lay the foundations for imaginative play when they are older.

Mops, brushes, and shovels appropriate to the size of the children and easily available are an important part of their social development. If they have a vacuum cleaner and a carpet sweeper they are fortunate indeed.

As I see it the use these children will make of their opportunities for domestic play might very well depend to some extent on the way in which their teacher spends some of her time whilst she is with them. By this I mean that she should make sure that the children, whilst playing alongside her, have the opportunity to see adult activities. My observation of this need arose from what I felt to the need of the adult too. Theresa O'Rourke† was one of my mature students on the Manchester course during 1962–3. Her final teaching practice was undertaken in a special care unit where all the children were speechless. In those times teachers did not have the classroom assistants that most authorities are now providing in classes where there are young children. Can you imagine spending a whole day with a group of children who made no noise, with whom you could not have a conversation about anything? The silence struck me immediately—her's and the children's. Whilst it is not a difficult task for mothers and others to make cooing and chuckling sounds to babies in prams, it is far more difficult to do the same with 'bigger' children, particularly when they are mentally handicapped. I had read M. M. Lewis's experiments with his own baby in the little book *How Children Learn to Speak*.‡ Briefly, these indicated that when he made sounds over a period of a minute in front of the baby the baby made sounds too; when he was quiet for a minute the baby made fewer sounds. He carried this experiment out over a 6-minute period, alternating the minutes where he used sounds with minutes of silence. It seemed reasonable to expect that if an adult in a room with mentally handicapped children, however handicapped, talked out aloud the children would not only make sounds but they would practise listening to a voice. What was the adult to talk about? That posed the question at that time in our knowledge about the development of these children in an educational setting.

It seems so obvious now. Mothers work in front of their normal children and often talk to them about their work. Why should not this technique be exploited in this particular situation? I suggested it to this student who

---

* Hayes, C. (1976) The Imaginary Pulltoy. In *Play*, J. S. Bruner (Ed.), Penguin Education.
† Deputy headteacher, Margaret Whitehead School, Salford.
‡ M. M. Lewis, *How Children Learn to Speak*. (This book is now out of print but may be obtained from libraries.)

Observing and teaching the young mentally handicapped child   57

was to perform a mother's task for a short period each day and to talk about it. The method was built in and extended in the work of those students who did teaching practice with very young children in the years that followed. I called it the 'mother's work' technique and during the course the students practised in groups with a tape recorder making 'running commentaries' about a wide variety of household tasks. This was a little artificial when the children were not there but the general effect was to focus the attention of the students on their own use of language and to evaluate it in terms of its appropriateness.*

In the years that followed, students working with the young mentally handicapped child were expected not only to think out a mother's task daily (and we saw no reason why we should not impose this special technique on the students) and perform it whilst the children were playing, but also they had to think out and write down in their notes the words and phrases they hoped to use. A talking adult will always draw some children around her quite spontaneously, even those who are mentally handicapped. If she were carrying out an activity that would normally go on in the home there would be a link of one kind or another in the child's mind. The responses of the children over the years was indeed most positive and convinced me, at any rate, of the value of the technique in this kind of education. However, teachers often have the image of what a teacher should and should not be doing. It does not always include sewing, knitting, making a sandwich, washing real clothes (structured, e.g. red socks and a red hat) in front of children.† Perhaps some will be persuaded to try out this suggestion and note the responses. They will not be disappointed.

This technique stimulates the children's curiosity, maintains their attention, and encourages them to imitate in their play the activities they see the adult carrying out. They will also join in the activity quite spontaneously and naturally when they are ready to do so. The teacher will find that talking in an ordered way (thought out) about the activity going on in front of her is a useful way of establishing communication with these little children.

I have tried to outline what I feel the young mentally handicapped child

---

* Unfortunately the academic nature of the training of present-day teachers of the mentally handicapped, and the lack of time afforded by the colleges to those students wishing to specialize in this sphere of education, give little time for such important and relevant experiences. Ten to twelve weeks' teaching practice cannot be considered sufficient to practise this vital communication skill. In-service Training Courses are probably improving the situation.

† Dorothy Jeffrees in her work with parents in the mid 'sixties wrote about the value of home activities in stimulating language. You can read about her work in: Jeffrees, D. and Cashdan, A. (1971) The home background of the severely subnormal child. *British Journal of Medical Psychology*, **44**, pp. 27–33. The Barnaby series of books (Jeffrees, D. and Cunningham, C. C., 1976) published by L. D. A. Wisbech, Cambs., takes the idea of familiar home activities forming a communication link between parents and child/teacher and child one step further. Important activities such as dressing and cleaning shoes are symbolized sequentially through pictures. Perhaps these publications remind us about the usefulness of the back chaining technique.

58   *Observing and teaching the young mentally handicapped child*

at school should be experiencing if he is to have a fully stimulating and appropriate education in the early years. Elsewhere you will find other suggestions for individual activities that can be carried out with him.*

---

*Stevens, M. (1976) *The Educational and Social Needs of Children with Severe Handicap*, Chapters 4 and 6, Edward Arnold, London.

5 Observing and teaching the adolescent

Since the writing of the first edition of this book a great deal of progress has taken place in terms of curriculum development in schools for the mentally handicapped (pp. 163–87). This applies particularly to the 'adolescent'. I have written elsewhere quite comprehensively about the kind of programmes and experiences I think that these young people should have.* Local education authorities have done a great deal through in-service training schemes to continue the development of a wide variety of activities in the schools—movement, games, outdoor activities including cycling, pony riding, camping, and nature study,† drama, woodwork, music, pottery, art, swimming, language programmes, reading activities (for those capable of achieving functional reading skills), needlework, gardening, shopping, dancing, and farming activities (where relevant in terms of the school's immediate vicinity). Most schools arrange regular visits to the library and it would be indeed rare to find a school where cookery was not carried out at one level or another.

However, rather less emphasis is still placed by the schools themselves and on in-service courses on making some kind of provision for these young people to have opportunities for self-organization and for their teachers and others to see their abilities in this feature of their life. Socialization comes about, to some extent, because we have the opportunity to choose our own activities and with whom we do them. Organizing the programme so fully that these young people have little opportunity to carry out their own 'thing' as it were, and to do their own thinking, means that they are being denied an important aspect in the growth process. Think of the isolated lives so many of them lead when they go home from school. Their school friends live so far away from them. Then you will

---

*Stevens, M. (1976) Education after 16 plus (Chapter 12). In: *The Educational and Social Needs of Children with Severe Handicap*, Edward Arnold, London.

† Barham, J. (1971) Nature study activities with severely subnormal children. *Forward Trends*, **15**, pp. 25–32.

Robinson, C. M., Harrison, J. and Gridley, J. (1970) *Physical Activity in the Education of Slow-learning Children*, Edward Arnold, London.

Heavey, R. (1973) *Creative Drama and the Mentally Handicapped Child*. Obtainable from Mill House School, Newton-le-Willows, Lancs.

Sherborne, V. (1973) Movement and the mentally handicapped child. *Inner London Authority Drama Teachers' 'Broadsheet'*. February 1972.

Nichols, R. and Mott, Eileen M. (no date given) *Individual Programmes Booklets* 1–5. Obtainable from Bennett House School, Radley Road, Abingdon, OX14 3RR.

Tilley, P. (1975) *Art in the Education of Subnormal Children*, Pitman Publishing Company, London.

60   Observing and teaching the adolescent

see it is of even greater importance that on several occasions each week (if we cannot bring ourselves to organize it daily for them) they are in an environment which caters for their spontaneous choices and needs. Gunzburg,* writing about the aims of education for these children, selects that first of all it must ensure that 'he is adequately prepared for his role in the community however modest this role is'. As I have come to understand it, through watching and being with these children for a long time now, the opportunities to mix freely with his peers and not just sit quietly alongside of them being 'good' for the adult, will be one of the steps towards having some form of social role in the community. He must have an opportunity to be himself too, to be accepted as he is and not only as others wish him to be.

The provision of an environment in which the spontaneous behaviour of adolescent mentally handicapped children can be observed, and taken note of, will present the adult with different problems from those present when thinking of young mentally handicapped children. Children of 12–16 years of age will have global developmental ages ranging from 4 to over $6\frac{1}{2}$. The range of their physical height will also be rather wide. Some children will be under 4 feet and others over 5 feet tall. Perhaps the teacher might need to remind herself that little harm can come from having all the materials readily available for the younger children available for this group too. What one can be sure of is that mentally handicapped children, just like normal children, will not use objects and other materials belonging to an earlier age stage if they have initially satiated their interest at the time when such materials were appropriate for them. If they do then the teacher needs to examine why they need the activity they are choosing or whether they are using it *qualitatively* in a different way from the way in which they previously used it. This is why we need to keep detailed records of these children and their activities—to serve as reference points for our judgements about them. The teacher also needs to encourage them to use more advanced material as well as to question continuously her own provision of activities.

As the children progress through the school or are transferred to another part of it or even to another building† they need more opportunities for creative work and new experiences of their own making.

---

* Dr Gunzburg whilst being a consultant clinical psychologist to a group of mental subnormality hospitals has in fact also been one of the leading special educators in this field of education for over two and a half decades. Most of his published material has been designed to enable other educators to do a better job on behalf of mentally handicapped children. Everything he writes is based upon practical experience as well as concern for the mentally handicapped. His work is translated into many languages.

Gunzburg, H. C. (1974) Educational planning for the mentally handicapped, in Clarke, A. M. and Clarke, A. D. B., *Mental Deficiency. The Changing Outlook*, 3rd Edition, Methuen, London.

† During the 1960s it was not uncommon to find mentally handicapped adults and children together in the same building. After the Mental Health Act (1959) local health authorities were responsible for building what were called purpose-built training centres for these two groups in separate buildings. However, this still meant that a child could attend school in

Observing and teaching the adolescent   61

Although these young people will be having real domestic experiences with their teachers during the week—washing, cooking, shopping, camping, going on picnics in the summer time—some of them will undoubtedly benefit from a period of free choice in which to reconstruct these real activities in a dramatic play situation. Play equipment should now be thought of in terms of the physical size of the children. It should also be considered in relationship to their increasing social development, that is to say in terms of their ability to play WITH and not only alongside of others.

Equipment must now be life-sized, e.g. real cups and saucers, real cutlery, tableclothes, etc. Most schools have 'flats' as part of the learning environment for these children. What I should like to see is that on some occasions these can be at the disposal of the children 'for play'. It seems a waste of space in overcrowded classrooms to use a corner to provide a 'home corner' when there is one already available in the school. Mentally handicapped children at this stage like to 'play' shops. Such shops should be appropriate to the height of the children concerned. They should contain everything that will make them realistic for the children—objects and substances for weighing, scales and weights, baskets, paper and cloth bags, handbags, purses, real money, aprons for the shopkeepers, and shelves on which to arrange the 'goods'. Adult training centres might co-operate here in building suitably sized and realistic equipment. One school I know had its own shop counter with fitted shelves and a door through which to enter made especially with 5-feet tall children in mind. Its use was most successful.*

During my experimental approach to training direct observational skills in teachers of the mentally handicapped from 1963 onwards,† we provided for the young people visiting our college one afternoon a week among other things a camp bed, a wigwam, and a blanket. Dolls in a variety of sizes were already part of the provision we made. All these materials afforded the group a great many opportunities for imaginative play as well as for group activity in constructing the wigwam and in folding the blanket. The children also enjoyed a table-tennis set. This really encouraged group play at a level appropriate to their physical size. I hardly need to write that tennis rackets and bats and balls will encourage a great deal of peer play that is acceptable in 'normal' society. Their use in developing hand–eye co-ordination can certainly not be overestimated.

When one visits schools for the mentally handicapped there is a great

---

the same building from (in some authorities) 3 until 16. After the Education Act (Handicapped Children) 1970 many authorities found ways and means of having the children in one building up to 12 and then transferring them into another for their later education. Local education authorities building new schools for the mentally handicapped have in some instances built separate buildings (units) for the various age groups, i.e. first, middle and upper schools with teachers as Heads of these 'Departments'.

* Mrs Davenport, Brentwood School, Timperley, Cheshire.

† Stevens, M. (1976) An experimental approach to direct observation of the play of severely subnormal children (pp. 127–9). In: *The Educational and Social Needs of Children with Severe Handicap*, Edward Arnold, London.

62   *Observing and teaching the adolescent*

deal of evidence that the value of art activities has now been accepted in most of them. In some, unfortunately, these are sometimes confined to specific periods with specialist teachers. Whilst the children undoubtedly benefit from such skilled help and produce valuable exhibits for the school, they also seem to need opportunities for creating more spontaneously; for showing what they can do unaided. However, if one looks for the opportunities for creative woodwork these do seem to be lacking. One reason for this may be that the majority of the teachers, in spite of the influx of men into this field of work after 1970, are women. Another may be that no one is willing to become responsible for seeing that there is always a sufficient quantity of soft wood with which to experiment. A further reason may be that often the adult can only see the reason for the activity if there is going to be a finished object at the end of the experimenting. Without specific help this is unlikely to occur except amongst the more competent children.

A woodwork bench with a firm vice (essential) and real tools will certainly give both boys and girls a wide variety of exciting experiences— experiences that many of them will not be afforded at home. Some of them indeed will produce recognizable objects of their own, however crude. Some will be seen as developing skills in the use of tools and in creating more and more realistic-looking models of what they wish to construct.* Varying shapes and thicknesses of wood will give the children ideas about what to make. Wheels, glue, and string will also stimulate them further in their experiments. An essential feature of class in which woodwork is allowed to take place is that it must be completely relaxed.†

I have described much more fully the wide variety of materials and special table games that can be provided to stimulate the imagination, the involvement, and the skills of this age group in my book *The Educational and Social Needs of Children with Severe Handicap*. However, I think that the following tables may still be justifiably included in this chapter particularly for the young student about to go on a first teaching practice or for a teacher having the first experience of a class of mentally handicapped adolescents. Imaginative and experienced teachers might gain ideas from these too. I know that in such an environment they will certainly learn a great deal about the children particularly if they take

---

* Crossland Ward, one of my former students and now a teacher in charge of an exciting creative area of a school (The Birches, Rusholme, Manchester), kept the spontaneous woodwork of a girl over the period of a year. Her attempts to improve her own ability to produce a recognizable figure were interesting indeed. Development in her skills in using the tools was also noted by this very creative teacher. George, a mentally handicapped man of 38 years, made a bird table after seeing his father make one at home. Two weeks later he destroyed it and buried it in the ground because he did not like it. He then began to make another one quite spontaneously with more skill. The observational notes I made at the time suggested that here was an example of a 'child' raising his own standards.

† In observing a group of 12–16-year-olds in a free choice situation over a period of 3 years some of them always chose woodwork for their afternoon activity. The tools were limited and often there were four or five children around the table—girls as well as boys. During that time I never saw a child injure himself or anyone else. An adult was always readily available to help but, in this early experimental situation, not to teach directly.

the trouble to use their observational skills to the utmost. Mittler in writing an article for the National Children's Bureau* states that educational psychologists might find it useful to observe children in a free choice situation as well as in the more organized test environment. Perhaps if they have the opportunity to organize their own free choice environment in a school they too will find my tables useful. Portable audio–video equipment will undoubtedly enable them to check over their own more subjective observation records.

The teacher will need to consider carefully the actual number of activities to include in the classroom at any one time. To a large extent this will depend upon the space available. It will also depend upon the teacher's skill in being aware of all the children in the group even when only one or two are being taught with a specific objective in mind. It might now depend upon an ability to direct the classroom assistant to more purposeful activity and involvement with the children.†

Some schools I know utilize the corridor space in their efforts to provide a wide variety of activities for the children. If a child cannot find what he needs in the classroom he might indeed find something to catch and sustain his attention in the corridor. Perhaps a TV 'theatre' in the corridor with a few easy chairs available might free the space often used for whole classes solely to watch TV. Twenty minutes of enforced viewing in an already much shortened morning of activity might be more profitably spent by the children if they have scope for a wider choice of activity. Viewing time at home will probably be quite substantial, particularly for the adolescent. At least he might have the opportunity to choose for himself whether or not he wishes to sit watching the programmes available to him in school hours.

In making these suggestions I am aware that some teachers will only provide the materials from one of the Tables. I would like to urge that most of the activities are provided AT ONE AND THE SAME TIME. If they are, one can be sure that the language of the teacher and her assistants will be positively about the activities rather than about how they, the children, should be behaving in a more limited situation. Much 'naughty' behaviour in the mentally handicapped adolescent seems to be a direct result of the inappropriate and often academic activities that are

---

* Mittler, P. (1974) *Concern*, No. 15 (Winter). National Children's Bureau Publication.

† This involvement even with the adolescent might be construed in terms other than sitting at the table occupying him with sedentary and often repetitive tasks. Whilst I am on the subject of sitting down I should like to help young teachers in the task of getting the very young mentally handicapped child to sit down near them, e.g. for short periods of time only. My observation so very often is that whilst the adult is SAYING 'sit down' she is often walking about the room and so are the assistants. If they all sit down and continue asking the children to come and sit down they will generally find that the majority of the children will imitate their behaviour and will in fact come in the direction of the voice. The rest can then soon be brought into the activity. The teacher will use a positive method here in using imitation as a source of the children's understanding. It will not work all the time with all of the children but it is worth giving the method a try. Experienced teachers will know this technique even if they have not shared it with their younger colleagues.

64   *Observing and teaching the adolescent*

often provided instead of creative ones that are being provided by teachers wanting to 'make them as normal as possible'. Wilf Brennan addressing the delegates to a conference organized by the National Council for Special Education in Bradford in 1974 reinforced my own practice and that of my best students when he suggested that these mentally handicapped people have plenty of time in adulthood to be subjected to the more formal aspects of education. As he saw it, as children they should have all that is considered to be the best in our primary schools of today— colour, texture, a wide variety of activities and experiences, and beauty of visual and auditory perception. We seem to have a long way to go in some of our schools.

Cutting out area

Safe scissors. Special scissors. Ready-made scrap books. Large pieces of paper on which to paste things. Pictures already cut out for pasting into books. Pictures to cut out. Boxes of pictures to sort into categories, e.g. clothes, shoes, slippers, boots, foods, men, women, children, babies, furniture. Home-buying catalogues. Glue. Brushes. Bits of material of different thickness, string, cotton, paper, cardboard, foil.

Painting, drawing, and writing area

Crayons, felt-tipped pens, thick pencils, ball pens, paper of varying sizes, colours, and shapes (round, square, oblong, triangular, diamond, octagonal). Paints (many colours), an assortment of brushes including those used by a decorator. Duplicated pictures for painting, colouring, and tracing over. Name tags. Envelopes, postcards (to motivate a child to send a card through the post to his family). Stencils of familiar objects. Think of these in the environment in home and school, in the hospital ward/ school. Outlines of familiar objects can be cut out of vinyl floor squares; the child then has two possibilities—a template to go round; a stencil to colour in; a stencil to take his pencil round *inside* the cut-out shape. Using the vinyl square is clean for the tiles can be washed quite easily by the children themselves whenever this is considered necessary. Apparatus to help the child 'keep inside' an outline (blocks of wood in ever-decreasing thicknesses to which may be fixed the already cut-out outline of an object. If the child goes off the edge his hand will quite naturally fall from the height of the block. The idea propounded by Kephart* is that as the child becomes more skilful and learns from the height of the block that he is going off the edge, he is finally able to colour in a shape that is on the paper without going outside the lines—an interesting teaching aid).

---

* Kephart, N. C. (1971) *The Slow Learner in the Classroom*, 2nd Edition, Charles E. Merrill Publishing Company, Columbus, Ohio.

Dramatic play and language stimulation through puppets

This might contain a puppet theatre (the teacher might use this with a group of children and then give the children the opportunity of using it by themselves in the free choice session), and puppets—glove puppets, box puppets, stick puppets representing animals in a favourite story, famous pop singers, the characters in a song learnt in the music session. Puppets representing the characters of a recent story told by the teacher.

Printing table

All kinds of printing equipment. Bobbins with thick paint to put on the end. Foam or felt letters or objects on large wooden stampers with handles. Toilet rolls and matchbox ends. Potato cuts. String prints on oblongs of wood fastened to leather handles (first designed by Margaret Baker, NAMH Course, 1966–8). Sticks for printing (commercially made).

Objects to excite curiosity and manipulation

Clocks. Alarm and ping clocks. Egg timers. Torches. Keys and locks mounted on a board. Bathroom scales. Opera glasses. Kaleidoscopes. Peep boxes (Simpson, P.; Southren, Anne; Gillham, W.). Old cameras. Tape recorders for use by the children. Magnets. Telescopes. Binoculars. Coloured slides of the children, the activities of their families and their teachers. Viewers and projectors. Springs.

Quiet activity area

Specially made books for the particular class (e.g. books of photographs showing the lives of the children and the adults whilst in school). Specially produced books with clear simple pictures (good models of these are the Barnaby Books). Specially chosen books to introduce all kinds of familiar items. Collections of pictures (these might be the photographs of the children in the class and their parents, photographs obtained from the press of the various aspects of life relevant to the lives of these children). Large table mosaics. Table games (see Stevens, 1976, pp. 134–6 just to start you off). Matching apparatus, lotto, small toys, animals, furniture and dolls, structural number apparatus, thinking games, catalogues, geo boards (cf. Stevens, again, 1976). Boxes of interesting objects to see, feel, and listen to. Holiday postcards.

Bit box. Creative materials. Language stimulation, number perception, etc.

To stimulate imagination and to give experiences of creating with a variety of textures—silver paper, cotton wool, string, cardboard, chocolate papers, cardboard of varying thicknesses, toilet rolls, rolls of other kinds,

66   *Observing and teaching the adolescent*

plastic bottles of all kinds (transparent and opaque), ice-cream cartons, yoghurt cartons, plastic egg boxes, paper egg boxes, pieces of bark, shells, tins and boxes of all kinds, ready cut out soft toys and doll shapes, table mat shapes, large needles threaded with silk and wools, purse shapes, thin leather, hessian, felt, suede.

Outdoor life table and indoor gardens

Small pets.

Sound area*

For free experimentation with sound by the child and sometimes with the involvement of an interested adult. One or two traditional percussion instruments, kazoos, combs and paper, musical boxes, clickers, bird shakers, tuned xylophones. Household items on string—spoons, forks, pan lids, etc. with hammers for striking. Hammers and a variety of objects to strike such items as wood, metal, large stones. Wooden spoons to clash, shoe trees to clash at each end (Ann Roe, NAMH Course, 1967–9). Coconuts to bang. Wire, elastic of varying thicknesses stretched between hooks and firmly fastened to the classroom wall. Shakers made from a variety of waste materials: dressed in animal and doll costumes of wool, fur, and satin these will attract the attention of the children. Rattles including a football rattle. Blowing instruments—recorders, whistles, mouth organs, melodicas. Empty tins to bang. Empty plastic boxes to bang—without a lid they make a wonderful drum. Gallon and two-gallon water carriers—again wonderful drum accompaniments to taped tunes. Autoharps. Maraccas made from papier mâché pasted over balloons; when the paper is hardened the balloon is popped and the hollowed shape is filled with cereals, e.g. lentils, beans, cornflakes according to the sound one wants the child to have an experience of. Tapes of familiar household and outdoor sounds. Tapes of unfamiliar sounds in order to get an 'error' response from the child; the 'error' response will tell you in fact what the child knows, what he understands about his imagination. Guitar, banjo, violin, accordion for strumming and playing and plucking. Tuning fork. A wide variety of bells at various pitches—think of size and material here. Simple record player and records. Large and small beach balls for patting sounds. Different kinds of paper and card to produce sounds. Piano freely available to the children.

Dressing-up area for dramatic play, and practice in dressing and undressing

In addition to clothes of all kinds (for all seasons/occasions) this might contain a wardrobe in which to hang the clothes on hangers, a set of

---

* Cf. Stevens, M. (1972) Music and the Mentally Handicapped: for the non-specialist. In *Educating the Mentally Handicapped*, A. Laing (Ed.), Swansea University Publications.

Observing and teaching the adolescent 67

drawers in which to put the clothes after they have been folded. A suitcase and hangers are useful as are the following: hats to suggest roles—soldiers, policeman's helmet, fireman's helmet, bus conductors, drivers, witches. A variety of outfits—cowboy's, indian's, nurse's, clown's, etc. Make-up including lipstick, powder, harmless creams, and perfume bottles, electric shavers. Masks of all kinds for 'fun' play.

Promotion of experiment and confidence

Skates (used most successfully in one school).* Ballet shoes and boxing gloves. Punch ball fixed firmly to the ground. A piece of rope. A tyre fixed horizontally to a piece of wood containing four castors (now available commercially but as I recall an idea of a student whose name I have now 'lost'). A real-size pram, trolley. All of this equipment will stimulate the children to play with other children, to use gross bodily movements, to use their imagination and to express themselves through gesture or through words.

An environment containing all or some of these aids will enable the children to show their interests, their difficulties and their imagination. If the classroom is thought of as a place where the children can choose and become self-directed, the teacher who skilfully observes will notice increased interest and concentration. She will have no need to organize her programme around the concept of half-hour sessions. She will rarely see behaviour that can be considered as 'naughty' (unless there is a child with an extra handicap of uncontrollable hyperactivity in her group), for the children are able to become absorbed in their interests which the teacher can then exploit in the learning situation.

Such an environment will also stimulate curiosity, and imagination. The children will become more alive. For a time, that they are handicapped to such a degree may hardly be noticeable.

---

*In the old Salford Junior Training Centre (pre-1971) when the headteacher was Mrs Littlewood, now headteacher at Werneth Grange, Hyde, Cheshire.

6 Observing in special situations

The ultimate aim in my mind in emphasizing the necessity for those working with the mentally handicapped to observe their spontaneous behaviour in great detail is so that the adult will make an immediate response to the child's communication—a response that is positive. Their communication might be in terms of movement or words. However, as I have pointed out in the introductory chapter, the act of observing is not an automatic skill. It is a complex and difficult activity. It has to be trained quite deliberately in those wishing to teach the mentally handicapped. I have suggested how I have gone about this training of staff in other chapters. When the habit of skilled observation becomes established the teacher will find little difficulty in using certain special situations to add to her growing knowledge of each child. Some teachers may even find that they can begin to use their observational skills more effectively and economically during what might be considered to be controlled situations.

Such situations might be the lunch periods, a bus journey, an expedition, in a cafeteria, in the cloakroom, or in an individual one-to-one teaching situation. No doubt you will think of countless other possibilities. The lunch period is most relevant since it happens so regularly and is a social occasion. Let us look at this period in terms of what we might discover about each child in our care. It is an occasion which might bring forth a surprising amount of communication between the child and the adult, and the child and another child, wherever communication is encouraged and approached in an informal way. It is a fruitful period in terms of revealing a child's level of development in a variety of ways.

Dr H. C. Gunzburg's Progress Assessment Charts* are well known in most schools for the mentally handicapped. These charts give pointers to certain aspects of behaviour expected at the table. Edgar Doll writing in 1947 produced his Vineland Social Maturity Scale. This scale gives us some information regarding the ages at which specific behaviour will/should appear in normal children. To some extent it is relevant in the education of the mentally handicapped, e.g.:

0–1 year	Drinks from cup assisted
1–2 years	Masticates food
	Drinks from cup or glass unaided
	Eats with spoon

---

* Gunzburg, H. C. (1966) *Progress Assessment Charts*. These charts, including a special one for children with Down's Syndrome, are available from Mind, 22 Harley Street, London, W.1.

Observing in special situations   69

2–3 years   Eats with fork
            Gets drink unassisted
6–7 years   Uses table knife for spreading
7–8 years   Uses table knife for cutting
9–10 years Cares for self at table.

If we examine these items and see the steady development of useful social skills with chronological age we need to ask ourselves whether we are providing opportunities for this development in a natural way both at home and in school. We need to work together with the home in order to ensure that the behaviour happening in school and at home (on the wards in hospitals, or in the hostel) parallels itself in both places.

Other points relating to the question of table behaviour might include:

(1) Does he/can he eat with his fingers if not fed by an adult?
(2) Does the child imitate the adult if she takes up a spoon to feed him (i.e. pick up his own spoon, push it into the food and convey it to his mouth)?
(3) Does the child sit easily and comfortably at the table? Would he be better if he had a cushion,* would he eat better if the height of the chair enabled him to 'look down' upon the plate?
(4) Does he bend down with his face near the plate (does he need glasses)? Can the bending habit be phased out by raising the level of the plate from the surface of the table? Can it be corrected by constant encouragement over a long period of time (i.e. a year)? Does he sit cross legged—is this a habit or does the child have a heart condition?
(5) What foods does he like/dislike?
(6) How large/small a meal does he eat? Does he bring a lunch to school? Is it a big one? What time does he eat it? What time did he leave home and what time did he have his breakfast? Does he have a drink of milk in school? Does he have this in a feeder cup, a beaker or with a straw?
(7) Does he try to drink/talk with his mouth full?
(8) Does he know the names of all the foods he is eating? Are the adults systematically giving him the names of the foods each day IN THE SITUATION? Can he recognize the foods in pictures? Have you made a daily menu book for him of the actual food he has eaten on each day of say, a week?

---

* I was visiting two little mentally handicapped boys in a local authority hostel over the period of a week in 1974. The first time I saw them at the table the nose of the younger one came level with the edge of the table—a table not specially bought to accommodate little children. I suggested that perhaps he might have a cushion to help him for I knew that his development in table behaviour in his own home was well ahead relative to his age and stage of mental development. I looked in the dining-room each day of my visit to see if the suggestion had been taken up. On my last visit 'they' would not let me anywhere near the dining-room but somehow I managed to 'lose my way there'—there was still no cushion and still no special table for little children! Fortunately they were going home the following day! I was extremely unhappy about this situation.

70 *Observing in special situations*

(9) Does he know the names of the food when they are presented in an unusual/different way? Thus sliced onions on a salad were not perceived as onions in that situation by a mentally handicapped man in his thirties, chips were not chips to an educationally subnormal boy of 11 when they were scalloped shaped instead of in fingers like his mum did them.

(10) Does he know the names of the foods whether they are cooked or uncooked?

(11) Does he ask for the salt and the pepper or sauce? Is he being encouraged to do this by example from the adults?

(12) Can he discriminate the salt cellar from the pepper container?

(13) Is he encouraged to put on his own salt/pepper/vinegar/mayonnaise/ sauce irrespective of whether he will put on too much/will make a mess on the plate?

(14) Is he encouraged to choose the condiments for himself? Can he ask for them?

(15) Does he eat quickly or slowly? Will he eat more quickly with appropriate encouragement? Will he 'get on with the meal' if he knows there is something he likes to follow?

(16) When using a spoon or a fork does he spill much of his food?

(17) When cutting with a knife does he cut everything or just some things (one mother reported to me that her son would cut meat but could not always cut toast)?

(18) When the skills of using a knife, fork, and spoon are achieved is he holding them in an 'acceptable' fashion? Is this like his family or not? Does he copy the adult in school in this or does he do what he sees in the home? Does he do both?

(19) Does he help to set the tables alone/with verbal instructions and a great deal of encouragement (remember the quality of the learning experience is of much greater importance than the perfection of the end result)?

With simple and repeated instructions from an adult who enjoyed seeing his pleasure in simple achievement, one very, very mentally handicapped boy of 13 was able to set several tables. The activity lasted 20 minutes. The instructions through words and gesture were as follows:

Put the knife here (pointing).
Put the fork here (pointing to the fork and the position it had to occupy).
Put the spoon here (pointing).
Now come to this side (of the table) (pointing).

Although this seems to be a tedious process it was a real learning experience for this child. It was an activity he could do; it was meaningful; he gained enjoyment from his achievement. His tendency to remain inactive in a free choice situation was offset in this structured and formal activity. Another child, on the other hand, set out cutlery on the table after an example of one place setting.

Observing in special situations   71

Since I originally wrote about the above behaviour, teachers have constructed pictorial aids to enable a child to match the cutlery appropriately. Some educational suppliers have produced plastic mats with place settings clearly produced on them for matching. I have recently designed a tea-time inset board of two place settings (cf. p. 50).

Planned expeditions on a weekly and even a daily basis are a feature of all schools for the mentally handicapped now—expeditions including short visits on a bus, as well as to cafés. Once more a skilled observer of children's behaviour will be able to build up her knowledge of the children in her group. Check lists are always useful to the busy adult working with children. I will present some to you for your consideration.

On the expedition
  (1) Does the child make himself presentable in terms of his dress when going out or have you to do that for him?
  (2) Does the child stop to receive instructions when told to by the adult?
  (3) Does the idea of going out excite the child? Does he look forward to it? How can you tell?
  (4) Does the child show fatigue after walking? What does he do if he is tired?
  (5) Are there some kinds of expedition which bring forth more response in terms of excitement and language than others? Which are these?
  (6) What motivates the child to hurry to see something?
  (7) Does it take longer to go a particular journey with some children than with others? Why?
  (8) Does the child take hold of the teacher's hand when walking? Is he independent? Would he be independent if the adult did not take his hand?
  (9) Does the child show any curiosity:
    (a) by looking at specific things?
    (b) by sustained attention? (One boy's attention was completely captured by the slow movement of the tortoise's head as it came out of its shell. He watched; he pointed; he wanted to go on looking.)
    (c) by comment?
    (d) by asking questions?
 (10) How does the child respond if spoken to by a stranger into whose presence he comes as a result of the expedition, e.g. waitress, bus conductor, museum keeper?
 (11) What words does the child use on the journey?
 (12) What kinds of comment does he make about notices on doors, walls?
 (13) Does the child know what is sold in different kinds of shops?
 (14) Does the child know where particular items are in a supermarket near his own home?
 (15) How does he respond to zebra crossings, pedestrian crossings, and traffic lights?
 (16) Does the child continue talking about the expedition when he has

72　*Observing in special situations*

returned to school/home? Does he do anything such as drawing spontaneously on his return?

(17) Do you send home a note to the parents of each child informing them of the expedition, what the child saw, what he said?*

(18) Is the child able to tell his parents about the expedition? What methods do you use to evaluate this?

Bus

(1) Does the child give his attention to boarding the bus quickly and speedily or does he have to be helped on the bus? (Would it be useful to gain the co-operation of the conductor in order that he will understand the situation?)

(2) Does the child know where to put a coin at the front of the bus if it is a one-man bus?

(3) What responses do you get from the child in a simulated bus experience in school—as a preparation experience before going/as a reconstruction of the experience afterwards?

(4) How does the child sit on the bus?

(5) Does he respond to the request by an adult that he should give up his seat to an older person?

(6) Does the child point to/name familiar objects, sights during the journey, e.g. types of cars/shops, kinds of people (policemen)?

(7) Does the child know that he has to take out money from his pocket to purchase a ticket?

(8) Does he know which particular coins to give from a selection of them or have you given him the correct amount as a visual experience (the money for each journey could be deliberately put into a separate packet/purse)?

(9) Does the child ask for the fare, say 'please' and 'thank you'?

(10) Does the child recognize the alighting point himself?

Cafeteria

(1) Does the child choose his own drink when given a choice, e.g. milk, tea, orange?

(2) Does he know that he should carry his drink to the table and sit before beginning to eat or drink?

(3) Does he carry his drink safely or is he unsteady in this?

(4) Can he carry a tray?

(5) Does the child know he has to have money ready when he gets to the end of the barrier and when he sees the cash desk?

(6) Does he know that money buys things? Does he know the common coins by name?

---

* By implication, teachers in other kinds of schools for normal children have to read in order to prepare their sessions adequately; they have to spend time marking and commenting upon a child's work. Teachers without these responsibilities might consider what their special responsibilities are regarding their work with mentally handicapped children. Home–school diaries might indeed take the place of marking.

Observing in special situations 73

(7) Does the child have money loose in his pocket, or if he brings it to school is it in a sealed envelope?

(8) Does the child know where to put the tray after he has taken his plate, etc. and put them on the table?

(9) Does a physically small but older child know that if he drinks through a straw he must first take the glass off the table and hold it low enough down his body to get the straw level with his lips?

I compiled these lists of basic behaviours from my own observations of mentally handicapped people in a wide variety of situations during 1961–6 in order to help my students think about their own behaviour in these situations. Since that time teachers in schools for the mentally handicapped, nurses in progressive mental subnormality hospitals, and instructors in adult training centres have compiled their own observation lists according to task analysis principles.* However, for those amongst my readers who are perhaps new to this area of special education, my original lists might enable them to have some appreciation of the very basic behaviours we need to look out for when we are with these children, particularly in the situations I have mentioned.

Criterion referenced scales† are now much more in evidence than they were 10 years ago in this field of education. This has been largely due to the fact that there has been more money to spend in the schools on such scales since the Education Act of 1970. Research workers‡ too have spent their time looking at the problem of helping teachers and parents to observe much more carefully. Criterion referenced scales enable anyone to record the present behaviour of a child in an organized way once the skill of observing is indeed established. The danger in using check lists in the first instance, as I understand my work as a teacher, is that one might be looking for a particular piece of behaviour one wishes to see and miss the behaviour that truly occurs.

---

*The breakdown of behaviours into the simplest components and the arrangement of these into a hierarchical structure starting with the easiest aspect of the behaviour and working through each one to the most complicated.

† Criterion referenced scales are lists of behaviours presented to the observer in order that he should establish whether a child can do something or not. They do not enable the observer to compare the child with other children as intelligence tests do. If they are completed at regular intervals, clear changes in the child's behaviour and performance will be seen. They are useful for teachers/parents and others to use particularly if they link up their findings with those of the psychologist assessing the child in a more structured test situation.

‡ Cunningham, C. and Jeffrees, D. M. (1970) *Parents Workshop*. Published by National Society for Mentally Handicapped Children, NW Region. Reproduced in Unit I-3 Appendix, Open University Course, The Handicapped in the Community.

Jeffrees, D. M. and McConkey, R. J. (1976) *Let me Speak*. Human Horizons Series, Souvenir Press (E and A) Ltd, London.

Kellett, B. (1976) An initial survey of the language of the ESN(s) in Manchester. In *Language and Communication in the Mentally Handicapped*, Berry, P. (Ed.) Edward Arnold, London.

7 Observing conversations

The records in this chapter are word-for-word transcripts of conversations with three mentally handicapped adolescents.* They will give you some idea of the way in which I tried to draw out their passive language. Few of us use all the words in our potential vocabulary. The same applies to mentally handicapped people. Reflect upon your own conversational experiences for a moment. You will then see that using your own passive language does seem, to a large extent, to depend on most occasions upon whether or not someone wants to talk to you, whether you have a mutual interest in the particular topic, and the trouble they are willing to take to listen to you. There are some subjects that we might not have touched upon in conversation for a long time. For the moment the words of the subject are lost to us. The flow of language from another person about this subject will inevitably remind us of the words we wish to use.

The 'seventies and 'eighties will undoubtedly see teachers and others using well-known language packages to stimulate receptive and expressive language. New ones will be compiled, especially with mentally handicapped children in mind. A great deal of thought will go into the production and publication of these 'structured' schemes. One of their main values it seems to me will not necessarily lie in enabling mentally handicapped children to communicate and understand better but in encouraging us to think about language in a more structured way. The lack of attention in schools over the last 25 years to 'grammar' as a subject, and increased emphasis on creative expression both in talking and writing, has clearly resulted in the fact that the majority of students coming into initial teacher training will not readily think in terms of subject–object relations, nouns, verbs, negatives, phonemes, semantics, etc. unless they happen to have a foreign language amongst their O or A results.† To some extent then the packages will bring them right into thinking about language systems in a structured way in the same way as reading books for young children force one's attention upon vocabulary control and the spelling constraints of our native language. Most teachers do not rely upon one scheme of reading. The same should apply with teachers of the mentally handicapped when they consider language stimulation. There is no doubt in my mind that the children need the fullest opportunities in real situations

---

*The tapes were played over and over again and the syllables/words/sentences as they were spoken by me and the children were written down. The task took 5 hours initially with a final check on all three transcripts, taking between 2 and 3 hours.

†Stevens, M. (1976) Implications of language research for teacher training. In Berry, P. (Ed.) *Language and Communication in the Mentally Handicapped*, Edward Arnold, London.

Observing conversations 75

to use their language. What is of even greater significance is that social situations must be created for this to happen. We might enable the mentally handicapped to use language in specific situations quite successfully. We also need perhaps to work just as hard influencing those he comes into direct contact with to think more about language, and to talk with him simply and directly and with some measure of real interest in him as a person. This task is *not* so easy to accomplish for an attitudinal factor is involved. Teachers will certainly have to think out ways and means by which to help classroom assistants, parents, nurses, hostel wardens, and perhaps even the community immediately round the school, become involved in the task of enabling a mentally handicapped child to enjoy a conversation.

As a background to the conversations I think I need to tell you about my aims. They were as follows:

(1) to discover the ideas of the young people concerned about work, in view of the fact that they were about to leave school within a week;
(2) to follow up their communication, wherever possible, immediately;
(3) to discuss their knowledge about a bunch of keys on a ring;
(4) to see if they could count the keys on a ring.

I have had conversations in a particular school* with eighteen school leavers. With few exceptions they were all able to have a conversation with me. The conversations lasted for about 10 minutes. I had never met the children before and asked for no information about them before we met. Each one came with me to a small room where we were alone. At the end of each conversation I played back the recording. Unfortunately, I did not have a second recorder recording some of the comments made by the young people when they heard themselves and when they heard some of the questions I had asked them over again.

The introduction of a bunch of keys on the second occasion of this particular experience was quite fortuitous. I was sitting in the headteacher's room when a boy of about 11 or 12 came in and picking up my bunch of keys said *'jail'*. He then began a sequence of dramatic gestures to tell me his understanding of the word. He needed no encouragement from me. As his imagination was stimulated by these objects† I thought I would use them in the later conversation sessions with the school leavers. As it happened this proved an interesting decision.

All the words spoken by the children are in italic.

---

* Robert Clive School, Shrewsbury. Headteacher Mrs E. Lord.

† I have stressed the importance of giving the children all kinds of familiar objects throughout their school lives in planning for the individual child (Chapter 12 in my other book). Presenting each child in a group (in a one-to-one situation) with an interesting object might bring forth all kinds of interesting experiences for the adult concerned if they only respond to the child—to his communication. If they record the responses and repeat the activity at regular intervals, important changes in response both of theirs and the child's will no doubt be perceived.

76   *Observing conversations*

David

Hullo, Peter.
Hullo.
What's your other name Peter?
David.
Oh sorry, David David?
Kenton.
David Kenton.
ye, yes, ye.
I met two Peters when I was here last time.
Yes.
Oh, (seeing him with a newspaper cutting in his hand) you are going to show me
something from Shrewsbury are you? Tell me about it David.
That used to be the coal that used to be.
Used to be what dear?
A coal.
No, a factory I mean well that used to be a mine.
A factory. Oh did it? Oh yes who?
Well, that used to be a man who used to be here.
Mm.
Because the the erm ... place.
Place?
Rose and Crown now.
They've turned it into the Rose and Crown have they?
Yes.
And what happens in the Rose and Crown?
Err, ducks and darts or something.
Oh darts.
Yes.
Oh yes, yes. Who plays darts?
Dad plays darts.
Does your dad play darts?
Yes.
I see, yes.
And what does your mum do?
She stays home.
Does she?
*Yes and she does all the shopping and when I gets home she's at home when I there,
see.*
Oh very good, that's very good. That's lovely David.
How old are you David?
Fifteen.
Are you, yes?
Yes.
Mm, mm.
When mm you go to work (pause) do you know what sort of thing you'll do?
A milkman's job I think.
Oh! (surprise in my voice)
Milkman's job.
You want to be a milkman do you?
Yes.
Why is that, why do you want to be a milkman?
*Because the man does the milk at school and we want to do the job with with the milk-
man does. Taking milk round to the houses.*
I see and do you think that you might be able to do that?
Yes.

Observing conversations 77

Do you know a milkman?
Ye.
'Cos you could sit beside him?
Yes.
And when he wanted you to put the bottle on the step,
Ye.
You could do that, couldn't you? Yes, that's a very good job, yes.
Yes.
My mom told me all about the job ... and mom says you you you you work with
milkman ... I said that's a good idea mom I said ... right I'm going to be a good
lad and do and do what the milkman tells me to do.
Mm. Good, yes that's very splendid. Yes.
Could you put on the tape recorder what I just said?
In a moment we shall do that yes, *yes*, we shall do that David in a moment but,
yes, I'm not very sure about that tape recorder, *yes*, so I don't want to keep on
turning it on and turning it off. *No.*
Perhaps, erm perhaps if I listen to all of you, *yes*, err in your class.
Yes.
Then we can all listen to it together.
Yes. Mmm.
Err, David, I wanted you to just look at these keys, *yes*, and err just talk about
the keys for a moment or two.
Yes.
Would you like to?
Yes.
Have a look at them then.
(looking)
Do you know how many keys there are?
(1–7 counted)
Yes, erm ... seven.
Now just have a look again.
How many are on there?
(1–10 counted, the word 'ten' pronounced emphatically to indicate the last number)
Mm, ten keys on that ring, yes.
You'd got three of them in your hand, *yes*, before you started counting, *yes*, let's
just check them again. I didn't know that I'd got ten keys. Let's just check. How
many on that one? *Two*, two, right.
(1–10 counted again, we did this together, both of us counting; David stopped at
ten)
Right, good.
Now tell me something else about the key ring.
Ahem, it it in the lock or it goes in ... opens the doors ... (some slight stammering)
Yes, yes.
Erm.
Do you think they're all for opening doors, those?
Yes.
Do you? Have a good look at them.
Are they all for opening doors?
Yes, they're all, yes.
What else, what else could these, these keys open?
What else could they open?
Err, cupboards.
Good, yes. Yes, these open, these open doors. These one, two, three, four, five of
the keys.
Yes, they open that or, err, that or the doors.
Yes, err. I don't know whether that would open that kind of lock.
That's called a lock, isn't it?

78 *Observing conversations*

Yes.
Yes.
What about these keys here?
What do you think these keys are for?
Er for the cars.
Yes, for the car.
One of those keys opens the door.
Yes.
Of the car.
I wonder if you can tell me which one there.
Ahem one of those or them.
Or that yes so what's this one for, this one with the black on it?
To start the car.
Yes, that's to start the car yes.
It goes. (makes a very good imitation of an engine tuning up sound)
Yes, yes, (high pitch) good you know it's got a special name, did you know? *Yes.*
   Do you know what it's called?
Er, it's a s s it's to turn the knob and it goes. (again repeats the engine sound)
Yes, it's called the ignition key.
Ignition key.
That's right, yes, that's what it's called, yes.
Anything else about the key ring? It's got something else interesting on it. (I was
   trying to bring his attention to the tiny torch on the ring)
Er, open the boot of the car, open the.
Oh good yes, the boot of the car, yes and also this one here, this. I wonder what
   this one opens. It opens the petrol.
Ye, petrol tanker.
Yes, the petrol cap. There's a little cap on it.
Then you turn it round.
Yes, that's right and you can put the petrol inside. Yes, that's right, that's good.
   Now is there anything else on that ring that you haven't told me about?
Err, have a look, err, y y you will open the garage. Yes, yes, you can open the garage,
   yes, with keys, yes.
That's right, that's very nice. (as next child arrived after the allotted ten minutes'
   talk)

After listening to David with his broad local accent I was immediately
reminded of all the mentally handicapped children I had recorded in various areas of Britain. Whatever the quality of their articulation, language
fluency, and vocabulary knowledge, an extended experience of their
spoken language on my part revealed their accent to me whether this was
in the heart of Lancashire, the Midlands, Scotland, or Manchester. They
had certainly picked up an accent spontaneously on their way through
life, for no one teaches accents. David had the definite local roll of an
'r' sound in his speech.

David, like many other mentally handicapped children I have talked
with, corrected me when I accidentally used the wrong name in addressing
him. The pronunciation of most of his words was 'correct' and on several
occasions he cut short my sentences and 'butted in'. There was only one
occasion when *he* initiated the next sentence, as it were, and this was when
he wanted to hear himself on the tape recorder. Perhaps I was wrong in
not responding immediately to this request in order to encourage more
questions from him. My genuine reason for not complying to his request,

Observing conversations 79

however, seemed to satisfy him. Olechnowicz in her book *Studies in the Socialisation of the Severely and Profoundly Retarded** states that when a child uses the word 'we', he 'has gained the ability to see himself as a social partner with others and has grown out of the stage of egocentrism in which all events are referred to his own person and wishes'. On one occasion David does in fact use the word 'we'. As I listened to the tape recordings of these three adolescents I could hear that David had the most fluency of speech. In retrospect I am wondering why I considered his conversation with me to be not as interesting as the ones I had with the other two children.

Substituting a word for a word that has been imperfectly learned/understood in order to retain the flow of language seems to me to be a feature of the language of the mentally handicapped as it is with young normal children. In David's case he seemed to substitute the word 'ducks' for draughts when he was talking about the Rose and Crown. I made a mistake here in not discussing the use of the word 'ducks' in this context with him. Abbreviations of two words in spoken English occur very often in David's language as they do in mine—words like I'm, that's, she's, and the possessive as in 'milkman's'. I think that in David's case the use of abbreviations was a fairly well-established speech structure. It was interesting also to note his use of stabilizers ('ers', 'ums', etc.), and to ponder on the possibility that he imitated mine.

I was interested indeed, as no doubt all of us might be, when I heard David describe the words 'ignition key' by an almost perfect imitation of an engine tuning up. When a normal baby points to an object and is told the name of it at least he is in a family that is observing him carefully. When the older mentally handicapped child symbolically 'points' to a word he does not know because no one has yet told him perhaps we are not so quick to supply him with the answer. We need to observe these cues for 'an answer' much more stringently if we hope to develop the vocabulary of the mentally handicapped children we know.

I think that you will agree with me that David's responses contained a good deal of grammatical skill† in spite of his occasional lapses in terms of function words such as 'the'. I think I can safely say that in no instance did David fail to maintain the meaning of what he wished to express.

Philip

Hullo.
Hullo Philip.
Hullo
Philip Whaby is it?

---

* Olechnowicz, H. (Ed.) (1973) Title in the text above. Obtainable *free* from The Day Centre of the Psychoneurological Institute, Warsaw, Poland. Send something to her as you cannot send money.

† Herriot, P. (1971) *Language and Teaching. A Psychological View*, Methuen and Co. Ltd., pp. 18–27.

80   *Observing conversations*

Yes.
Philip! (high-pitched voice to catch his attention because he was looking down; perhaps he was looking at the keys in the middle of the table)
Yes.
Are you going to leave school soon?
Yes.
Are you, and Philip, where will you go when you leave school?
I going to the adult centre.
Are you? You're going to the adult centre?
Yes.
I see, and what will you do there?
Em, y'make stools and sto....s.
Making stools and some chairs.
Stools and chairs, yes, what else?
Er, some logs.
Rugs? Yes, *logs.*
Logs.
Rugs?
Yes, some logs you know scraping logs.
Oh, logs. *Yes.* Sawing logs you mean.
For what for?
Err.
What do you do that for?
Because, erm (pause) *make chairs.*
I see yes, sawing wood really.
Yes.
To make chairs.
D'you know logs are from trees aren't they? I remember some time ago seeing a lot of logs in a river.
Oh.
And they were floating, floating on the river these logs.
Oh.
And the logs are the trunks of the trees aren't they?
Yes. Yes that's right mm, mm.
So you know what you are going to do. Are you leaving school next week then?
Yes. I think so, yes.
Will you be sorry to leave this school?
Yes.
Why will you be sorry?
Er. (looking down at the table)
You can look at me while you are, yes that's right.
Why will you be sorry?
Em, 'cos I like this school.
You like it, yes, you like it.
Why d'you like it tell me, why you like it?
Er, I do some woodwork.
Oh, because of woodwork. You like woodwork? *Yes.*
What have you been making in woodwork?
Make some signs.
Signs, what for, what have you made signs for?
For, for the races.
For the what love?
Races, for the sports.
Oh, for the sports, for the races.
Oh I see, for the races and the sports. That's very splendid, yes.
Have you made a tennis bat?
No.

Observing conversations 81

'Cos I saw one boy this morning, *Oh*, making a table-tennis bat. You know, *Oh*, what table tennis is?
Yes.
Do you play table tennis?
Sometimes.
Sometimes, where, where do you play?
Er.
Where do you play table tennis Philip?
At home.
Do you? *Yes.* At home? *Yes.* Who with?
My dad.
Yes, who else?
Err, erm, my sister and my mam.
Oh very good yes.
How many sisters have you?
Only one.
Oh, only the one sister, *yes*, only the one yes.
And is she older than you Philip?
Yes, she's eighteen now.
Is she?
Yes.
I'm, I'm fifteen.
I see you're fifteen, *yes*, and she's eighteen, *yes*. Mm, so she's older than you, *yes*.
And what does she do, does she go to school or work?
She goes to work, (me interrupting 'does she?') *up Telford.*
In the telephones.
Up Telford.
Oh, up Telford, yes Telford's a place isn't it?
Yes.
I haven't been to Telford.
Oh.
I don't know Telford 'cos I don't live round these parts.
It's by the hospital.
Is it? By the hospital, mm.
Yes.
Mm, right.
Philip, I would like you to look at these keys and I'd like you to tell me about the keys, *oh*. Tell me anything you like.
Mm.
You can take them up in your hand if you want to.
Er, this to open.
Yes this to open.
The door.
Ahem, this is a w whistle.
Is it a whistle? (a surprised tone of voice because I was interested in his perception of the object)
Yes.
How do you know, why did you say it was a whistle?
Err, you have, you have to blow it.
Well, if you blow it d'you think it'll whistle?
Yes.
Well you try, (I was smiling here) you try.
Oh, it won't. (inaudible)
It isn't, is it?
No.
What else could it be then?
Err.

82   *Observing conversations*

If it's not a whistle, what else could it be then, what else could it be?
Err.
I agree it looks like a whistle. The shape is like a whistle, isn't it?
Yes.
I think that's why you said it was a whistle, because of the shape. You know how
it is, we call this (going round the shape with my finger) the shape, don't we, like
this you see, but it isn't a whistle. But what is it?
A light.
Yes, (very positive tone) it's a light, yes.
Do you know another name for it?
Err, to flash.
A flash.
A flash, yes, a light, a flash, what else? (animation in my tone)
A torch.
Very good. So you know three names for it—a light, a flash and a torch. And some
people call it a flash, err, a flash light.
Yes.
Yes.
And some people call it a flash light. They might do. They could call it a flash light
but it's a torch, a little torch, isn't it?
Mm.
Alright, look at some of the other keys.
Erm this for, erm, open de rrr shed.
Opening the shed?
Yes.
Open the shed?
Yes.
I see. Have you got a shed?
Yes.
I've got a shed and a greenhouse.
Oh, a shed and a greenhouse.
Yes.
I see. What do you grow in your greenhouse? (excitement and anticipation expressed
in the tone of my voice)
We grow some lettuce, cucumber.
Oooooo, yes.
Tomatoes, err, yes.
I'm growing some tomatoes this year for the first time and I've got about, ooo, I've
got about twenty little tomatoes. Tiny little ones, you know. Green they are at
first, aren't they at first. Are yours green?
Err.
At the moment?
No, *Yes.*
Yes, aren't they green yet, err?
Yes, they're green, they, err, turns to red.
Yes they do, they,turn to red. You're absolutely right, they turn to red. What makes
them turn to red, d'you think?
. . . to ripe . . .
Pardon?
To ripe.
To wipe?
Yes.
I see, when they're red and before you eat them your mum wipes them, does she?
Yes, wipes them.
Yes.
But it's the sun I think isn't it, that, *yes,* the sun and that makes them, turns them
red, doesn't it?

Observing conversations   83

Yes.
The sun and that.
But sometimes you can put them, you can, in the sun or you can put them in a
    drawer *or* and that makes them ripen, doesn't it?
Or in the freezer.
Well, you put them in the freezer afterwards, don't you?
But...
Oh yes.
They won't go red in the freezer will they?
No. (imitation of my tone in his inflection of this word)
Anything else about those keys?
Errm.
Open the door and open the shed and open the garage.
Yes, open a garage, open a shed, open the door.
Yes. Anything else it might open?
Err. This to open...
Something smaller than a garage, or a shed, or a door to a house, anything else
    that it might open?
Errm mm, mmm mm open a back door.
A back door, mmm. Which way do you go into your house, the back door or the
    front door?
I think the back door.
Do you?
Yes.
When you go home you go in the back door do you?
Yes.
Why? Why do you go into the back door? *Err.* Why? Why don't you go in the
    front door?
I don't know.
(I laughed and smiled)
You always go to the back door do you?
Yes.
I see.
Mm.
I never go in the back door unless I've got a lot of shopping and it's near to my
    car but I usually go into my front door.
Yes.
Mm.
Anything else about the keys. What about this key?
Can you tell me what that was for? (something inaudible) *Err.* What else could that
    be?
Er, open a car door.
Well, it's not to open the car door but it's for a car, isn't it?
Yes, I know a boot. ('I know' was spoken very quickly and 'a boot' emphasized)
A boot?
Yes.
Oh, have you got a car?
Yes, yes, we have we haven't err taxed it yet, oh, *taxed it yet.*
It isn't taxed yet.
No. Oh, it isn't taxed, I see, it isn't taxed yet. *No.*
What does that mean when you say it isn't taxed yet?
What does your dad have to do to tax it?
Err.
Err, get some money.
Oh yes, he has to pay some money, that's right.
Yes, well that's the key that starts the car, isn't it?
Oh, yes.

84   *Observing conversations*

Yes, there's one thing I want you to do for me Philip,
What's that?
and then I'll let you hear yourself on tape.
Yes.
And that's—I want you to tell me how many keys ... there are. How many are there?
(1–9 there, ten, eleven, twelve, thirteen)
Thirteen keys, well actually Philip there are ten keys on the ring, three there,
   (4–10).
There you see, you counted the torch, didn't you?
Oh yes.
And then you went on counting.
Right, Philip that was VERY nice.
Goodbye, Philip.

Philip was a young man with Down's syndrome. He was tall and perhaps had a rather shy personality. Perhaps it was the situation with a new person—a real-life situation in other words—talking with new people. From time to time I could detect a slight stammer in his speech. I equated this to the stammering that young children do when they are first becoming fluent in using language and paid no attention to it. It occurred when Philip was using longer sentences to express his thoughts.

Philip used a great many 'ers' and 'ums' in his responses. They seemed to afford him time to think of the words he was going to use. His sentences were said slowly on most occasions. His articulation needed attention. On some occasions I did not catch his words though this might have been a measure of *my* inattention in the actual situation. When I played back the recordings I could not understand why I had not discriminated every word immediately. At the beginning of the conversation I mistook the word 'logs' for 'rugs' and I did not catch the word 'races' (p. 80). I was interested to note here, however, that Philip must have seen from my facial expression or perhaps other bodily gestures that I had not understood him. He immediately gave me another word 'sports'. I wonder where he had learnt that language behaviour from.

On one occasion I missed his word 'ripe' and followed it up with an idea about 'wiping the tomatoes' before eating them. Fortunately we soon returned to the discussion about ripeness. Perhaps such a mistake on the part of the listener might be a function of not listening carefully enough to the meaning of the whole idea being expressed. Perhaps it might suggest that the child needs some extra speech help with specific sounds. Perhaps adequate feed-back, in terms of the child being allowed to listen frequently to his own conversations from the tape, would act as a 'remedial situation' for him anyway. For, as Herriot writes 'language behaviour needs feed-back. We need to hear ourselves talking in order to articulate adequately!' To my knowledge few schools for the mentally handicapped have made special arrangements for each child to have the opportunity of listening to his own 'talk'. There will always be a shortage of speech therapists. Instead of continuing to complain about the fact, we might begin to view the matter from another angle and ask ourselves the question 'are we spending enough time enabling the mentally handicapped to acquire the

Observing conversations 85

skill of language behaviour in social situations as well as in what might be described as "remedial ones" (taped feedback in language laboratories)?' Whilst Philip's natural speed of talking was fairly slow his 'yeses' and 'ohs', interspersed between the words of my explanations and questions, made for a certain quick speed of word exchange on many occasions. On replay I noticed with some regret that I did not always give Philip enough time to finish his sentence, e.g. (p. 83) 'er, this to open'. 'Yes, this to open——'. His answer, 'the door'. Had I given him time he would undoubtedly have completed the sentence himself. The skill of pausing, hesitating just long enough when talking with a mentally handicapped person is a difficult one for us to acquire. I have been theorizing about this feature of the teacher's language behaviour for many years now and helping my students to understand the implication of it. In spite of a lot of personal practice I can see from this tape that I have a long way to go yet in order to perfect such a skill.* Another of my faults was in some instances telling Philip too much about something that he was interested in to the extent that he could not 'get in' as it were with what he wanted to say, e.g. when I was talking about the sun ripening tomatoes. However, he prevailed in the end and forced his own idea upon me, 'or in the freezer'.

Sheila

Hullo.
Hullo. Hullo, and what's your name?
Sheila.
Sheila. Sit down Sheila. Sit down.
Sheila Davis. (teacher brought her to me)
And how old is Sheila?
How old are you Sheila?
Thirteen.
How old? (I did not catch the answer)
Thirteen.
Thirteen.
Yes.
Are you, you're a nice big girl for thirteen.
Sheila, would you like to come a little nearer to the table?
Mm.
Yes. (I showed her what I meant there by 'that's right')
Now, we are going to have a nice talk. Sheila, *Yes,* when you leave school where will you go, (hesitation) when you leave school?
Leave school?
Yes.
When you LEAVE school. *Leave school?* (inflection indicated question) Yes, when you go away from school.
Where will you go? (hesitation) Do you know? *Yes.* You will go to work, won't you?
What will you do when you go to work?
Telephones.
The telephones? (high pitch with surprise)

---

* Another thought occurred to me whilst writing this criticism and it was that I had not been in weekly contact with the mentally handicapped during the year of the recording. Skills do need constant practice as we all know.

86 Observing conversations

Yes.
What will you do on the telephones?
Ring mummy up.
Ring mum up will you?
Ring mummy up, yes.
And what will you say to her?
Hullo mum.
Go on, tell me some more.
Alright mum, alright.
Yes, yes, go on tell me some more.
How's Mary?
Who's Mary then?
My sister.
Oh, yes, she's your sister, yes, tell me about Mary.
She's going school now.
Is she a little sister?
Yes, oh.
She's going 'n school.
Yes, which school? What's the name of the school . . . d'you know, (hesitation) d'you
    know the name of the school, tell me.
Margaret.
Is that the name of your sister, Margaret?
(she nodded)
Margaret's the name of the sister and yes. Tell me your name again.
Sheila.
That's right Sheila. Sheila, yes, very good.
What's that for?
What do you think it's for?
Tape. (it sounded like 'pape')
Yes, it's called . . . d'you know what it's called?
No.
It's called a microphone.
Oh, what d'you do?
What d'you do?
Yes.
Well, what are you doing now, with me, (hesitation) tell me what you are doing
    with me.
Talking.
You're talking with me, right and as we're talking, Sheila?
Yes.
It's going, it's going through there.
Yes.
And right into the tape there, and then, when I've finished talking with you I'm
    going to let you listen to it. Then you'll hear yourself talking on the tape, you
    see, you'll hear yourself talking, O.K., right, well now, anything else you want
    to tell me about your mum?
Yes.
Go on.
She goes to work sometimes. Theo's.
Yes.
What kind of work does she do?
Ah, she's doing the beds and washing up and . . . put the dinner on.
Puts the dinner on, yes.
And mums takes me home sometimes.
Your mum takes you home sometimes?
Yes.
Do you live in the hostel then?

Observing conversations 87

Yes.
But she takes you home at weekend. Does she take you home every weekend?
Yes, mum.
You dried your hair very nicely with the hairdrier yesterday, didn't you? (no answer)
Yes, had you been swimming? *Yes.* I've got a nice hairdrier at home and it's pink
and it fits, you know, you you held it in your hand didn't you, like this. Well,
the one that I've got fits right over your head like that (gesture) and you sit on
a chair and you press a little button and the heat comes on and it blows your
hair dry, doesn't it. Yes, it does, doesn't it? Sheila.
Yes.
You see these keys here?
Yes.
Well, I want you to tell me about the keys. We'll have a little talk about these keys.
They're my keys. Can you tell me anything about them? (hesitation) What can
you tell me about them?
Keys in the doors when you.
Yes, keys on the doors when you ... when you ... what?
When you're in the car when you.
Yes, yes, in the car yes ... which do you think's the car key, from there can you
see the car key? (hesitation) Which one do you think is the car key?
This one.
Which one?
This one.
Well, take hold of the key. You've not got hold of the key, you've got hold of the
ring. Where's the key that you're talking about? Oh, that one.
Yes.
Oh that. I see you think that one's the car key.
Yes.
I see, I see, yes well actually it's this one. This one with the black on it, that's the
car key. What kind of a key could that be for? What would that open d'you think?
A car.
Um. Welll, no I don't think that would open a car. What else could it open? What
else could it open that one? (hesitation) *Um.* Can you see something in this room
that it might open?
Mm. (hesitation)
I can see two things that it might open. It won't but it could. (pause) What are those
up there? (pause) What's that called on the wall?
Wall.
Yes, what's that on the wall called?
Light.
No, on the WALL. (stress on the word wall)
Where's the wall.
(she pointed)
Yes, that's right.
There's something on the wall. Do you know the name cupboard? That's a cupboard,
isn't it? That's right. Well, these are cupboard keys. Now then, tell me about these
keys here, what do you think these keys open?
A door. (said in a sing-song intonation)
Yes, a door that's right a door. (I imitated her sing-song intonation) Which door?
Which door, which door do you think ... well, which door? (she pointed) Well,
not that door. That door would have a bigger key, wouldn't it? (one could see
the lock for a large key. I was showing her a yale lock key) But which ... why
do you think I have these keys, they're all my keys. So what do I use this one
for?
Open the er cupboard.
Opening what?
When you open the cupboard.

88   *Observing conversations*

Well, well this is the cupboard key, those are the cupboard keys but what are these keys for? What would I want these for, (hesitate) mm?
Don't know.
Can you think?
No.
Why, they open my, (hesitate) *door* ... of my, *house.*
That's right the door of my house, otherwise I can't get in, can I? (raised intonation to encourage and stimulate attention)
Why do I lock my door, why do I lock the door of my house?
I don't know.
What love?
I don't know.
Why do you think I lock the door of my house? (hesitation)
To stop open it.
To stop opening it.
Yes, the draught.
And the draught.
Yes.
Ahaa yes. I also lock it so that nobody else can get in except me and my husband, yes.
Yes.
What's your husband's name?
What's my husband's name?
Yes.
His name is Lionel.
Lionel?
Yes.
What's your dad called?
Eric.
I see, yes, my husband's called Lionel, Lionel Stevens, Mr Stevens and your dad's called Mr ...?
Eric.
No, he's not called Mr Eric. You're called Sheila ...?
Davis. (inaudible to me in the real situation but not when I transcribed the conversation from the tape)
What darling?
Yes, I call him daddy.
I know you call him daddy but yer mammy doesn't call him daddy. She calls him Eric doesn't she, but what would I call him? I wouldn't call him daddy and I wouldn't call him Eric.
I'd call him Mr ...?
Davis.
Yes.
Is your name Sheila Davis?
Yes.
That's right, I'd call him Mr Davis I would, yes, Mr Davis.
Does your dad work, Sheila?
Yes.
What does he do then?
Now?
Yes.
He's, he stays at home in bed sometimes.
He stays at home in bed, does he?
Yes.
Why, isn't he very well?
No, he had he had the bed on fire.
Oh, he had the bed on fire, how did he manage that? (surprised voice)

Observing conversations   89

How did he manage that?
Dunno. (a laugh or two from me)
Did he, was he smoking in bed?
Yes.
Perhaps he was smoking in bed was he?
He was dead.
He was what?
Dead.
Dead?
You mean he, you mean he, you haven't got a dad now?
No, he's dead.
Oh I AM sorry Sheila.
Did he burn himself to death then?
oh ... o ... o ... (sympathizing tone)
He had acc...ent.
He had an accident?
Yes, he had acc...ent.
He was dead on the bed.
Oh, dear yes, I see. So you haven't got a dad?
No.
Oh I arh sorry Sheila, yes. Shall I tell you something?
Yes. (animated tone)
I haven't either.
Oh.
I've no dad. Still I'm an older lady, aren't I?
Yes.
So I wouldn't need a dad?
Do you have a mummy or a granny?
No, I've got no mummy and I haven't got any granny, no, no mummy and no granny.
   Have you got a granny?
Yes.
Mm.
But, you've no dad, I see yes. Well, I'm very, very sorry, Sheila.
Aaah. (Sheila imitating the intonation of sorrow I was trying to convey in my voice.
   Her imitation told me she had observed a change in my tone. Of course it didn't
   tell me that she had understood my feeling for her)
'Cos you're a young girl and you need a dad, don't you, yes you do.
Have you got brothers?
Yes, John.
Yes.
He's married.
Oh is he?
Yes.
He's a dad.
How many children has he got?
Garry and Stephen.
Garry and Stephen, so how many's that then?
One, two.
Yes, he's got two.
Sheila do you think you can tell me how many keys there are on that ring?
Mm. One.
You'll have to pick them up I think.
Yes.
Yes.
(counted 1–10, hesitations in between all numbers and a great deal of fumbling with
   the bunch of keys)
Ten keys. You're absolutely right. I don't know how you got it but you're right.

90   *Observing conversations*

There ARE ten keys. What do you think this is, erm, Sheila? (I pointed to the little torch on the ring).
Hearing.
What is it? Yes?
It's a ...
Can you tell me what it is?
No.
What do you think it does?
What does it do?
Ahaaaaa, when you put it in the ear.
What love?
When you put it in the ears.
Oh, when you put it in the ears. You mean a hearing aid. (hesitate) No, it isn't. No, it's not a hearing aid.
It's a ... mmmm ... look! (I flashed it)
What came on then. Did you see the light? *Mm.*
Did you see a light? There, did you see the light?
So what is it then, if it's a little light? What is it if it's a little light?
One when you put the light on in the night.
Yes, it's called a ...
A.
What do you think it's called? It's called a torch.
Torch.
A little torch ... yes.
It's so that I can see where the lock is to put the key in the door you see.
Very good Sheila, do you want to listen to yourself now?
Yes.

Sheila was initially perhaps the least fluent of the three young people I talked with. This may have affected once more my not waiting for her to respond before saying something else to her—to stimulate her as it were. The possible justification for my language behaviour in this situation was that at least in listening she was receiving a model of language fluency. As I got to know Sheila better I began to assume that her lack of knowledge of certain everyday words, words that you would expect her to know, e.g. cupboard, wall, and torch was because she lived in a hostel during the week and only went home at weekends.* Perhaps the school needed to take this into account when thinking about increasing her vocabulary content.

One of the facts that struck me as I was replaying this particular tape was the way in which almost imperceptible ways of communicating to them suggest a non-equal relationship. Thus I say to Sheila 'You'll hear yourself' instead of 'We'll hear ourselves'. If 'we' is a difficult concept for the mentally handicapped to grasp (Olechnowicz, p. 79) then we must be quite sure that both the word and the concept are indeed introduced to the children in a wide variety of social situations where we all are involved—they are doing things with us rather than we are doing things for them or to them.

Another instance of implying a non-equal relationship was when I committed a fault common to all of us in this field of education from time

---

* This was because she lived at too great a distance from the school to travel daily.

to time. I asked her teacher how old Sheila was instead of asking Sheila directly herself. In reality I WAS in fact asking Sheila, but the words I used implied that I was addressing someone else 'And how old is Sheila?' I immediately corrected myself and said 'How old are you, Sheila?' Later on in my conversation with this young lady I commented 'you're a nice big girl for thirteen'. Perhaps I was surprised that knowing she was sixteen she gave the answer 'thirteen'. These children very often don't know their ages as they grow into adulthood because they are not told their new age often enough every year—we are assuming that they add one to their last age. More often than not they don't.

In thinking about Sheila's contribution to my thinking about observing the taped spoken language of the mentally handicapped, I was interested to note that *she* initiated the change in direction of our conversation on two occasions. She also asked three questions. I never explored her ideas about work after her initial response 'telephone', but she obviously knew the meaning of the word itself for she described the work her mother did. I was interested also to find that whilst using the hesitation technique might be useful once the child has the words in his passive vocabulary, no response to the hesitation will possibly indicate that the child has in fact not got the word in the first place in his language repertoire—in Sheila's case the words 'cupboard', 'wall', and 'torch'. Skilled judgement is indeed needed to choose when to use this technique or to give the child the word.

'What is it' or 'what is this' are very common phrases heard everywhere in classrooms in schools for the mentally handicapped—very often the question is put to the children before they have been told the word by someone and have had a discussion about the 'object' appertaining to the word. Of less frequent use is the phrase 'What does it do', yet this is likely to elicit far more interesting ideas from the child as well as encouraging him to use verbs or adjectives.

In thinking about the function of the word 'yes' in the context of my conversation with Sheila, I have concluded that I used it to give me time to think out simple words to offer to her in explanation for something she wanted to know as well as a commonly used reinforcer in conversational terms. As we would expect, Sheila had the concept of her sister having a name but not of a building—her sister's school. The possibility occurred to me that we should teach the children the names of their own school first and then the names of the schools attended by their brothers and sisters. We all influence each other in our use of words during a conversation. It would seem I was interested to observe that at the end of the dialogue I reverted back to Sheila's use of the words 'mummy' and 'daddy' in spite of the fact that I had tried at the beginning to get her to use what I consider to be a more 'mature' word, 'mum'. In fact she did use this word some seconds after I had used it. This indicated that she was listening attentively to me as does her use of the word I had 'taught' her—'cupboard'—several times in the conversation.

If we now take a rather general look at the three conversations one or

92   Observing conversations

two more points might be of interest. All the children used at least one sentence of eight or more words during our conversation although this seems of less significance than the fact that we learnt things about each other during our discourse. All the children omitted words from sentences but then so did I. Spoken English is full of such occurrences whether we happen to be 'normal', highly intelligent, or mentally handicapped. Some of their omissions included verbs, and function words such as the definite and the indefinite article. There were no instances, however, where we did not understand each other. Whilst the speech of Philip and Sheila was not always clearly articulated there were very few moments when I did not fully grasp the actual word they had spoken. All three asked me a question using question word language structures. These related either to me or to something they wanted me to do. They had indeed discovered the function of language.

In each conversation I took the opportunity of modelling language by giving them a piece of information. I cannot know whether this was new information to them or not. Sometimes this took the form of giving them a new word—'ignition' key in the case of David—or talking to them about something—the floating logs, the hair drier, my habit of going in at the back door, my not having a dad, and so on.

Whilst I never referred directly to a child's error or asked the child to say it again in terms of correct pronunciation nevertheless I did provide a more correct model of the word/phrase almost immediately afterwards on most occasions. I also used the child's name frequently in order to gain either attention and rapport on meeting them and getting to know them, or to indicate to myself that I was going to introduce something new into the conversation....

Shortly after examining these transcripts I came across an article describing the attempts made by the National Association for the Teaching of English to interest teachers in their own techniques of teaching English in all its forms in the secondary school.* I can recommend the article for we have much to learn from each other. The article was about the techniques of training teachers' observational skills in a specific area of the curriculum and in encouraging teachers to observe their own language behaviour in the classroom. The author writes, 'It is valuable but difficult for teachers to tape their own lessons. Only secure teachers were prepared to play the tapes of lessons to each other.' I hope I am secure in presenting you with this very small sample from my enormous collection of conversations with mentally handicapped people.†

---

* Extract from *Language Across the Curriculum; Guidelines for Schools* by Mike Torbe. Ward Locke Educational Publishers in *Times Educational Supplement*, 8th April, 1977.

† I started taping my own conversations and some of those of my students with mentally handicapped people when I entered the field of mental subnormality in 1962. I have used them with students in the University (Manchester Advanced Diploma Course for Teachers of the Handicapped 1964–75) and on initial courses of special training for teachers of the mentally handicapped. They have also been used very much on in-service courses for teachers, nurses, houseparents, and others all over the country. During the early 'seventies

Observing conversations 93

As we shall have seen after reading the transcripts, a transcript can never fully convey or recreate the nuances of the communication between the two people concerned. It cannot reflect the bodily and facial cues that we all know are so much a part of the social interaction in conversation. It cannot record the smile exchanges, the warmth, the inflections, the intonations. It cannot indicate the enjoyment of each other, the impatience I sometimes felt with myself for not always giving the child enough time to think out a response, and my nervousness in a new situation with the child, lest I failed to interest him at his level and allow him to do his best with me and thus retain his confidence.

However, there is no doubt in my mind that if we record ourselves in such situations uninhibitedly with mentally handicapped children we might find that:

(1) We become more aware of our language habits.
(2) One of the functions of the repetitions is to keep the interactional flow between us in a manner similar to that we adopt when talking to a non-handicapped person—through using stabilizers, 'ers', and 'ums'. The repetitions perhaps act as language patterns too.
(3) Another function closely allied to the one above might be to give ourselves time to find something else to say that is meaningful to the child, or to think out whether to pursue his lack of the 'correct' response to our questions in another way. I have written the word correct in inverted commas because as teachers we should be more interested in the response rather than in whether it is correct or not. Piaget has been teaching us this for a long time by his scientific method. Paul Berry in his discussion about 'error' in language reinforces this point in a more specific context. Repetition might also 'cover up' silences in a dialogue.
(4) Perhaps we must begin to consider more carefully the CONTENT of their ideas, when as adolescents they use more complex language forms such as longer sentences or questions. We might have become too concerned and then inhibited about the effect of our questioning techniques—whether we get a one-word answer or not. Perhaps we have failed to observe the role being played by their comprehension and interest in motivating the quality of their language structures. By giving them objects, and pictures of objects, instead of talking more with them about their families and immediate relatives and neighbours, we might prevent them from expressing themselves in more complex terms. We might also forget that to a large extent it is PEOPLE that the mentally handicapped are interested in. The 'I said to her and she said to me' type of social life is going to be the social milieu for many of them in the future. If we ignore this fact

---

I devised a simple guide for my audiences regarding how to listen to specific recordings. I have described one of these guides in my chapter 'The Implications of Language Research for Training Teachers' in Berry, P. (Ed.) (1976) *The Language and Communication in the Mentally Handicapped*, Edward Arnold, London.

94   *Observing conversations*

because it has not been our experience we might ignore them altogether in terms of their being our social partners in a conversation. We might too readily assume they have little to contribute to our lives. It might mean that our expectations of their correctness of expression will be too demanding and they will fail to become motivated through our implied lack of confidence in them.

(5) An enormous amount of intellectual effort will be needed by some of us to adapt our language behaviour to them in order that they can use theirs more effectively. In helping them to achieve fluency as adults I firmly believe that we must do this for them—adapt our language structures—rather than adopt an attitude which connotes, 'Well the real world will not be doing this so why should I'. Most of them any way will be in a world of planned dependence.

(6) Whole chunks of our language will surely have no meaning for the mentally handicapped person however skilled or well intentioned we are or however hard we try to arrange it otherwise. We shall certainly discover in talking with them (note the 'with' and not 'to') that it is indeed difficult, but not impossible to stem the automatic (creative) flow of speech that we have developed in our path towards fluency of spoken expression. This will inevitably be so if the mentally handicapped person as an adolescent or an adult has achieved fluency. We shall certainly forget to be aware that what we say is not all understood more than when we are in a situation when there are constant hesitations and a lack of response on the part of the child.

(7) It is difficult for some of us to model language with the child, i.e. present a continuous flow of talk where we are telling the child something arising from something he has said; where on occasions during the modelling we shall be indirectly correcting his mistakes. Most of us will find it easier to ask questions of our conversation companion—THIS model of asking questions has certainly been assimilated only too well by older teachers from schools when formal communication, and the 'question, hands up, and answer' method was the order of the day. Younger adults might find informal communication much easier, particularly if they have attended schools where the conversational flow between teacher and taught has been the method used rather than the 'hands up and answer the question' type of approach. I have seen this approach used in schools for the mentally handicapped in the last 5 years in the mistaken view that this is treating them more normally.

(8) We must give the mentally handicapped adolescent much more opportunity than we do at the moment in our schools to have conversations with us in the same way as we would have a conversation with a friend, i.e. sitting in armchairs and talking freely. In this way they will be afforded the much needed opportunity to practise a skill—the skill of language use. On reflection the three conversations I had with these particular children were to some extent not as fruitful as they might have been if I had not set myself specific goals to achieve in too short

Observing conversations 95

a time (10 minutes each). Parents, members of the community with time to spare, and classroom assistants might all be encouraged to talk with individual children in the older age ranges. They will all need guidance but taped recordings will not only be useful for discussion afterwards but they will act as feed-back material for each child as the need arises.

(9) We start thinking more about what happens to these young people at 16 when the majority of them leave school before they have achieved verbal fluency. Most of them are forced into the work-bench situation where their attention is often wholly captivated by the task in front of them and where often the opportunities for practising their language skills daily are minimal. I am aware that sometimes work bench conversations are forbidden.

My intention in presenting language material in the way I have is to encourage others to explore the INTEREST of talking at length with mentally handicapped people and record the experience for feed-back. Research workers following a similar approach themselves instead of observing teachers talking with the children in group situations in classrooms might indeed discover the most fruitful techniques we can adopt to enable them to communicate in spoken language more easily.

Perhaps my material can be used for language analysis by students. It takes time to transcribe conversations such as those I have included. However, they will afford students an opportunity to evaluate not only the language of the individual child but also of the adult. They might look for the following:

(1) when does the length of sentence increase?
(2) how many omissions are there?
(3) when does the child change the conversation himself?
(4) how many different words does the child/adult use?
(5) how many words contain more than two/three syllables?
(6) how many pauses were evident in these particular samples?
(7) jot down the one-word/two-word replies of the child.
(8) measure the length of time the adult expects the child to listen to the longest 'chunk of language'.

Perhaps my material will reassure parents and others that all but the profoundly handicapped child will in fact be able to speak and hold a meaningful conversation, however simple, as they grow up, unless that part of the brain controlling speech is damaged and unless the physical organs of speech are malformed.

8 Observing in a one-to-one teaching session

It is now generally recognized and accepted that the child who is mentally handicapped needs short, systematic, methodical, individual sessions with an adult as frequently as the organization of the school allows. Since 1970 local education authorities in most parts of the country have appointed classroom assistants to help teachers, particularly in classes for nursery and junior age children. This means that all the children should now be receiving a share of individual attention from the teacher in a one-to-one situation. It is wonderful to see the teachers of these children with a companion but I do know from my work with students during 1961–71, when classroom assistants were not the rule, that most of them on teaching practice were able to demonstrate their ability to work with two or three individual children each day and to do this in a systematic fashion throughout each week. Clearly, it all depended on their provision of appropriate activities and absorbing teaching aids to engage the interest of the other children. Sometimes the whole organization would be upset by one disturbed child but generally speaking the technique was possible and successful in terms of the teachers getting to know children.

The number of sessions spent with each child individually will undoubtedly depend upon the skill of the teacher and her commitment anyway to the concept of such a relationship. It will depend upon the length of time she spends with each child. As I have come to understand this more fully, it will differ according to each child's needs and stage of development. It will also depend upon the amount of preparation the teacher has carried out beforehand and how precise she is in her assessment of what the child needs from her in this situation. When I wrote this particular chapter in the mid-'sixties there was little to help the teacher find a starting point for her work. Innovation in training students, in deciding upon what we were going to do with individual children, and in providing specific aids was the order of the day. Whilst students on 1-year courses had given some thought to the individual within the group as it were, few of them had worked in a one-to-one teaching partnership with a child.

It was only when the 2-year courses started, in Manchester (1965) at any rate, that students were given a real opportunity to find out whether they liked working with individual children and using their observational skills to decide from day to day what they would do with them. These students had four teaching practice periods in 2 years of training. They lasted for 6 weeks each. During the first two periods students practised in two's. They arranged their day so as to have experience of both group and individual work. As far as I am able to judge, this method did in

Observing in a one-to-one teaching session 97

fact enable students to begin to understand the varied needs of mentally handicapped children. Without such opportunities I doubt very much whether an inexperienced teacher would be able to pin-point precisely the child's strengths and weaknesses or to achieve proficiency in observing.

The following notes, taken from a student's teaching notebook in 1966/7, are still interesting for me, for they seem to illustrate an important concept that I have been trying to convey throughout this book—that is to say we observe the child and 'follow him'. As we shall see from the second part of this chapter this does not mean that we have no responsibility in deciding beforehand what we might wish him to learn. It does mean, however, that we must develop flexibility in our approach to him—for our planned decisions could be wrong. Such an approach exploits what is in the child. It depends on our belief in him too that there is in fact something on which we can work positively.

Session 1

GOAL—To work with the Cuisenaire Rods with Pamela.

REASON—She has shown tremendous interest in the Cuisenaire apparatus, sorting out the rods and making patterns with them in the free-choice sessions.

METHOD—Give Pamela the box of Cuisenaire Rods and observe first what she does with them. If there is any number concept at all, work on this, asking Pamela to take a rod and put it next to a number of rods to make the same size, i.e. 'Can you find two sticks which are as long as this one when put end to end?' Record all patterns Pamela makes on paper.

MATERIALS—Cuisenaire Rods, pencils, and paper.

EVALUATION—I gave Pamela the Cuisenaire Rods and she first took all the black rods out one at a time and laid them on the table next to each other. Pamela then said, 'Let's make a house.' She collected all the black rods and built them up into a house. Then she knocked them down and took the orange rods and the yellow rods out on to the table, first fitting the black rods back into the box correctly. Pamela laid the orange and yellow rods on the table alternately. When she had used all the orange and yellow rods alternately she added five red rods at the right-hand side of the orange rod. 'It's a pattern,' Pamela said. She then asked if she could paint a pattern, so I suggested that she copy the pattern she had made with the orange and yellow rods. She started to do this very well, but suddenly she went all over the paper with yellow paint and covered up the pattern. I decided that this was the time to stop as Pamela had worked with the Cuisenaire Rods for a quarter of an hour and I thought this long enough for one time. Pamela had difficulty putting the yellow rods back into the box: she couldn't fit them at first. I helped her and she soon realized on her own the way in which they went back into the box. Perhaps it is easier for her to fit the longer rods.

98   *Observing in a one-to-one teaching session*

Session 2

GOAL (1)—To continue working with the Cuisenaire Rods and record patterns which Pamela makes with rods.

REASON—Pamela has shown a marked interest in the Cuisenaire Rods and formed some very interesting patterns last time.

GOAL (2)—To show Pamela how to do blot painting.

REASON—She loves painting and making patterns.

METHOD—Give Pamela Cuisenaire Rods and record patterns which she makes on graph paper. Try out a number of simple experiments with her, asking Pamela to find a number of rods the same in length to certain other rods. Afterwards give Pamela a sheet of paper and show her how to do blot painting. I will do one first to show her what I mean. Splash different colours of paint on to the paper and fold paper down middle whilst paint is still wet.

MATERIALS—Cuisenaire Rods, graph paper, paint, and paper.

EVALUATION—I asked Pamela to build the rods up on the desk in height succession. I showed her what I wanted her to do and she started with the smallest, the beige rod, but when she got as far as the yellow rod Pamela knocked them down and said, 'Let's make a garage.' She arranged six blue rods to make a 'garage'. She then took two more blue rods and arranged them. She said this was the Parish Church. Then Pamela said she would make my house and arranged black, orange, and beige rods. She then took ten orange rods and placed them all together. She said this was a 'pattern'. Pamela loves painting and enjoyed splashing the paint on to make the blot painting. 'It's a butterfly,' she said.

Session 3

GOAL—To continue work with Cuisenaire and do potato printing.

REASON—To follow up the patterns Pamela makes with the Cuisenaire Rods and to do potato prints because Pamela enjoys making patterns.

METHOD—Give Pamela the Cuisenaire Rods and record carefully what she does with them spontaneously. I will ask Pamela if she can build up the rods in order of size. Record way she builds them up. Prepare paper, paint, and water for potato printing. Ask Pamela what she would like to draw on the potato and cut out what she suggests on the potato. Show Pamela how to paint with the potato on the paper.

MATERIALS—Pamela could not build the Cuisenaire Rods in the correct order of size. I asked Pamela what she would like to make with the potato prints and she said 'a flower and a parakeet'. I cut out a flower and a bird and Pamela put paint on these and printed them on to the paper. When she had put the flowers on the paper Pamela took the green paint and painted stems on the flowers and leaves. She said it was a garden.

Observing in a one-to-one teaching session 99

Session 4

GOAL—To record more patterns with Cuisenaire Rods and to make a model of a church.

REASON—Pamela attends the local Parish Church and yesterday she said she would like to make a church.

METHOD—Record all spontaneous patterns which she makes with rods on graph paper. See that Pamela puts all the Cuisenaire Rods back in the correct places in the box. Prepare boxes and Cellophane paper for church model. Also scissors and glue. Suggest that Pamela cuts out windows and sticks Cellophane on to give the effect of glass. Prepare paint for Pamela to paint church.

MATERIALS—Cuisenaire Rods, graph paper, crayons, boxes, Cellophane, Sellotape, paper, glue, scissors, and silver paper.

EVALUATION—When Pamela was selecting the boxes for the model, I sneezed. 'Bless you, oh Miss G. you've got a cold.' Heard children singing *'This old man'* in the Hall, began to join in. I drew lines on the cardboard Pamela had chosen for her to cut along. I showed her how to join the four walls together with Sellotape. She asked if she could paint the church white as their church was coloured white. She painted it white saying, 'One wall, another wall, roof,' and so on as she painted it. We left the church to dry and will finish it next time.

Session 5

GOAL—To finish church model.

METHOD—Show Pamela how to cut out windows and stick the Cellophane paper on. Pamela wants to make a cross and a flag on the roof. The flag can be of colourful material stuck on a match-stick and I will draw a cross for Pamela to cut out. Pamela might be able to draw her own cross. This can be covered with silver paper. I will draw a line for the door and Pamela can cut round this line and paint the door.

MATERIALS—Paint, church model, Cellophane paper, silver paper, cardboard, and material.

EVALUATION—Pamela tried very hard to cut the windows out for the church model, pulling all sorts of funny faces because the cardboard was stiff. I held my hand over hers and this made it much easier for Pamela to cut. I showed her how to stick the Cellophane on behind the windows with Sellotape. Pamela found two pieces of cardboard and covered them with silver paper. She stuck these together to make a cross which she stuck over the door. She then painted the door blue.

Session 6

GOAL—To make a dress for Pamela's doll.

REASON—Pamela asked me if she could make a new dress for her doll.

100   *Observing in a one-to-one teaching session*

METHOD—Let Pamela select material to make the dress with from the material box. Draw the outline of the dress on the wrong side of the material so Pamela can cut along it with pinking shears to prevent fraying. Show Pamela how to use thimble. Pamela can sew the dress together using small tacking stitches. Talk about sewing as she does it, i.e. seaming, tacking, etc.

MATERIALS—Cloth, needle, thread, thimble, pinking shears.

EVALUATION—Pamela cut the dress out very evenly along the outline I had drawn. I fastened on for her, showing her carefully how to do it with two or three overstitches. She sewed the dress up with very neat small stitches and followed the edge all round until she had about 2 in. left to sew, then the stitches went a little crooked. She took the clothes off her doll and said, 'Let's try it on.'

The notes show how the teacher took the child's *spontaneous* interest in the Cuisenaire Rods (found in the quiet activities corner during free-choice time) as her starting point for individual sessions with Pamela. This teacher's reference to the way in which the child handled them and lacked interest in what she (the teacher) wanted her to do, reveals that she was at the level of representing with them imaginatively well-known objects—a garage, a church, and houses. She liked making patterns with the rods.

Sessions two and three show, too, how the child's expressed desire to paint patterns in a previous session was followed up and responded to. Her teacher provided her with the new experience of using paint.

Pamela's expressed wish to make a church had stimulated her teacher to collect the materials for making a model with her. The comments show Pamela's ability to communicate, her use of certain words and the way in which the teacher enabled her to choose the boxes for the model. They also help us to understand some of the methods used by the teacher to give guidance where it was needed. For we see in the notes that she prepared the materials in such a way as to ensure success in achievement that is meaningful to the child, e.g. 'Pamela cut the dress out very evenly along the outline I had drawn.'

The reason for selecting this particular description of individual sessions is to show how ably the student followed the CHILD'S lead and interest. The number apparatus was available in this school and was found to be a useful piece of teaching equipment. The rods could be used for pattern making, for emptying and fitting back into the box, and for imaginative construction. Thus Robert aged 15 years (mental age 6 years) was asked by the teacher what he could do with the rods. 'Show me what you can do with these, Bobby?' was her request. He immediately set to work and made a model. He told his teacher that it was Batman's Cave. 'What else can you make?' 'Batmobile' was his reply and he represented this with his rods.

These records describe how a young student teacher observed the child wanting to make things with the rods. She did not push her to a stage she was not ready for, i.e. making her count them, making up sums with

Observing in a one-to-one teaching session 101

them. I had countless other interesting examples of how students using their own initiative and observation skills worked successfully with individual children. On many occasions they followed the lead given to them by children in the long free-choice sessions to develop an interest in the individual session. We all have much to learn in knowing exactly what to do with each mentally handicapped child. Each new one we meet will be a different experience for us. We shall find that each has need of different experiences.

Systematic, individual sessions spent in:

(1) using the children's communications and visible interests;
(2) introducing them to new situations both in and out of school;
(3) encouraging them to look at, manipulate and to experiment with materials and games* of all kinds;
(4) talking, reading, and singing to them, and telling them stories† sometimes using puppets will bring their own reward to the teacher.

Especially will this happen when, with experience, she can see where the original spontaneous activity of the child might lead in terms of the total development of each child's abilities.

In order to develop such an approach and make it a part of one's professional skill, the teacher needs to be certain that she always has available and close to her and the child 'waste' and creative materials of all kinds including glue, scissors, paints, and crayons, for she will never know when she will need them. So much individual teaching going on in the schools today is concerned with commercially produced teaching aids and 'academic' learning that sometimes bear no relationship to meaningful experience or to the directly observed needs of an individual child. At the end of the session neither child nor teacher has anything to show for the time that has been spent together. On most occasions precise records of the child's response to the aids are non-existent.

Since writing this description of a student's efforts to teach in a one-to-one situation a great many changes have taken place in the schools for the mentally handicapped. More money has also been available. This new situation has not meant, however, that the schools have been invaded with ready-made assessment materials to enable them to find their starting point with a particular child. Most teachers are still relying upon development scales and of course this is sound practice. Most of them, however, do not always contain the stages of behaviour in small enough or precise enough detail. It seems that work on assessment is being developed all over the country but it has not yet reached the publication stage. This is a pity for we need whatever is available to enable us to focus our attention more specifically on what a child needs as part of his special education. Research workers at the Hester Adrian Research Centre are to some extent

---

* Stevens, M. (1976), Chapters 4, 8, 12.
Jeffrees, D. and McConkey, R. (1976) *Let Me Speak*. Human Horizon Series. Souvenir Press and Academic Ltd, London.
† Fitch, J. (1969) *Story Telling for Slow Learners*. Published by National Council for Special Education, London.

102 *Observing in a one-to-one teaching session*

now ahead in their attempts to provide teachers with guidelines regarding the individual young child.*

Two pieces of work interested me as a teacher some 4 years ago. I could envisage that both would extend observation skills in a rather specific context. They would also encourage teachers to devise remedial programmes for the children in their classes. They were useful for children with intellectual levels of under 1 to about 6 years. I want to spend time sharing some thoughts with you regarding the way in which I used these. One was the Language Imitation Test (LIT) compiled by Paul Berry (previously a research worker at the Hester Adrian Research Centre and now a Senior Lecturer at the Fred and Eleanor Schonell Research Centre, Queensland University, Australia). The other concerns a scale devised by two American psychologists, Uzgiriz and Hunt, used by my colleague Olwen Gregory, and interpreted for teachers by me in 1973.†

The Berry Language Imitation Test (1971) caught my attention because it was compiled especially with teachers rather than psychologists in mind; it afforded an experienced teacher the opportunity to produce possible programmes for individual children—programmes that were indeed specific to an individual and not programmes that all individual children were processed through at their own level, although undoubtedly the ideas that were contained in the programmes could, with slight alterations, be used with other children or with groups. It aroused the interest of a great many teachers I lectured to in aspects of language that hitherto they did not seem to have been interested in to any depth.

The LIT contains seventy-five items so a score can be obtained. Whilst the score is not so important as an examination of the way in which the child has responded to each item, nevertheless a change in the score over a period of time will indicate changes, however slowly. Some teachers like to use a scoring technique.

The test begins by asking the child to say the same as the teacher in terms of words. There are twenty-five words. By using the particular words chosen the teacher is able to see which initial sounds are giving the child any trouble (with the exception of V, Z, X). These twenty-five words are then used throughout the test with the addition of 'function' words—'the', 'is', 'isn't' and a few extra nouns and a present participle, viz. 'being'. The main theoretical theme of the test seems to be that when 'imitating sentences, words, sounds, a child must bring into operation his knowledge of language. The test has been tried out on a normal, ESN(M) and ESN(S) population of children. The results have indicated that when a child imitates sentences or word strings he does not simply repeat them in a parrot fashion. Indeed, he uses the rules he has learnt about language to help him imitate. When his rule system breaks down he makes errors. It is the error pattern of a child in an imitation situation which tells us a great deal about his language development.'

---

* Cf. Jeffrees, D. and McConkey, R. (p. 101).

† Stevens, M. (1976) *The Educational and Social Needs of Children with Severe Handicap*, Chapter 4, Edward Arnold, London.

Observing in a one-to-one teaching session   103

The test examines language skill from a very basic level to a fairly complex mature level. There are six sub-tests measuring a variety of aspects in language development. The test does not enable the teacher to convert the scores into language ages. Some might dispute its usefulness because of this for we are so used to the conversion of score into ages concept. However, if we think of the test as a diagnostic test when we are more likely to be considering the kind of teaching materials we should be providing for the child.

The six sub-tests are as follows:

(1) Measures basic articulation and sound imitation. (It might also enable the teacher to hear which part of a word the child is hearing, viz. the beginning, middle, or the end. I can see possibilities in experimenting with putting phrases of varying lengths before the word that we want the child to imitate, particularly with young children. This might act as a kind of 'lead in' in other words, as an attention device.)
(2) Helps us to discover if the child can produce whole words.
(3) and (4) These tests examine the level the child has reached in forming sentences with correct word order ... using two-word/three-word/six-word sentences followed by the child's ability to use the question and negative forms of these longer sentences.
(5) Test to see how child is able to control organized word strings.
(6) A sentence completion test testing the child's control over meaning. It also gives the child an opportunity to end the sentence in one or more ways. (We often found that if the child did not end the sentence in any one of the expected ways his response could lead us on to a conversation about his recent experiences, e.g. 'Blood is ——.' The answer one child gave was 'coming your hand'. Enquiry on the ward he lived in revealed in fact that several weeks beforehand he had indeed cut his hand.)

I think I can say quite fairly that the majority of teachers of the mentally handicapped and perhaps teachers of normal children too with few exceptions do not cultivate the skill of listening to language analytically. Neither do they spend sufficient time considering the part a structured approach to *listening* should play over a long period of time in the early years of a mentally handicapped child's life. Language becomes so automatic by the time we are adults that we rarely listen to the way in which we are using words. This test, therefore, seemed to me to be useful in enabling teachers and others to gain some language sensitivity skills. It is useful in that it encourages us:

(1) to think about language structure and to think about language more analytically;
(2) to practise some degree of objectivity in looking at a child's current achievements;
(3) to see how the test results could be used to plan more precisely for individual children;

104   *Observing in a one-to-one teaching session*

(4) to see how such a test might encourage us as teachers to devise suitable teaching aids, games, and materials.

By far the most important reason for using this test is that it demonstrates a useful and essential concept—a concept needed by all teachers working with children with learning difficulties of whatever degree of difficulty. It encourages us to see how important it is to look very closely at children's 'errors', and it encourages a positive approach to looking at everything the child gives and using this for his benefit.

Piaget in his clinical method has been teaching this for many years but it is obvious that it is not easy for teachers to discard the models of the past in their own childhood where the correct answer was the 'thing' to achieve. A measure of inhibition of spoken language on the part of all teachers is necessary if we are to practise more successfully using errors as a starting point for our teaching, whether in the testing or natural contact situation.

In describing his test Berry states 'Not all errors are bad. Some indeed show that the child has understood and "processed" the language. This is especially so of the child who reduces the language presented to him and at the same time retains its meaning and form. Although the child may imitate only three words of the input (e.g. "the man is eating the cake" to "man eating cake") he shows a great deal of linguistic maturity and is clearly at a much later stage of language development than the child who parrots the final three words of the example. In other words this is an example of two imitations of three words; the first shows a great deal of linguistic development the second shows very little.' (From *Administering and Scoring Procedures for the LIT.*) Berry concludes his description of the test instructions with a scoring procedure which can be useful to the teacher.

The other test that caught my imagination (for I had been Piagetian orientated in my thinking since reading Woodward's work of the late 'fifties*) was the Uzgiriz and Hunt Scale used by Olwen Gregory in the Day Centres for the Handicapped in Glasgow. I will do no more than refer very briefly to it here for I have described it in more detail elsewhere.†
The scale covered the main aspects of what we might be looking for in intellectual development in the first 2 years of life. It was something, therefore, that could very well be used to observe older profoundly handicapped children in a more systematic way or very young mentally handicapped children who had not yet reached the stage of imitation of vocal and gestural movements. The scale is now being used in a research project with the profoundly handicapped by Tom Foxen. His work is described in a paper obtainable from John Penfold (Ed.), Northern Counties College, Newcastle-upon-Tyne.

---

*Woodward, M. (1959) The behaviour of idiots interpreted by Piaget's theory of Sensori–motor development. In *British Journal of Educational Psychology*, **29**, pp. 60–71.
Woodward, M. (1972) *The Development of Behaviour*, Penguin Books, Harmondsworth, Middlesex.
† Stevens, M. (1976) Cf. pp. 47–55 in ref. p. 102.

Observing in a one-to-one teaching session 105

During 1974 a local education authority in England* gave me the opportunity to organize a full week of in-service training in a hospital for the mentally handicapped. I worked not only with the teachers but also with the children. We decided to focus our attention on the importance of observation in teaching but observation in specifically devised situations. The situations we chose included testing the children with the Language Imitation Test and two sections from the Uzgiriz and Hunt Scale. An educational psychologist Mr John Presland also taking part in the course devised a comprehension test for the teachers to use. He showed them how to use the test and how to convert the raw scores into language comprehension ages. Working from 9 a.m. until 4 p.m. with an hour off for lunch and discussion from 4 p.m. to 5 p.m. was a marathon for all concerned. The whole school had to be reorganized so that the teachers could participate as fully as possible in the course of training. Students on an Advanced Diploma Course from a nearby College of Education† came in daily to help out when teachers left their classes. It was an exciting week and so valuable.

The course was not carried out as a research project but as a possible in-service training technique. The headteacher of the school whose idea it was, chose the children she wanted us to work with and test. In terms of the Berry test she chose children already able to imitate vocally and verbally. What she did not know was the extent of their responses or the difficulties the test would highlight.

A short description of the method that was used will put you more clearly in the picture. Small groups of teachers worked with me, sometimes watching me demonstrate the two tests I have mentioned and then trying them out in front of the group with individual children; other groups worked with the psychologist. All teachers worked with both of us during the week and so saw all three tests and the children's responses to them. We tested together 18 children on the Imitation Test and 11 on two sections of the Uzgiriz and Hunt Scale. Mr Presland and his group of teachers tested 49 children. His test examined imitation, understanding, and spontaneous speech. The materials for the test were all available in a school environment—chair, table, ball, spoon, cup, bed, window, brush, feet, hair, etc.

The Uzgiriz and Hunt Scale covers six aspects of intellectual development in the sensori motor stage (0–2 years). These are as follows:

(1) looking and permanence of objects;
(2) providing for movement with a purpose;
(3) development of a schema‡ in relation to objects;
(4) development of causality;
(5) the object in space;
(6) development of vocal and gestural imitation.

We decided to use Series 3 and 4 with the teachers (Table 8.1).

---

* Warwickshire. † Westhill College, Birmingham.
‡ Schema—this is a sequence of motor/mental actions.

Table 8.1 Adaptation of the Scale for Teacher's Use. (Cf. Stevens, M. (1976) *The Educational and Social Needs of Children with severe Handicap*)

16 items

3. *Development of a sequence of motor/mental actions in relation to objects*	(1)(2) Holds, mouths, brings before eyes to look at	Bell in case
(1) Development of mouthing	(3) Hits, hits objects on surface, shakes, waves, hits two objects together	Striped beaker
(2) Visual attention to	(4) Examines object	Six 1″ bricks (2 yellow, 2 white, 1 red, 1 blue)
(3) Simple movements towards	(5) Slides objects on surface, crumples, stretches out object, tries to tear	Shopping basket
(4) Interest in		Velvet mouse with sequin eyes
(5) Development of complex movements towards	(6) Drops objects systematically, throws object, puts another object in it, builds with blocks, drives car on surface, makes doll walk	Transparent egg box String
(6) Development of letting go		Foil Pearl and gilt necklace
(7) Development of ideas based on social learning and	(7) Demonstrates drinking from a cup, wearing a necklace, hugs doll or animal, listens to musical toy	Squeaky rubber lamb Red car Doll Doll's hat Doll's shoes
(8) Development of social interaction	(8) Shows object to a person; points to another object in association	Tambourine
(9) Recognition and naming	(9) Names object	Large/wooden/plastic spoon
4. *Development of Causality*	Give each toy listed in turn and demonstrate. Leave toy to see response of child. Repeat action. Observe. Note down the quality of the response. Set off clown and train out of sight. Children need a great deal of experience with these causality toys. It will usually be *given the adult present*	Rocking musical clown
(1) Repetition of actions producing interesting result		Humming top
(a) shows interest		Policeman on wheels. Press down on hat to activate
(b) moves arms vigorously		Jointed dog on stand. Press base to move dog
(c) repeats actions to keep objects going		A train which moves when buttons at side pressed
(d) grasps objects		A jolly clown with cymbals plunging action to set going
(2) Uses the gesture of the activated object		*Stevens* Live and learn toys
(3) Starts movements involved, touches, looks for way to activate object		Lipstick. pedal bin. Torch.
(4) Recognizes person in causing action recognizes reason for action searches for independent causes		Pull down musical box
(5) Gives to person. Explores way. Tries to activate object any way. Tries to copy		Weebles at the park

Observing in a one-to-one teaching session   107

I chose these two sections because they were simple to set up, and I felt that they would bring forth interesting responses from the children. All the adults concerned would be able to use the toys suggested in front of colleagues without too much stress. The toys were laid out in the order in which they appeared in the lists on tables concealed behind a screen. One toy at a time was presented to the child. If the toy following the one on the table needed that one to make the play more effective, then it was left on the table as the child was handed the next one, e.g. the basket and the bricks. We did not have a technician but we taped a great deal of the work we carried out to use in the discussions that followed work with each child. All the teachers in the group recorded in detail all that they were able to observe. We need to remember that this was the first time these particular teachers had been expected to use their observational skills in such an intensive manner. Unfortunately we did not have video equipment to record the experience. After two demonstrations each teacher tested a child in front of us all. Whilst this was going on I recorded the response of the child to the items and later on compiled further suggestions for each child tested. A 5-day course was not sufficient to train observational skills, interest teachers in language, AND compile specific individual programmes for the children we tested.

The notes that follow will give you some idea of the suggestions I made after the course for following up the observations we made. Unfortunately there was no follow up in terms of the teachers use of these suggestions, but I am presenting them because so many of the individual programmes one sees described are in much more general terms than some of these.

With reference to the eighteen children doing the Imitation Test this, as you would expect, was much easier to give, to record, and to observe. As each child tested left the room we listened to a playback of the tape recording and checked our own recordings of the responses made. It was not difficult in this active situation to involve all the teachers in lively discussion. There were no long drawn out silences such as one often hears in more formal lecture type in-service courses.

On my return home with the individual LIT forms, scrappy notes, and often incomplete tapes I decided to devise programmes for the children concerned even though I knew I should probably never see them again or their teachers. At least in doing them and sharing ideas others could improve on what I had suggested. Such an attempt would be yet another way in which the concept of planning for an individual child in a systematic way could be practically demonstrated.

The suggestions for the first three children described were based on some of the responses to the Uzgiriz and Hunt Series 3 and 4. The rest are referring to the results observed on the LIT.

June (10 years)
Needs eye test. Teeth bleeding. Spastic. Tended to focus on an object *at the side* of her. Explore this by presenting her with objects in different positions and note the response carefully. Not able to do imitation test but uses language seemingly

108   *Observing in a one-to-one teaching session*

in a delayed imitative fashion. No nurse was present but other adults were during the Uzgiriz and Hunt Session with her.
e.g. Language heard during session:
Here Y'ar.
What d'you want nurse.
Where's it gone.
He ya nurse.
Nurse, what do you want.
Anymore nurse
Thank you
Thank you
Where's the car nurse (referring to student)
Eh come on. After putting a doll on pulling toy. Gave the doll her leg (it had come off in the play)
'Here singing' when given tambourine.
Teacher: Stand up and sing. She did. She tapped the tambourine.
Given swing. She imitated the word 'swing'.
She did not have any understanding of how the causality (Series IV) toys worked except the top. (note age)
Complete sequence of purposeful activity noted.
(1) Got up from chair.
(2) 'Wee wee', she said.
(3) 'Does the doll want a wee?' I said. I said, 'take the doll for a wee'.
(4) She took the doll off the table and put it on the truck.
(5) She returned to table to get doll's leg (it had come off in play), the hat, and the shoes.
(6) She put the leg near the hole on the doll's body.
(7) Dropped the wellingtons and hat on to cab of truck.
(8) Returned to table, said, 'There y'are, eh, come on.'
In another report she was said to have poor co-operation. She passed a few items only at stage 1 level (under 1 year) in the comprehension of language test (Presland).
Suggestions. Using June's enjoyment of the tambourine, use rhythm in singing songs about June:
(a) what she is doing;
(b) what she has been doing.
Keep a book of these songs to ensure that:
(a) the words introduced are noted and repeated;
(b) continuity is maintained.
Understanding needs fuller investigation. Instructions about her clothes when dressing, the table and eating activities, toileting, etc. (her life) might be compiled:
Pull June's/your knickers up (down)
Take June's/your socks off
Put June's/your foot in (shoe).
Instructions could refer to her actions on a doll the same size as herself. She needs to be taught the words referring to people: boy, girl, teacher, lady, man, nurse.

Christine (17 years)
Eye test needed? Drugs?
Understanding level, 1 year. Christine built a tower of five bricks. She began to make noises when playing with the string with the teacher. Christine wound string round beaker till it fell over. She put the string in the beaker. Later she pulled it out of the beaker.
'Gone' games. Could be played with relevant language. String, nylon scarves, into beakers, boxes, bags. 'String gone', Christine. Perhaps better still, 'Christine——string gone'. Christine wrapped the silver foil round the beaker.
Other 'gone' games. Wrap up objects in a variety of papers, cloths, etc. When asked to 'pick it up', Christine picked up yellow paper. In using the causality toys Christine

Observing in a one-to-one teaching session 109

was shown how to press the bulb which made the 'frog' jump with her foot. (Quick innovation by teacher.) She began to stop the moving policeman from falling off the table.

Suggestion. Christine needs encouraging to keep hold of objects in order to explore their qualities. Can we look at the possibility of interesting Christine in:

(1) Things to wear. Use these as play materials, e.g. hats of all colours, shapes, sizes, textures; scarves of various kinds. In playing with these with an adult and perhaps another child, concept building of 'in', 'on', 'round', 'off' will be introduced.
(2) Things she uses to wash herself with: soap, toothbrush, flannel, toothpaste, toilet paper roll.
(3) Things we eat, things we use to eat with. Simple real cooking.
(4) A handbag and its contents.
(5) A shopping bag and varieties of objects: grocery items, greengrocery, hardware/kitchen items.

Although Christine is profoundly handicapped she is 17 and looks like a young lady. Exploring objects and playing with them with an adult who is going to talk positively with her should enable her to develop her powers of communication.

Pamela (18 years, profoundly handicapped, ambulant)
We had placed the toys for Series III and Series IV behind screens. Pamela knew they were there.
Some responses observed.
Cup. She said, cu—cup.
To basket. She put it on her arm.
String, she was looking for her 'beads' to thread (had seen her doing this in class).
Association.
Bricks. Able to build to five when it was started off.
Look. Here y'a
  'Put it on your neck'
Necklace. Put it on herself, (neck, arm) to
'Look' 'Take it off'
Tambourine. She laughed.
Doll. She said 'comb'. Combed doll's hair. Pulling hair up and saying 'oo here ya' to the lady.
Bell in cage. Gave it to me.
Causality Toys.
Clown with tambourines. She stood him upside down.
Weebles Playground. Banged a 'Weeble' on table (a little oval shaped figure). 'You shouldn't have done it.'
Swing. Swing broke. Clapped hands when swing was swung. She gave the swing to Mr L. in order to get another toy. She had observed the giving of the toy to me by Mr L. and the return of each toy behind the screen.
Musical Top. Explored it to see how it worked.
  Banged it first of all.
Anticipated moving policeman falling off the table by stretching well over the table from chair. Did not see how it worked.
Jumping Frog. Took the bulb and squeezed it. She gave the bulb to three of us to squeeze.
Toys with wind-up action. Wanted my keys.
In view of her appearance and growth we decided to see her response to a handbag and its contents.
Scarf. To instruction 'Put it on your head' (because she had gestured with hands to teacher's head) she put it round neck.
  She put a hat on. Then she took off the hat to comb her hair when she discovered the comb. Took out mirror and put it in the right position to look. Could not manage comb and mirror together. Combed my hair.

110 *Observing in a one-to-one teaching session*

Found keys and screamed 'Look'.
When fastening handbag she said, 'Come on.'
She used a raffia hat as a string bag (*Association*).

Me. Have you got all your things in (the bag). I had a scarf on my knee. She looked round to see if I had it. 'Toilet,' she then said.

Words collected in the session.
Look cu—cup
oo
Here ya
Take it off
Comb
No
Come on
Toilet

Giving objects to her. Say:
Here ya bag.
Here ya comb.
Here ya scarf.
Here ya keys.

Suggestions for follow up from these words already known and *objects she was interested in.*
Teacher points to object and says
'Look bag.' 'Look keys.'
'Look comb.' 'Look scarf.'

'Gone' game. Objects present then put away. No bag, no comb, no scarf, no keys, etc.

'Come on/go back' game.
Come on Pamela.
Come on 'Names of children in the class'. When she says 'come on' (name of child), child comes out from group to a given spot or chair.
Teacher plays first:
Come on Pamela, etc.
Go back Pamela.

Other two-word possibilities.
Comb hair.
black (hand) bag
scarf on
scarf off
necklet on
bracelet off.

Associative play. Give Pamela play objects relevant to her adolescent years. Dressing-up (party and dresses) modern shoes. Make-up corner, handbags, boxes in a shop, baskets, necklets, bracelets, hats, etc.

Gerrard (12 years)

Did not like the teacher or me to touch his left hand. Has he had it hurt?

Brick. Banged the brick on table. Shook it in right hand.

Cup. Took it up and 'drank' it. Banged cup on table. Picked up brick and banged it. Watched left hand.

Basket. Bricks and cup banged on table softly, loudly.

Bricks. *Hand-watching behaviour left hand.*

String. Took it in right hand.

Foil. Looked at me in glasses. Took foil. Gave it to examiner (a teacher). Put foil to mouth. Took foil ball and gave it to examiner.

Necklet. Shook it. At this point in time he knew the objects were hidden.

Lamb. Smiled. Put it into mouth, the long end sticking out.

Observing in a one-to-one teaching session   111

Car.   Banged it on table. Threw it in such a way as to let it fall upside down on·table.
Clapped hands.

Doll.   Picked up wellington boot when I put it down.

Tambourine. Tapping the inside with left-hand fingers. Banging tambourine on table. He let it drop. Let it drop on skin. Then fell on the other side.

Finger-watching. Picked up tambourine, dropped it six times from an angle then another three times. Finger-gazing.

Spoon.   Banged on table. Let it drop. Held it by the bowl. Tapped handle on table then the bowl then the side of the bowl. Put spoon in his mouth. Dropped spoon into tambourine. Took up lamb. Dropped lamb systematically.

Hand-gazing behaviours.

Rocking Clown. Banging the clown on the table. Put clown's head (hat) in his mouth. Banged clown.

Swing. Smelling it. Clown was still ringing. He looked from it to swing. Banged 'oval-shaped' men on table two in hands. Dropping them. Holding swing. Teacher pushing it. Banging the swing on the table.

Musical Top. He pulled up the plunger 1 inch. Turned it over on side. Teacher set it going. Stopped it with four fingers of right hand. Waiting till it stopped. Teacher helped him to get it going. Made two sounds (indescribable).

Moving Policeman. Press action on hat. When wheels underneath made sound he picked it up and looked underneath. Banged policeman on table gently. When policeman sent towards him he smiled. Left hand in mouth.

Frog. He imitated the rhythmic jumping movements with his body. Gave the bulb to him to squeeze, to make the frog move. He shook it.

'Man' on the swing. He made a loud noise. Tapped left hand on table. Clapped at this spectacle. I wonder if the clapping meant that he wanted to go to swing in playground. Was he remembering.

Clown with cymbals. Imitated the banging of the drum on the table.

Suggestions. The systematic dropping of car and tambourine suggests that perhaps we could start from there and introduce all kinds of other toys that drop and do something.

There are three occasions when Gerrard imitates movements:
(a) nodding head as clown;
(b) jumping movements of frog;
(c) banging of drum on table.

(1) Think out imitation activities/games for him to SEE and then carry out in front of a mirror, e.g. combing hair, washing face, cleaning teeth, eating something sticky, nasty (grimace).

(2) Using a large doll or another child/adult, put the beads/scarf round the doll's neck. Put the hat on the doll. Put the gloves on. Feed the doll. Give a drink to the doll. Put the basket on the doll's arm.

(3) Do something with your fingers, e.g. clap, walk over the table with your fingers (quickly, slowly). Put the palms of your hands flat on the table, then flick up the fingers saying 'up' then put down flat again. You can do this slowly, quickly, softly/loudly down. Make up little songs for these hand activities.

(4) Let balls of all sizes, colours, textures fall and roll; bounce—differences in bounce.

(5) Using rolls of cardboard (toilet roll tube) qualities of noise when they fall on to hard floor, wood, foam, a cushion.

(6) Tins that roll when they fall. Cable drums and reels.

(7) Continue to play with the tambourine; cars of different sizes, colours, shapes. Make a large car with him to sit in.

(8) Sing to him every day. He imitated singing sounds at beginning of session, when bell sound heard. Singing might encourage him to make more sounds. Check hearing.

112 *Observing in a one-to-one teaching session*

Jane (9 years, imitation test score 21/75)
Needs plenty of opportunity to learn how to put two words together.
Play with toys carrying out actions:
  (a) doll sitting, 'hello doll';
  (b) doll falling, 'bye-bye doll';
  (c) doll standing;
  (d) doll gone.
Play with toy animals. One kind at a time (e.g. horse, cat): dog walking, dog hiding, dog jumping, dog gone. Think of other 'gone' games in action using the animals and other suitable objects.
Use the following pivot function words with another word. Use the objects first of all, then use pictures, e.g. poor dolly (baby, lady, doggy): big, more, pretty, my.
See doll, see dog, see Mason (a teacher), see table, that doll, that man, two forks, two knives, two cups, two plates, two brushes, etc.
Jane needs help with 'd', 'm', 't', and 'p' sounds so the *objects* on tables need to be chosen to allow her to *hear* these sounds clearly pronounced by adults.
Table 1: Doll, dish, dress, dog, domino, drum, duck, donkey.
Table 2: 'm' words.
Table 3: 't' words.
Table 4: 'p' words
Table 5: A mixture of objects with 'd', 'm', 't', and 'p' words.
  Remember the 'gone game' Mr Presland suggested to us. I have modified it and structured it for the *individual* child:
  Teacher takes off one object at a time and hides it: 'doll gone', 'dish gone', etc.
  Then let the child do the taking of the object and teacher says: 'doll gone', 'dish gone', etc.
  A variant on the game above, still using two-word sentences, might be to put the object with the initial letter d, m, t, or p (for Jane) INTO something and say: 'doll in bag', 'pencil in bag', 'ball in case, box, or bowl', 'tie in box, or bag', etc.
  A useful tip for young teachers when preparing such an exercise is to have a dictionary at hand when looking for suitable nouns (names of objects)—somehow just sitting and thinking them out takes longer. Julia Malloy's book *Teaching the Mentally Retarded Child to Talk* contains useful lists of nouns in alphabetical order. One of the major considerations with children living in the hospital situation is to ensure that the words given are relevant to the life they lead in the hospital and to the objects they see around *them* and have to come into contact with, e.g. pills. This means that the teacher ideally needs:
  (1) to spend a day or two observing the life of the children when they are 'at home' on the wards.*
  (2) to write down the words she *sees* around them in terms of names and actions.
Do you ever bring a pet into school just for a day, e.g. a dog, a cat, a rabbit? I know of one Special Care Unit where they brought in a sheep, calf, dog, and rabbit at Harvest Festival time. The photographed response of the children to these animals was very positive.

Gaynor (10 years, imitation test score 2/75)
Understanding level in experimental comprehension test, 1 year.
Made following sounds and combination of words spontaneously: B, bye-bye, uh, yea, dolly, there you are, da, wha, ha ha, oh–ah, oh, they are, ta ta, there are, look at that. Give Gaynor *daily* 20-minute sessions where five items are put before her.

---

* Teachers having children in their classes who live in local authority or voluntary hostels perhaps need to see this as a vital part of their job too. Some regular interest from teachers might improve the living conditions for these children in a variety of ways. Teachers could organize short courses for hostel staff in order to help them provide positive leisure time activities for the children. They might also go to tea.

These should be interesting items and not only toys, e.g. an onion, a carrot, a cake, a pillow, a cup. The teacher says: 'Gaynor, this is a —, this is a —, this is a —, to each item. Then ask her:
    (a) to give (name of teacher) the —, the —, the —, the —;
    (b) to point to items (teach pointing).
Play with the items, talk about them, do something with them, talk about them and tell Gaynor what you are doing as you are doing it. Encourage Gaynor to copy your actions, e.g. pretend to: peel an orange, cut a cake, drink a cup of tea, put your head on the pillow. Make sure G can see your face and mouth, when you are talking to her. When you see from your observation records that G is able to show you the items introduced in the first session introduce five more items. See if she imitates the words immediately after you say them or some time afterwards. Think up 100 relevant items. Keep the groups of inedible objects in separate boxes for future use. Take note of the initial and penultimate sounds of each item. Be sure to introduce her to all the sounds.

David (13 years, imitation test score 60/75)

Comprehension level, 4 years.
Spontaneous conversation, 2–3 year old level.
David needs a great deal of tape recorder work in a one-to-one situation to extend his vocabulary and to improve his articulation. If you talk to him about his life, his interests, and a word is intelligible but not articulated well you can use this word quite naturally in another sentence following on from his. When the tape is played back to him he will then hear the correct word. I am sure that some of the articulation difficulties of these children is due to the fact that they have never indeed heard a clear pronunciation of the word in the first instance. David needs to be given special pictures or films (of interest to him personally) where he can hear the passive negative being used to describe them, e.g. 'the man isn't being hit by the boy'.
Slides of hospital life of relevance to the child could be shown whilst you give him specific sentences about them using language structures he needs to experience. In David's case for example:
    'The wheelbarrow isn't being pushed by John.'
    'The child's hair isn't being combed by a child.'
    'The spaghetti isn't being eaten by Jane.'
Then, ask David questions; for example:
    'Who is the wheelbarrow being pushed by?', etc.
This will help David to *listen* to the correct language forms.
    Daily practice with David will need lots of pictures and slides. You could make stand-up models with him too.
    Four sounds seemed to need attention: k, l, d, and j (dier as in sol*dier*).
Collect objects/pictures containing initial/final k. Place these in a circle and play the game 'Spin the Pointer'. When the pointer stops David has to say the name of the object or picture. Play this game with the four sounds needing attention. Play 'Spin the Pointer' with a mixture of sounds, when you feel David has mastered each sound. Using the tape recorder, record for David ten words beginning/ending with each of the following:
    (a) k
    (b) l
    (c) d
Method of recording: say a word, e.g. beginning with 'k'. Pause for 8 seconds then say another word and so on. The pause will give David the opportunity to imitate the word as he listens.
    It was interesting to note that in the Sentence Completion Test his spontaneous response to 'Blood is ...' was 'coming your hand'. He had had a cut attended to some days/weeks beforehand. This suggests a further exercise to play with David to encourage his growth of spontaneous conversation: begin sentences and let David complete them. Vary the form of language used to begin the sentence.

114   *Observing in a one-to-one teaching session*

This example reinforces my impression that all the verbal responses of the children are relevant to *them* and meaningful to them. *We* have to sort it out and understand. We have to be the communication 'translators'.

Geoffrey (14 years, severely handicapped, in a wheelchair. Imitation test score 51/75)
Tested only on stage 1 of understanding, because a good proportion of it involved the child in movement.
Needs practice on hearing the passive negative. See games for David (p. 113). Modify games to cater for Geoffrey's interests.
A hundred picture cards or photographs. Go round outlines in black felt-tip so they can be seen clearly. Mount on card. The cards might contain:
  (a) Sentences for the teacher to say out aloud to Geoffrey with the last word missing. Geoffrey should gain the cue from the picture. Each picture should be talked about in a 'running commentary' fashion beforehand. Try not to ask questions. The 'running commentary' or modelling of language will probably stimulate spontaneous responses from G.
  (b) Sentences beginning with a noun (for the teacher to say) and a verb:
    'Coffee is ...',
    'Leaves are ...',
    'Hens are ...',
    'Dogs ...'.
These games will enlarge G's vocabulary because of the naming. Geoffrey might need an attachment to his wheelchair so that the picture being shown is at an angle and not flat on his table. Find out the optimum distance for this to be placed so that he can see clearly—the distance could be stated on the back of the pictures, e.g. When using these pictures with Geoffrey—put on specially made stand at ... inches away from his face. Other instructions could be added to cater for the specific difficulties of other children.

June K. (Imitation test score 69/71)
Examples of sentences spoken during slides shown:
  'He's putting on his shoes. He's going to work.'
  'Cleaning the grass.' (mowing)
  'In there.' What window 'It's long.' (hair it was)
  'Down her dress frock.' (draught)
  'I do know.'
  'Our'
  '... washing her face, washing it.' (referring to face)
We had a conversation with June about the hospital life slides shown on a back slide projector. She needs plenty of opportunity to have conversations with you showing her slides of *familiar* scenes. She needs to carry out more 'grown-up' activities, e.g. cooking, washing-up. During the imitation test I had to use a number of strategies to help her 'inhibit' a verbal response before I had completed the copy. 'Be quiet' before *each* copy to be imitated brought the desired behaviour.
  In view of the score and the kind of mistakes (including the difficulty with inhibiting) I think that J needs practice in listening and paying attention. Difficulties in paying attention appear to be the cause for missing out words heard (drugs?). Make a special set of tapes for her to use individually. Speak slowly and clearly on them, leaving a 30-second pause in between each instruction. Sit at the back of J and record her responses on the first occasion. Sit *with* her after this and carry out the instruction on the second, third, fourth occasions. Using this method could be considered the teaching part of the exercise. Then allow June to do it by herself again. Compile more instructions of longer lengths. Taped instructions will encourage June to listen without the added attraction of the adult's facial expression.
Possible ideas for first tape.
Have ten real objects on the table (of interest to her).

Observing in a one-to-one teaching session 115

Instruction: 'Point to the ...' Repeat for each object. Remember to pause for 30 seconds in between each object.
Second tape: Have ten stand-up cut-outs of people from magazines (photographs of real people she knows would be better), mounted on card and pasted to a block so the picture will stand firmly.
Instruction: 'Point to ...' 30-seconds pause in between. Each figure should be pointed to at random in the line/circle/square arrangement that you make for her.
Third tape: Have the same cut-outs of people and an equal number of objects (articles to wear, to eat, to play with, etc.)
Instruction: 'Put the ... (name of object) in front of/behind, etc. ... (name of person on cut-out).'
   Subsequent tapes could contain all manner of instructions using these same objects and persons. The instructions would contain nouns, prepositions and verbs and they could very well increase in length up to, say, three ideas. I would like to suggest that June should be taught when you don't know the name of something you must say to Mrs ... 'What's that called?'.

Joy (Imitation test score 23/75)
Refer to the notes on Cheryl for 'two-word' games (p. 116). Joy imitated two words from an adult's spontaneous speech, i.e. 'go now', but did not imitate two words in the LIT. Needs practice with the games suggested (p. 112) using words helping her with 'g', 'p', 'k', 'j' sounds. 'p' seems to cause special difficulty if you look at her imitation test record sheet, e.g. pencil, pushing, sleeping.
Note how she tries to say 'p'. Give her the experience of the 'p' sound on your lips.
Joy was stimulated to use some passive knowledge of words when she saw objects. Using these words make up some games where you can help her to put another word to the one she knows:
'swing', 'duck', 'baby', 'yes', 'donkey', 'handbag', 'feet'. Did she say? 'sit there, good girl' (Imitative speech, a continuously heard phrase. It perhaps needs eliminating from your own language and substituting with a variety of more interesting phrases.)
Have a number of handbags:
   gold handbag
   black handbag
   shiny handbag
   old handbag
Talk about them and play the game 'What's in my handbag?'.
Have 5–10 different items in each handbag.
Instruction to Joy: Say aloud, 'What is in my handbag?' If she says a word describing something in the handbag give it to her. If she says another word jot it down and follow it up at a later date. If the item should be in a handbag respond by making sure it is next time. This is a useful game for a small group of children too. The aim is to stimulate passive language within them, not to have a correct answer. It is a creative approach to language with an emphasis on finding out what the child knows.
Have a model of a swing and little figures in cardboard:
'boy swings, girl swings, lady swings, man swings, boys swing, girls swing, ladies swing, men swing.'
Sing to a rocking rhythm 'boy swings' (soh–doh), etc.
Have a movable baby doll to do actions (for a boy have Action Man):
'baby sit, baby eat, nice baby, baby cry, baby drinks, pat baby, poor baby.'
Try to give her a new group of objects once a week. Collect and record the words she uses spontaneously. Talk about the objects. Talk about the words she gives. There is no *correct* answer. Get to *her* meaning and use the words she uses in a meaningful way.
Her articulation might be improved if she has the opportunity *to hear* clearly the sounds in a one-to-one play situation with a talking adult.
Sounds not consistently known are 'p' and 'j'. The only alphabetical sounds not

116   *Observing in a one-to-one teaching session*

tested in the sound and word imitation tests are 'v', 'x' and 'z'. Give her an opportunity to copy words containing these, e.g. van, box, buzz.

Cheryl (Imitation test score 14/75)
Hearing? 'Boccle' (milk)
Suggestions to teacher: Forget to say the phrase 'What's this?' to everything. You are often asking for an answer before you have taught (told) the child something. *Try to talk about* her experiences and yours about:
(1) objects
(2) happenings
(3) pictures
(4) your life
See the games suggested for Jane. Objects will be different for Cheryl.
These two children could perhaps work together.
Needs teaching two word sentences: compile fifty words in the life of the ward and school to teach Cheryl, e.g. toast gone, nurse gone, teacher gone. Use other words besides gone. Look at the slides of making beds, washing, dressing, eating, toileting, looking at television.
(1) Make a list of all the words you can see on each picture.
(2) Look at the list and put the words into one-/two-/three-/four-syllable words, e.g. spa-ghet-ti is a three-syllable word.
(3) Look at page 1 of test sheet and note that Cheryl has difficulty with the following sounds: de, k + (hard c), j (end of soldier), sm, sl, sh.
Play the 'gone game' with objects containing these sounds in various positions in the word (don't be afraid to use the real things of life, e.g. a carrot, something smooth, etc.). Later you will discover if she knows which object has gone and if she can name it.
Cheryl needs to be sitting fairly close to the adult in order to see her face.
Can you obtain a set of special earphones and trainer so that Cheryl hears the sounds more clearly?
From the list of words you have selected from the hospital life slides (which collection of course you will now use with the children and also add to):
A. Select one- and two-syllable words in which the sounds, causing difficulty for Cheryl, appear.
B. Make up games with these words to play with Cheryl. Talk to her using these words in a variety of ways (perhaps one word in any one/three days). Remember you are going to add a doing word (e.g. gone) as well.
Make sure she is looking at your face when you are talking to her.

Jonathan White (Imitation test score 75/75)
Uses stabilizers 'er, er' when thinking of the next word/idea. As Jonathan is partially sighted, it might be useful if a whole tape (2 hours) of stories, for Jonathan especially, could be compiled. The stories could be made up about the life in the hospital, the life of his teacher. Think of any topic. Then make up the story spontaneously using simple words and easy structure. Think out beforehand one or two *new* words to put in the story to enlarge Jonathan's vocabulary.

Catherine Hawkins (Imitation test score 28/75)
Comprehension ⎫
Imitation ⎬ 3 years
Spontaneous   2–3 years ⎭
Hearing: does it need testing?
Tendency to whisper: *needs to learn how to 'voice' words.* 'g' is a voiced consonant. If we help her with games on 'g' it might be useful for practising 'voicing'.
Play the Girl Game.
Say to her 'Go and get the Girl Game', then she has the opportunity of hearing 'g'. Let her feel the movements in your throat as you say this.

Cardboard cut-out of a girl 9–10 inches tall. Six envelopes each containing cut-outs of different sets of clothes and shoes:
(1) for winter
(2) for summer
(3) for wet weather
(4) for swimming
(5) for sleeping
(6) underwear
One envelope containing parts of body—hair, eyes, arms, legs, etc. to put together on cut-out.

A large dice could contain pictures of a body part on each of its faces (other dice faces could contain pictures of clothes). As the dice is thrown the cut-out parts can be placed in the appropriate position on the cut-out doll.

Needs practice on two-syllable words. Use the list compiled on the slides for Cheryl. Needs lots of practice on action words.

Method:
(1) models available
(2) pictures
Look at the model as it is arranged, e.g. doll at table, nurse near a bed. Talk about what the doll (nurse) is doing using the 'action' words respectively. Then say to child 'Tell teacher's name/me if child is ready for 'me') all about the doll/nurse man/lady', etc.

Illustrated action words from child's life*:

pulling (knickers up/down)	sitting down ⎱ (from table)
pushing (sleeves up)	getting up ⎰
washing (face, knees)	sitting on (the toilet, chair)
drying (hands)	sleeping
getting (into)	eating
getting (out of)	drinking
taking off ⎱ (clothes, names of all	
putting on ⎰ these with pictures)	

Slides of these could be made using Catherine (repeat with a boy) as the 'film star' in the photograph. 8 mm film might be even more effective.

A useful piece of apparatus to use with Catherine might be a 12 inch × 12 inch peg-board. Cut-out figures in action could be drawn and mounted on the dowelling that fits the holes of the peg-board. The models would then be more easily handled. Stories could be illustrated in this way too. As the story is unfolded a model is built up in front of the children.

Eugene (15 years, imitation test score 8/75, profoundly handicapped)

Comprehension	1–2 years ⎤	
Imitation	1 year ⎬	Presland Comprehension Test
Spontaneous	1 year ⎦	

Imitation test:
Note his use of words within his 'doing' experience. Suggests he can do more. Also conversation with me about the slides suggests that his spontaneous conversation can be developed from familiar life scenes:
milk, watch, boy, man, tea, Paul for pencil, eat, eating drink, Stevens, eyes.

Eugene needs to be introduced to objects that are in *his* environment. Look at *his* life:
(1) in bed: bed, pillow, sheet, pyjamas (top, bottom).
(2) getting up: action words such as sitting up, legs out of bed, etc.

---

* Some of these activities are readily available in jigsaw form from Reeves Educational Supply firm. They were compiled by a Swedish teacher. We now need short film loops to show such activities.

118   *Observing in a one-to-one teaching session*

(3) washing:	soap, towel, toothbrush, face, neck, hands.
(4) dressing:	shirt, pants, trousers, pocket, jacket.
(5) meals:	plate, cup, knife, fork, etc.
(6) evening activities:	Do you know them?
(7) school activities:	...
(8) weekends:	Do you know what he does?

He also said: 'some boys in there', 'shirt on', 'boys in there'.
Needs a stimulating programme with same kind of games as Cheryl and Jane. The objects need to be of interest to *him*, his interests, his *physical* age, such as 'gone games' using words in (1)–(8) above. With Eugene there should be two sets of objects for sound imitation games. He has one set in front of him and the other set is on a table in front of him. As the teacher removes one he has to give her the one gone from his set. As he does so the teacher can tell him the name of it. A lot of work is possible using this method. (1)–(8) suggests the kind of objects and names to include.

Whilst working with Eugene it occurred to me that the word 'say' (e.g. say desk, boy, girl) might 'get in the way' as it were of imitation. The child might not understand the word say. Other words that might be used to gain a response are: tell, speak, talk (aloud).

Another interesting method might be to put the words, phrases on tape at 15–30-second spaced intervals. The child's attention will then be on the sounds and not on the movement of the tester's face and voice.

Eugene was hearing the last sounds of some of the words
(e.g. ar = car ake = cake sh = push).
This poses the question: What kind of remedial game/experience could help him to hear from the beginning?
Another useful idea after working with Eugene
To have causality toys for testing young people over 14 years of age instead of toys:

(1) torch
(2) switch that turns on a light
(3) circular switch that turns on air
(4) magnet
(5) button to press to cause a bell to ring
(6) musical box
(7) retractable tape measure
(8) laughing box
(9) tape recorder

Stephen (14 years, imitation test score 25/75)

Presland Comprehension: 4 years
Spontaneous ⎫
Imitation   ⎬ 2–3 years

Needs practice with sm, j, sh sounds: games and songs containing these sounds, e.g. The smoke goes up the chimney just the same.

Do daily work on the hospital life slides and slides you bring in about your friends, your families, your holidays. You might collect 5–6 slides from each of your colleagues or friends and sort them into topics. Stephen needs much encouragement to *use* the language he has. You need to talk to Stephen regularly about the slides and to encourage him to listen and not to copy what you say.

Stephen (Imitation test score 27/75)

Stephen began copying the words before teacher had finished the copy. This constituted a difficulty so we played a game with him: when we put our hands on the table then he could say it. He was able to imitate two words—in three-word sentences he said the last two words. To extend his language abilities a number of games might be devised:
(A) Perform a number (100) of interesting real actions in front of Stephen. During

Observing in a one-to-one teaching session   119

the performance say 'I (or your surname) am putting the ...', 'I am washing my hands'.
(B) Work with a small group of children including Stephen. Tell one of the group to do something: put objects in a box, a paper-bag, a handbag, a pocket. As Stephen is performing the action say 'Listen Stephen!'
   (1) 'John is putting the ... in the ... What is he doing Stephen?' Then repeat it with him (not as a test but as a game).
   (2) 'Mary is picking up ...'
   (3) 'Mary is drinking coffee/tea/cocoa/milk/water'
   (4) 'David is combing his hair'
   (5) 'David is brushing his teeth'
   (6) 'David is cleaning his shoes'
   (7) 'David is washing his face'
   (8) 'Mary is clapping her hands'
   (9) 'Mary is stamping her feet'
   (10) 'Mary is scratching her knee/nose/face/back'
   (11) 'Mary is nodding her head'
The performing children will catch attention because Stephen knows them and will give him an opportunity to listen to the words and the structure.
(C) (1)–(11) could be repeated with *two* children doing the actions. The verb form changes (is/are) and there are plurals.
(D) The actions above (B) and (C) could be repeated using slides of the actions, preferably with the same children carrying them out.
(E) The above using pictures.
(F) The above getting Stephen to tell the children what to do (this stage will come much later).

Jack (Imitation test score 15/75)

Find objects beginning with m, p, w.
Object play. Include objects having the above initial m, p, w, sounds. Have a hundred useful objects. Say: 'This is a/the ...', *telling* the child and talking about the object, so that he has the *opportunity* of hearing initial sounds of names of objects plus new names of the objects. Then after presenting 3–5 objects say: 'Show me the ...', 'Point to the ...'.
   Play my game of *'Shine Spy'*. Tell him to shine the torch on whatever item you tell him (door, window, ceiling, floor, a child, a part of the body). This is a good game for a small group too. A darkened room is best. An alternative way is for the child to shine the torch on something he wants and to tell you what it is. Once more accept (and record) his answer. Supply the object when you play the game again or immediately if it is to hand. It can be played in the music session. The torch is passed round the group to music. When the music stops whoever has the torch shines it on the items placed in the middle of the ring either on an item he then names, or an item he is told to name.
Domino game using 'sh' objects/actions:

shake	shell	shirt	dish	wash
sheet	shelf	shoe	push	ash
sheep	ship	shoulder	fish	

Make dominoes of stiff card. Put the child's name on the back of the cards. They are then his and he can carry them about in his pocket.
Domino game with 'd' illustrations:

doll	dress	drink
donkey	dustbin	dot
dish	doctor	dough (let him experience)
deer	dog	domino
desk	dig	dragon
dinner	duck	dolphin

120 *Observing in a one-to-one teaching session*

Make up special stories bringing in words with sh/d, e.g. a story/song about a donkey, a dragon. The stories should be illustrated by pictures, puppets.

To arouse interest and listening concentration:

(1) Put an interesting object in front of him. Stand behind him as he sits (tell him about the object in this way so that he is not attending to the movement of your mouth).

(2) To encourage him to listen have a set of pictures of objects. These should be objects you have which make a sound. Use sets of three. Let him listen to a sound and then point to the picture of what made it.

(3) Have two boxes, each one containing the same sounds (say three to choose from at first then five). Facing him, play a sound. Keep hand on the lid of his box. Then tell him to find the same 'thing' in his box and make the sound/noise. Repeat with the next sound. Let him do it and you 'guess'. The same activity can be carried out using taped sounds and pictures. The sounds you use could be those heard on the wards/in school/in the grounds.

David (10 years, imitation test score 44/75)

Comprehension age: 4 years

Imitation ⎫
Spontaneous ⎬ 3 years

David seems to need a lot of opportunities for practising the language he has 'inside of him'. Talking regularly with him about the models he makes should give him these opportunities. We let him play with the fairground toys, the roundabout, etc. because of his immediate interest and the causality toys including torch, tape recorder, switches, etc.

Samples of spontaneous language:

'They've fallen off'; 'They've gone down the'selves'; 'That's the roundabout'; Counted 1 to 4; 'Swing'; 'See-Saw'. He made the man go up and down and said: 'In a bag', 'orange', 'fish', 'haddock to', 'the man is eating—fish'.

Pronunciation of vowels needs attention. Some letters causing possible articulatory difficulty are r, s at the *end* of a word, k, sh, j (as in sol*dier*).

David seems to need his own store of objects/pictures to help him with these sounds and some one-to-one attention where he *hears* these sounds clearly and sees how they are formed. Note when he leaves off the *end* letter of a word.

Pictures of toys with r. Julia Malloy in *'Teaching the Retarded Child to Talk'* has obviously consulted a dictionary to find suitable nouns under the various letters— tedious but useful, for it is always difficult to think spontaneously of the words we need:

r	*k*	*ending*	*s*
roundabout	king	stick	shirt
rat	key(s)	kick	shovel
rain	kettle(s)		shoe
rug	kitten(s)		shirts
road	kitchen		shovels
roof			shoes

What nouns begin with 'k' (1) on the ward, (2) in school? Compile a useful list of basic words for David to use; introduce him to interesting adjectives to use with these words. Make up songs using these words/stories:

big roundabout
quick roundabout
grey rat
ugly rat
dirty rat

The big big roundabout goes round and round, round and round, round and round (repeat). The big big roundabout goes round and round. Today, today, today.

Observing in a one-to-one teaching session   121

Story (with stick puppet aids). A grey rat, an ugly rat and a dirty rat lived in a ...,
and so on. The importance of *making up* the songs and stories is to communicate
to David that they are for HIM especially.

Paul (12 years, imitation test score 57/75)
He had his own very pronounced local accent.
Paul needs practice in listening to the:
 (a) question forms of sentences
 (b) negative forms, e.g. isn't
 (c) passive forms, e.g. the car is being pushed by the boy
 (d) passive negative forms, e.g. the car isn't being pushed by the boy
He had difficulty in pronunciation when he had to imitate girl, car
cf. Yes/no answer to picture cards, David (p. 120).
His understanding is at the 5-year level. Spontaneous language can be fostered
through his teacher providing him with interesting activities and some specific
remedial attention, as outlined above, to introduce him to more complex language
structures.

Although there was no intention on my part to analyse the experience
once the course was over, after 'living with the results' and making up
the programmes for over a week as it were, I became curious in the quan-
titative results of that week even with its many snags in terms of planning
and lack of follow up. The results were as follows: Under the guidance
of Mr Presland 49 children were in fact tested. (There were 74 in the
school.) Eleven of these children had no score in any area tested—imitation, understanding of instructions, or spontaneous speech. Had there
been time each of these children should have been given the Uzgiriz and
Hunt experience with me, in order to assess their preverbal level of understanding and response. Twenty-three children had no score for spontaneous language, and twenty-three had no score for imitation. Four children had a major discrepancy between their understanding levels and their
ability to use language spontaneously. This seemed to suggest that each
of these children needed intensive remedial language work in terms of:

(1) further diagnosis and assessment of the possible cause for this;
(2) an attempt to motivate spontaneous language through enrichment ex-
    periences;
(3) an attempt to analyse the present relationships in the child's life in
    order to 'improve' them. One 14-year-old had been in hospital for 9
    months. Perhaps the shock of being admitted, although he had regular
    visitors, was responsible. Another child of 12 had lived there for 7
    years and had had no visitors. Can we wonder he did not talk. The
    other two, 15 and 18 respectively, had been in hospital for 5 and 3
    years and both had visitors. Some examination of the family and the
    reasons for their placement of the child in hospital might offer a clue.
    It was not my brief on this course to investigate this but the teachers
    would certainly wish to know.

If we look at the results in another way, 25 children were functioning
below a 3-year-old level in comprehension, 14 between this and up to a
6-year-old level, but almost 50 per cent of this small number (49) could

122 *Observing in a one-to-one teaching session*

not imitate. Perhaps one of the major concerns in helping teachers working in mental subnormality hospitals should be to devise some kind of detailed sequenced approach to teaching imitation when this is obviously the precursor of the spoken word. The adults concerned should certainly remember that they should be imitating the movements, however slight or strange, of the children. In this way they will be catching the attention of the children; they will be teaching them to imitate and this is a necessary first stage in the sequence to their doing it themselves.

Some note, perhaps, should be taken in compiling such a sequence of the kind of REAL activities the child sees around him in his life IN AN INSTITUTION so that the adults can use these particular activities in their imitation of them. In order to do this efficiently they will certainly have to spend some time observing the child in his 'home' on the wards. In order that the nurses understand some of the gestures and movements of the children and in order that they can extend their imitating they will have to spend time too, observing in the school so that 'home' and school work together.

My particular groups of teachers and I were able to work with thirty children in the week. I have already presented you with the programmes I finally prepared for the teachers in order to demonstrate that these do need careful planning, and an analysis of any test/activity you carry out with the child.* Eighteen children between 9 and 17 years were given the imitation test. I shall just give you the raw scores for unfortunately I do not have the original scoring and observation sheets:

2 scored 2 and 8;
2 scored 14 and 15; } out of a possible score of 75.
3 scored between 21 and 25.

All of these seven children were able to imitate sounds and some of them whole words. All of them had articulatory difficulties and some of them were unable to discriminate specific sounds and would therefore need special attention to enable them to hear and ultimately produce these particular sounds. Those children scoring 21 to 25 points needed special help to use two-word sentences and also three children scoring even up to 41 points:

4 children scored 42–57;
4 scored 58 and 75.

They needed a wide variety of experiences and games to extend their vocabulary and to use language socially.

Other thoughts occurring to me after this experience involved a change in the kind of objects you might present to an adolescent profoundly handicapped child who was still at the sensori-motor level of development. Here I am thinking of objects other than toys—food, fruit, clothes, an old typewriter, etc. Who knows what qualitative differences in the kind

---

* Stevens, M. (1976) 2nd Edition, Chapter 12.

Observing in a one-to-one teaching session 123

of sensori level of behaviour they might stimulate the child to use. No harm could possibly come from such a practice and the child would certainly be having a new experience in the 'test' situation. In using the imitation test it seems important to record on the form any spontaneous speech the child uses, for we might find that after being told something he will imitate what we have just said even if he has not imitated all that we have asked of him in the more formal situation.

Perhaps we also need to devise a method of recording observation of specific spontaneous gesture on the part of the child for the gestures the child uses are very often 'standing in' for the words he has never been told but wishes to use. Such an exercise would make one more aware of the words these children need to be taught specifically in their particular environment—to understand/to say. The following groups of basic common words might be considered useful in the hospital situation:

man, woman, baby, boy, girl, nurse, doctor (photographs of real people in the hospital);
bed, pillow, sheet, blanket;
bus, car, bicycle, motor bike, lorry, ambulance;
mirror, table, window, chair, television, clock, door;
toilet, bowl, soap, water, flannel, paper, brush, comb, towel, toothbrush;
pants, vest, trousers, shirt, shoes, socks, pullover;
pants, dress, skirt, vest, socks, stockings, shoes, boots, jumper cardigan, gloves, scarf;
egg, bread, cake, sausage, chips, tomato, beans, apple, orange, banana, tea, milk, biscuit, cocoa, coffee, glass of water;
knife (knives), fork(s), spoon(s), big spoon, little spoon;
pepper, salt, sauce, plate, cup, glass, saucer;
parts of self—fingers, toes, leg, back, shoulders, hands, feet, thumb, head, nose, ear, neck, mouth, arm.

Concentration on games, matching cards, lotto, etc. in which these basic need words were well to the forefront of the teachers' minds, would help these children in learning about their particular world.

One cannot participate in such a concentrated period of work without being stimulated to consider its implications for further courses of a similar nature, in school with teachers and children instead of behind a table on a platform with a sea of faces in front of one. The whole experience suggested that:

(1) Arrangements could be made at least once a year for all the children in a school to be assessed by teachers interested in such a procedure. Two such teachers in a school of 100 children could in fact complete the task in a fortnight. Alternatively, a group of teachers working intensively for 3 days might perform just as good a job.
(2) Between 1 and 2 hours per child would then be needed to write up a report and suggest an initial programme on the basis of it. The programme would be a written one.

124   *Observing in a one-to-one teaching session*

(3) A member of the staff with special talents could perhaps be appointed:
  (a) to make specific teaching materials from the teachers' specifications;
  (b) to design materials from observed needs;
  (c) to be responsible for a developing resources bank/library;
  (d) to keep records evaluating the material.

The last suggestion is made because the nature of the individual difficulties are such that commercialized material is so very often irrelevant. There is certainly a need for teaching aids such as I have described here and elsewhere to be made by the individual teacher as part of her commitment and responsibility in her work with mentally handicapped children. She has always to remember that she has no scripts to mark, and no preparation in terms of reading material and reconstructing it for her pupils' assimilation. Her preparation will certainly lie in other directions. A resource bank is certainly a positive step and one I suggested after this experience was over.

9 Keeping records

The importance of observing individual children in a number of situations and of jotting down, for future reference and for descriptive report-making, what one sees and hears, without making personal comments or drawing conclusions, has been emphasized. The teacher of mentally handicapped children needs to train herself to observe the individual child and his activities in a special way. She also needs to habituate herself, because of this special training, to observe something about *all* the children in her group each day, whilst participating in and providing for their activities. She also needs to keep *brief* records of these observations. A recording habit, which need not take up more than 10–20 minutes of the teacher's time each day, could become a useful guide to the children's development, to their immediate needs, as well as to their changing interests. It will also provide the teacher with a record of her own *active* part in the children's education.

One has constantly to remind oneself that the memory does not serve us accurately for long, particularly when we are dealing with human beings. In view of this fact, systematic record-keeping ought to be thought of as being another important aspect of special education. There are many methods which teachers use to keep systematic records. Teachers need to devise their own methods which are relatively non-time-consuming, non-cumbersome and yet give them the information they need at the flick of a page of their notebooks.

I have used the following method as a teacher for many years.* I have also encouraged young teachers in training to do the same. It is not only a simple method but one that ensures that a teacher to look deliberately at each child every day.

Each teacher should have an exercise book, preferably of the spiral ring type. With the exception of the first page, the pages will be cut back an inch on the right-hand side so that the names of the children, written alphabetically in register form down the left-hand side of the second page, can be seen when the remaining pages, containing the notes, are turned over.

---

* Since writing the first edition of this book I have devised a notebook that not only enables the teacher to record her observations about each child but also to record how she bases her day's teaching programme on *some* of these same observations. It is described in my second book Appendix 2. I will add that a very useful little book *Record Keeping in the Progressive Primary School* by Peter Rance (1972; Ward Lock) was published in the 'seventies'. I was delighted to see that some of the ideas propounded in the first edition to this book were used to support the need for teachers in the primary school to keep systematic records.

126   *Keeping records*

As the teacher begins to write her notes alongside the name of each child she is forced to recall something about that child that has caught her attention. Whenever there is a blank in her mind she will know that she has not really observed the child and so must make an extra effort the following day to make sure she watches more carefully. Of course, she will not complete the space alongside the name if, indeed, she cannot remember the activities of a particular child. The importance of writing these notes lies in their relative accuracy and not in simply filling up spaces in a notebook. The habit of writing about each child daily, however briefly, will encourage the teacher to look at all the children.

In addition to the names of the children the teacher should add some inch-wide columns alongside them and a wider column on the third page with the following suggested headings at the top (Fig. 9.1) The teacher will devise more suitable headings as her own knowledge and experience increases.*

Page 2   *Page 3*

Name of child	Date of birth	Life age	Mental age	IQ	Social age	Family details. Number of brothers and sisters. Names. Father's work.	Other information
Mary							
John							

Comments

FIG. 9.1

The size and order of these columns may vary and it may be of more use for the teacher to name the last column—*Other information*—taking up the whole of page 3. This page would contain information which the teacher needs to keep well to the front of her mind all the time and even to memorize. Comments on the parents' current attitudes to the child; on the present problems of the parents; about the child's need to wear glasses (the busy teacher can easily forget); the fact that the child had attended ESN(M) school or a Special Care Unit before admittance to the particular class; family relationships; that the child has a twin sister; the reading age, if it exists; the language age; or the extent of his knowledge of social sight words would be included under this heading.

The rest of the pages in the book might be used for daily jottings about each child. The top line of each page will contain the date so that the teacher then has an easy method of referring back to the happenings of each day. Comments written at the bottom of the page could act as a valuable aid to the teacher in enabling her to keep a record of the use she had made of her observations. These might be in terms of how she had

* Stevens, M. (1976) Appendix 2.

Keeping records 127

followed up a child's interest, helped a child over a difficulty, or what new materials she had provided for the group or an individual child the following day on the basis of her observation of need for a particular experience.

Two lines per page for each child would ensure that the teacher has enough space to write down her comments. They would also remind her that these should be brief and would only describe the most outstanding points and the ones she thinks would be useful to her in her teaching and understanding of the child. If she has tried to train her attention by watching the activities of the children in the special observation sessions already described, she will inevitably find this becoming increasingly easy with practice.

Examples of the kind of observations which were recorded for 3 days about a group of children will give a clearer picture of what is considered useful.

The records, made by Lillian Prendiville, a mature,* experienced student in training in 1964, will give you some idea about the kind of jottings she made every day and the use to which she put them in planning her work, providing materials, and in getting to know the children. This teacher was considered exceptional—she was on teaching practice and she had a tremendous capacity for hard work as well as a genuine interest in the children. The records which have been chosen are unedited.

They are written here in continuous form, but it must be remembered that they were actually written in her notebooks as suggested previously (see Fig. 9.1). Comments were added on the last four or five lines of each page.

The life ages of the children in this group were $7\frac{1}{2}$–12 years. Their mental levels were said to be 2–3+ years. Difficulties, in addition to mental subnormality, included those due to emotional disturbances and to physical disabilities—epilepsy, defective vision and hearing, overweight, etc. There were four mongol children in the group and one child who was microcephalic. Two children were particularly withdrawn and several children were obsessionally clean—they did not like soiling hands or their clothes when they were playing. Several children were considered by the teachers who knew them to be rather spoilt and overprotected. All this information was inserted against the name of the child concerned, in the column headed 'Other Information'. The names of the children have been changed. Their ages were:

Jimmy	10 years	9 months		Alan	10 years	11 months	
Mary	11	„	9	„	Robert	11	„	0	„
Jean	12	„	2	„	Janet	10	„	10	„
Tony	10	„	11	„	Graham	11	„	11	„
Michael	10	„	1	„	Colin	11	„	11	„
Bobby	12	„	0	„	Peter	11	„	3	„

---

* She has just retired prematurely to be with her family after becoming headteacher to a progressive school for the mentally handicapped in Chester. I am grateful to her for the notes she made, and I have used them to illustrate this chapter on keeping records.

128 *Keeping records*

Joyce	9 years	1 months	George	11 years	10 months
Margaret	7 ,,	7 ,,	Brian	9 ,,	8 ,,
John	9 ,,	5 ,,	Vera	10 ,,	10 ,,
Louise	10 ,,	0 ,,			

First Day

Jimmy went over to sand. Stood and looked at it. After a couple of minutes looking at other children playing, he found the large beach ball and walked around the room most of the morning, carrying it. Repeats phrases he hears.

Mary was busy at the music table during activity time. She played the dulcimer. She would not leave this to listen to story.

Jean absent.

Tony spent the morning at the woodwork table. He put two pieces of wood together to make a boat. He wanted another piece to make a bedroom on it. There was not a piece small enough. He helped Alan saw a piece for it.

Michael fighting a lot with other children mainly over possessions and toys. Responds to individual attention. Played well in shop.

Bobby played in the water all the morning. He drools a lot. Turns away if spoken to.

Joyce played at music table. Spent a long time painting. Mixed all colours together.

Margaret played with dolls. Wheeled doll to shop. Played shopping.

John absent.

Alan worked at the woodwork bench. He found a long and a shorter piece of wood. I said, 'What will you make?' He said, 'A bed for the dolly.' He tried to secure the smaller piece of wood to the end of the large one. I helped him with the first nail and put on the other bed end. He did the others.

Robert spent most of the morning at the water play.

Janet took the wrong towel when I took her to be washed. She did not recognize her own name when shown it.

Graham absent.

Colin played shop with Dennis.

Peter absent.

George played in the sand. Played at the water tray. Splashed Jimmy whilst there.

Brian played in the sand. Watched the boys at the woodwork table.

Vera played with the small doll. Went to paint table. Rubs paper with the brush. Does not look at paint when dipping in brush.

Comment on Day: The children had been used to formal work. They did not move about much. Several *asked* if they might play in the sand or cut out, etc. The boys were very busy at the woodwork. They are unused to the tools. Will need watching carefully until they become used to them.

Third Day

Jimmy blew balloons today. He talked more too. He wet the sleeves of his shirt in the water tray. I took it off and put it to dry by radiator. He came to me several times and said, 'Can I put my shirt on?' I said, 'It's still wet.' When I put it on he said, 'It's dry now.' Also said, when putting it on, 'What a naughty temper, naughty temper, Jimmy.'

Mary played in the sand making sand-pies and flattening them, then filling the bucket and turning them.

Robert enjoyed the singing session today. Sang *Boys and girls come out to play*. Joined in and enjoyed bubble play and painting. Got paint spots on his shirt. I must make him an apron. I note he is made to wear a bib at lunch time.

Janet played in shop. Using scales. She weighed real fruit in the shop. We weighed oranges. I explained that we buy one orange, two oranges, etc., but we buy one pound of apples. Janet only speaks in whispers.

Graham absent.

Colin played in the Wendy House. He went on with this when it was story time. I told the group the story was to be about a rabbit. Colin heard and pointed to a small picture of a rabbit on the wall. I suggested that he brought it to show the children. He then joined the group.

Peter absent.

George at woodwork table trying to saw—with knee on table keeping wood steady. I showed him how to press on it with his hand. Seemed ungainly in co-ordination. Noted that he used his left hand to saw, right one to hold wood. I took him to other end of table. He changed saw into right hand and managed to saw more easily.

Brian played in the sand. Dragged the sand from three sides of the tray towards a large pile at his own side. Mary threw sand at him. When Brian came to the sand, she threw some at him; he threw a lot more at her. She came to me and pointed to the sand on her head and dress but did not speak.

Jean absent.

Tony absent.

Michael tried out all the activities. He played shop for quite a long time and he used the scales today. He screams for possession of toys and equipment but is easily diverted to something else when necessary.

Bobby responded well to the *bubble* play today. He did not master technique of blowing them as he blew too hard. Was very excited at watching others blowing. Words tumbled out, 'Look at it, Bubble, Look, look.' I blew some for him, saying, 'Blowing, Catch, Gone, Burst, Bubble.'

Joyce absent.

Margaret absent.

John absent.

Alan shows an interest in painting and did clear round shapes all over paper. When I asked him about these he said *seeds* and pointed to his tray of cress seeds on nature table. I played some tunes today to a small group of children. Alan sang *Pop goes the Weasel.*

Louise following me around the room. Blew bubbles but went away when more children joined in. Standing by Janet in shop but not playing actively.

Comment on Day: The class teacher was not in today. She has brought the milk in each morning this week and put it into cups for some children, giving it out with straws to others. Today I put it on a table hoping the children would leave their activity and come to get their milk themselves and drink at the table. It was a complete failure. Some took their milk to the activity tables, others did not come at all. On Monday I will sit them down in a group and give out the milk at a definite time—and then clear it away completely. I shall then be able to discover who can drink from a straw and who has to have a cup. See if the latter can learn to use a straw. I must also put names in shoes so that I will know them when we change for Movement. I will check names in washroom.

Fifth Day

Jimmy played in the Wendy House. He fetched some sand and put it in a cup, stirring it with a spoon. He tipped some on to a tea plate and pretended to eat with a spoon. He piled the dishes together and lay down on a large doll's bed. Does not like other children to join him.

Mary did not take part in movement until almost the end of the period. When children rolled on the floor she joined in. Perhaps this type of exercise does not make demands on her weak legs. I will try to include more of this type of movement in future sessions. Mary hit several children today. Also threw sand and water.

Jean. When Jean played in the water tray she picked up a large funnel and putting the wide end into the water, she blew through the tube and into the water making loud bubbling.

Michael wore policeman's hat. Talked about, 'Send for the police, come to John's house, 999,' etc. This lasted for two minutes. Spent rest of the morning serving in the shop—wearing policeman's hat.

130   *Keeping records*

Bobby came to woodwork table and used the hammer. Banged the wood and table indiscriminately. Gazes round room whilst banging. He refused to touch bottle and straw this morning. I must try feeding cup.

Joyce enjoys stories. Constantly asked, 'Can we have a story now?' She often goes to the quiet corner and looks at books. She showed me the characters in a Beacon book and identified them as Mr Lob, Mr Dan, etc. I sat down and read the story to her, talking about the pictures.

John returned to school today. Quiet. Looked at the children in the room. Occupied with the torch and found switch to change colour of light. Interested in the hamster.

Alan played at rolling pastry, folding it, squeezing it and rolling it again. He cried when Mary took the rolling pin.

Robert at the blowing table. Pours bubble liquid from the other basins into his own until it is full. Knocks it over as he dips in bubble wire. Does not want other children to dip in their bubble wires.

Janét absent.

Graham absent.

Colin still spending time in the sand, digging with spade and making mounds of sand, then shovelling the mound away to the other side of the tray and going over to the other side and repeating this.

Peter absent.

George rolled and folded over pastry. Long time at woodwork table, banging not nailing.

Brian made pastry today, cutting and putting pies in a row. Played in shop filling a large paper bag with fruit and vegetables and then tipping them back into the boxes. Repeating this.

Vera painted. Covering paper with paint outline of any kind. Spent a lot of time following me about the room.

Comment on Day: The children were very noisy today. Mary has hit several children and there have been numerous quarrels for possession of toys and equipment. Water and sand have been thrown. I feel the children are beginning to come to life, so to speak, and are trying out different things and wakening up to the presence of one another. They seem to have spent too much time with a *sitting at table* method of learning. Now, perhaps, there will be a period of noisy communication as they realize they can express their feelings. Organized cupboard space.

In looking at the comments made by this student on her first day of teaching practice with a new group of children one gains a preliminary picture of the class. Some children were playing constructively and imaginatively—those in the woodwork corner and those playing with dolls and the shop. Others were having sensory experiences in the water, and the sand. Two children were playing together. The phrases 'Played in the sand', 'Played in the water', 'Played in the shop', would have given a more useful picture if the question 'How?' had been answered by the teacher in writing up her notes. Let us look for a moment at the variety of ways in which children might use water and sand. In keeping records, teachers need to give more specific detail. It takes no more time than making a general statement. Specific comments tell us so much more about the child's level of development and interest.

Water

Licking, lapping it, drinking it. Banging it. Splashing it. Throwing it. Pouring it over oneself. Pouring it over others. Pouring it out of vessels if the adult fills them. Filling and emptying it. Pouring it through funnels, sieves,

Keeping records   131

tins with holes in, toy tea-sets. Transferring it from one object to another. Washing dolls. Washing objects. Washing clothes. Paddling in it. Blowing through straws and rubber tubing. Blowing table-tennis balls across the surface. Blowing boats across the surface. Mixing it with sand, paints. Washing dishes. Mopping up. Cleaning the tables with a cloth. Washing the floor, i.e. mopping. Making dams in streams.

Sand
Eating it. Touching with hands. Poking fingers into it. Poking toes into it. Burying hands in it. Burying feet in it. Throwing it. Blowing it. Throwing it over or at another child. Filling but not emptying. Filling and emptying. Knocking down pies made by adult. Making sand pies. Moving sand. Carrying sand in buckets, other vessels. Imaginative use of sand—'it is a custard pie'—'it is a meat pie'. Mixing sand and water. Burying toys in the sand. Making castles, dams, etc.

The descriptions of the wide variety of activities which children can undertake with basic sensory play materials will give some idea of the extent of the development of the play that can be expected when they are provided with them. They also show how the phrase 'Played with water' tells us relatively little about the stage of play development reached by any particular child or about his understanding of the nature of the material he was using.

The teacher's comments at the end of the observations serve a useful purpose. They show how much encouragement the children needed to choose their own activities in view of the fact that they had not previously been allowed to do this. They also show that the children felt, temporarily, a little insecure. This was shown by their *asking* if they could do something. It was understandable because they had a new teacher. She was introducing them to something new.

The records kept on the third day of the teaching practice show how Mrs Prendiville provided other round objects for Jimmy to work with. On a previous day he had held a beach ball and carried it around the classroom. They were also more detailed, particularly with regard to 'How' the children played with the materials she provided. They tell us by purposeful suggestion (see Colin and the rabbit), that she had not quite realized that this particular child might perhaps have benefited more by being allowed to continue with his own activity in view of his social and intellectual immaturity (under 2 years). We can also see how she had not yet understood that such abstract thinking about apples sold by weight and oranges sold separately would not have been achieved by the child concerned. Perhaps it would have been more beneficial if she had given the child the words in the situation, 'You are using the scales today', 'You are weighing', 'Look at the skin of the oranges' and asked questions about the weighing activity.

We see how she guided George in the woodwork corner and how she learnt that, apparently, he had not yet achieved hand dominance. We also see that she did not become overanxious when the children were 'rough'

132   *Keeping records*

in the sand. The interest and spontaneous follow-up by Alan in his drawings of 'the seeds' shows that when the teacher does something interesting with the children the activity will be remembered by some of them and might be developed—in drawing, in painting, in making a model. It certainly shows that Alan had been thinking about his experiences.

If we look carefully at the comments at the end of the third day, we see that the student had not asked the class teacher for a list showing which children used cups, and which used straws. We can also see that, perhaps, she was expecting too much of the children when she invited them without due warning, or a movement towards the milk for them to imitate, to leave their own absorbing activities to come immediately to get their own milk. She was, however, experimenting. She was learning about children as a teacher. She was certainly caring about them.

The last set of records describe how stimulating, permissive, and interesting for the children the classroom was becoming day by day, for we read about the pastry, the torch and the policeman's hat. The children who played with the pastry were helped later on by their teacher to make real tarts and sweets. We also read about the growing awareness on this teacher's part of the importance of letting the children express their feelings. She was not afraid of these. She understood their importance in the children's development.

These examples show quite simply the kind of useful everyday records the teacher might keep in rather a systematic fashion as part of her work. They indicate how this student's skill grew in providing imaginative activities for the children, in adapting these to meet the needs of some individual children, and in generally getting to know the children she had in her class.

10 Role of the headteacher in encouraging record-keeping

Not all teachers, even devoted and dedicated ones, are sufficiently self-motivated to keep records such as have been suggested, without the continual encouragement, guidance, interest, and support that a good headteacher can provide. Perhaps the time has not yet arrived when teachers can be left completely alone to their own devices with classes of children—hence class-record books inspected by headteachers and visits by inspectors of all kinds. Yet in a field of work demanding the utmost skill and professional integrity from their teachers, the idea of the need for some 'checking-up' on what is carried out with the children is not yet fully realized.

Whilst headteachers in schools for the mentally handicapped cannot (indeed, should not) generally expect records about *subjects* and *lessons*, they can, nevertheless, play an important part in encouraging their staff to keep records about the children. Such records should be seen by the head weekly or fortnightly. The contents of the notebooks could be discussed at regular staff conferences.

Another feature of the headteacher's role might be in arranging monthly conference meetings with the staff and other specialists to discuss individual children. At such meetings reference to the records kept by each teacher would reveal to other teachers knowledge concerning the needs, difficulties, interests, and development of each child. Reading them out to colleagues would enable them to get into the habit of specific, rather than general, description of a child's activities and behaviour.

Another aspect of the responsibility of the headteacher in encouraging staff to keep records is that in which communicating with the parents is concerned. Progressive schools for the mentally handicapped are indeed communicating with the parents on a regular basis now but the idea is far from being accepted in all schools. The home diary scheme, originally described by Dale in a book on the education of deaf children, was first adopted in the north-west by Miss Buckley, Head of Ings Lane School in Rochdale. She later described the experience to my students. One student decided to try out the idea on her final teaching practice. In essence it involved the teacher and the parents writing to each other in a little notebook about the activities of the child and the behaviours observed both at home and school. A major problem with the mentally handicapped is their inability (until they are often in their teens or are adults), to communicate to other people what they have been experiencing. One can see, therefore, the difficulties confronting both teachers and parents. To some

134   *Role of the headteacher in encouraging record-keeping*

extent the home diary scheme has alleviated this problem wherever it has been used.

The interest of the other students in Ann Southren's diaries from her teaching practice was such that we adopted the practice for all students on following teaching practices. Thus an idea spread. However, as I have already said the practice is not established in all schools. I know that this causes many parents anxiety, especially when they hear from other parents how valuable such an exercise can be. It does seem to be another of those extra little responsibilities for the headteacher, i.e. encouraging some form of regular direct communication between home and school. It makes such a difference to parents having a mentally handicapped child. Some teachers fill in the home diary in spare moments during the week and send them home on Friday; others take each child in turn and encourage them in one way or another to tell them what they want them to write home to mum and dad. Some write a page, others write a few sentences. Perhaps the latter is all that is needed to support and inform a mother with a handicapped child. Another positive aspect might be argued to encourage this scheme and this is in the case where the parents of the ESN(S) child are ESN(M).* Such diaries, if printed, might encourage such parents to have a use for their own continued reading and writing practice.

When I am on the receiving end of complaints from mums and dads regarding the fact that the teacher of their child does not use this method of communication in their area I always suggest that THEY can start the ball rolling by buying a notebook and sending it to school with the first message. As I see it the responsibility of the head in all this is to see that once established the habit should not be discontinued or become sporadic because of a teacher's personal problems. Someone at least should keep up the communication with the family. With adequate safeguards some of the classroom assistants, particularly those with a full nursery nurse qualification, might very well take on the task from time to time. Keeping the communication lines flowing seems all important for it might act as a vital support system in such a family.

Whilst I am writing about communication between home and school I would like to say that it is extremely important that the parents should know the names of the child's teachers and immediately they change the names of the new ones. One of my mums told me that for several weeks the behaviour of her very handicapped child visibly changed when she arrived home from school. Worried about this fact she rang up the school. She discovered that her child had had a change of teacher. Most schools for the mentally handicapped have a regular stream of students from nearby colleges of education. They usually stay with the class and it is the custom of some colleges to allow the student full responsibility for

---

* Bayley, M. (1973) Mental Handicap and Community Care. *A Study of Mentally Handicapped People in Sheffield*, Routledge and Kegan Paul, London.

Role of the headteacher in encouraging record-keeping   135

the class.* Once more it is important that the headteacher records this fact for the parents so that they will be aware of changes in their child's life, some of which will have an effect.

In the following chapters I have suggested the teacher keeps a summary of her daily notes on some form of record card. Such cards might be kept in the headteacher's office and might be available to all workers concerned in helping the child and his family. Copies of these would accompany the child if he attended another school, or if he went to a hospital school for short- or long-term care. Once more the headteacher would need to take on the responsibility of ensuring that the cards were up to date, were based on objective data from the teacher's personal notebooks, and were filled in systematically. She would certainly need to encourage her staff to be specific in their remarks or to 'justify' more general statements with examples.

---

* In view of the current serious lack of time for preparing for teaching practice on many of these courses I am not so sure that this practice (cf. Stevens, 1976, p. 251) should continue. Class teachers need to be involved in the 'training' of these new special educators from the Colleges of Education.

11 Cumulative record cards

With practice, then, the teacher should become skilful in observing children and in keeping records. The value of keeping personal records will be minimized, however, if there is no method of transferring and taking stock of the knowledge collected about each child. One method of doing this might be in completing specially devised Record Cards. These would be cumulative, the information on them increasing year by year.

Teachers in schools for the mentally handicapped need information about all aspects of the child's development and his difficulties from other specialists and from parents in addition. This idea cannot be stressed strongly enough or repeated too many times if the job is to be done satisfactorily. Therefore, information needs to be collected carefully from all those knowing the child and assembled in an orderly fashion on specially prepared cards. These would include a wide variety of useful items for consideration. They would be available to all coming into contact with a particular child and forward looking schools might even trust parents to see what is written in the records since both are working positively for the child's good.

Little information has filtered through in the past 10 years about the record-keeping systems in schools for mentally handicapped children. Cummings (cf. p. 20) seems to be one of the few research workers taking an interest in this aspect. His results were not too encouraging. However, I think that if records were in a form understood by all teachers, children and parents would invariably gain. Perhaps the detailed record cards presented as examples will act as a stimulus to those intending to compile and print their own. They certainly will convey what I consider to be important pointers in gaining a comprehensive picture of a developing child.

The cumulative record card system should facilitate the collection of information and enable the teacher to receive and to pass on whatever has been discovered about a child considered useful in his education.

The professional exercise of writing up record cards might be carried out at the end of every term. The cards should be available for the teacher to feel free to consult and to add important details to the growing knowledge about each child in her care. As I see it, teachers in special education should be prepared to spend not fewer than three long sessions during the year on this particular aspect of their job. Some might even consider this amount of time too little. I think I can say without any hesitation now that this should be looked upon as an extra-curricula activity and not one that is done whilst the children are present. It could be looked upon as another feature of the special educator's responsibility and com-

Cumulative record cards 137

mitment—a feature for which a higher salary is being paid. Perhaps the most important factor is that this aspect of teaching should be given an absolute periodic priority in the teacher's thinking.

The following set of cards* includes sections needing to be completed at regular intervals by a variety of people—the doctor, the psychologist, the social worker,‡ and the school welfare officer. It also includes sections which make use of the teacher's own daily records, helping her to order her thoughts. The headings may be useful in suggesting the most fruitful lines along which the teacher can learn about the children and, at the same time, contribute to other people's knowledge of them. There are eight sections.

Many of the items are self-explanatory. They have been included because inquiring teachers will find little difficulty in gaining the information *over a period of years* as part of their relationships with the children as well as with those who know them. If teachers possess this knowledge they will be in a better position to provide for the development and education of each child. Many of the items are a result of the author's own experience as a teacher. Some items were added after discussions with students training to be teachers of the mentally handicapped. The contributions made by these students are considered to be particularly valuable as most of them had had some experience of teaching before training and had some curiosity and insight into the kind of information a teacher might need.

---

*These could be printed officially by a local education authority (with necessary amendments or additions), in which case each section could be in a different colour for easier reference. They could be duplicated by the teachers themselves to meet specific needs.

‡ Although there is no official machinery whereby a family with a mentally handicapped child now has a social worker (as pre-1971), many families see this as a backward step in the services supposedly giving support to families with a mentally handicapped child. Most of them only see a social worker when there is a serious crisis. Perhaps they need one all the time!

138 *Cumulative record cards*

Section 1: General Information

Name......................... Date of birth....................

Address...................... Tel. No. Home ....

.... „ „ Work (Father)............

Date .... „ „ Work (Mother)..........

Address......................

....

Date ....

Address......................

....

Date ....

- -

Name of Schools attended...

....

....

Transferred from: .... Date ....

....

To: .... Date ....

....

- -

Permission[a] for my child:

  (i) to be photographed*

 (ii) to go out of the school on expeditions

(iii) to go swimming

(iv) to have an anaesthetic in an emergency

[a] delete where applicable

Signature of parents ....

....

Date ....

---

* New teachers will be surprised to see this item. We had to 'battle' very hard to treat taking the children's photograph naturally in the early 1960s. You see most photographs were in medical books to show examples of cases of this or that condition. We wanted a normal approach to a child having his photograph taken—as a child. Parents keeping photographs of their children year by year can see development in a number of ways.

Cumulative record cards 139

Section 2: Home Environment. The Child at Home

(Entries in this section will be based upon information gained from the teachers' personal interviews with the parents, from informal home visiting, from talks with any other person knowing the child in his home situation.)

Father's work (times of working):

Mother's work (times of working):

Child's position in the family:

Names of brothers and sisters:

Ages of siblings:

Other adults living with the family (e.g. grandmother, aunt, etc.):

Date Date Date Date

Material living conditions of home:

Safety arrangements in the home (e.g. fireguard): (All items to be dated.)

Eating arrangements in the home:

Food preferences:

Food dislikes:

Toileting arrangements for the child (this might include name of person generally responsible for child at toilet):

Play space available in the home (state if child is allowed to use):

Date Date Date Date

General appearance of child (with regard to clothing, cleanliness, etc. of body and head; is clothing old-fashioned in style, appropriate to physical development of the child, tidy, repaired, etc.):

Date Date Date Date

Arrangements for identification (e.g. bracelet):

Sleeping arrangements for child (e.g. does he share a room/bed with another person? With whom?). Does he wear a 'restrainer'? Does he have a toy?

Date Date Date Date

At what time does the child go to bed?

Date Date Date Date

Do his parents go to bed at the same time as the child?

Date Date Date Date

140   *Cumulative record cards*

Are any rituals carried out in connection with bed time (e.g. dummy given, toys taken to bed)?

Does he have a biscuit in the middle of the night; a drink?

Quality of sleep (indicate difficulties if any exist):

Date   Date   Date   Date

Baby-sitting arrangements (if any):

Date   Date   Date   Date

                                        Date   Date
Sign for using toilet: ....
Word for using toilet: ....
Sign for feeling ill: ....
Word used for menstruating: ....
Name by which child is called at home:.........   ....

Coach arrangements:

Date   Date   Date   Date

Is he met by mother/other adult (whom?)?

Date   Date   Date   Date

Is he brought to bus by mother? How far does she have to walk?

Date   Date   Date   Date

Does he show pleasure on meeting mother/other adult? How?

Date   Date   Date   Date

Is mother ever late?

Hobbies and play interests (television, books, modelling, helping mother, listening to the radio, toy sets, etc.):

Dated comments:

Parents' interests:

Does parent meet other parents of handicapped children?

Does parent know of sources of help (e.g. wheel chairs, special nappies, attendance allowances, Joseph Rowntree Fund)?

Have the parents visited the nearest adult training centre, hostel, hospital, school as part of their concern for the future? Has the school made arrangements for such visits?

Cumulative record cards 141

Any reported undesirable/peculiar behaviour in the home?
Description   Date

Major conditions in home (epilepsy in a parent, diabetes, general backwardness, illiteracy, nervous breakdown, marital disharmony, etc., illness of any kind):

Dates

Who informed the parents about the child's defect?

Date

Attitude of child to school, as reported by parents or other relatives:

Date   Date   Date   Date

Attitudes of parents towards child as seen in the home:
(Notes should indicate the degree to which parents will allow the child to do things for himself/cover up for the child. They might also include the fears of the parents with regard to the child; particular difficulties in the home, e.g. overcrowding; whether the parents keep the child quiet; whether the child tries to rule the parents; aspirations for the child.)

Date   Date   Date   Date

Attitude of child towards parents (give examples to indicate; give dates):

Attitude of parents towards school:

Dates, comments:

Holiday arrangements:

Visits to home by welfare officers, teachers, headteacher, physiotherapist, health visitor.

Dated comments:

(Whole card devoted to this.)

Counselling and information
(This section should indicate the kind of encouragement given to the parents and, where possible, the reasons for this. It should also include the specific information that is given and any behavioural objectives suggested.)

Date   Date   Date   Date

142 *Cumulative record cards*

Section 3: Physical Care and Health

(The information contained in this section should be available to the teacher. Information should also be given by her. It should be based upon information given by the doctor, by the parent or gained from own observation—weighing, measuring height, when child has a cold, etc.)

Name of private doctor. . . . .
Clinical category (where applicable, e.g. microcephalic) . . . .
Specific physical handicap (if any, e.g. spina bifida, cerebral palsy, epilepsy) . . . .
. . . .

Physical examinations
Date   Remarks/advice to teacher   Doctor

Vaccinations
Polio: date   Diphtheria: date   Whooping-cough: date
Smallpox: date   Measles: date

Illnesses (hospitalization/operations to be indicated)
Date   Illness   Result and recommendations

Years	5	6	7	8	9	10	11	12	13	14	15	16
Weight												
Height												

Examination: eyesight
Date   Result   Recommendations to teacher *(this will include information about the wearing of spectacles, provision of special furniture, special lighting, etc.)*

Date by which habit of wearing glasses established . . . .

Examination: hearing
Date   Result   Recommendations to teacher   Examiner

Date by which habit of wearing hearing aid established . . . .

Examination: dental
Date   Result   Recommendations to teacher   Taken by

Cumulative record cards 143

Medication
Date   Reason   Prescribed by   Administered by   Changed by   Comments

Date of commencement of menstruation . . . .

Comments

Date of achieving satisfactory standard of feminine hygiene care . . . .
Date of commencement of voice breaking/spontaneous erections. Reactions . . . .
Date by which use of handkerchief is spontaneous. . . . .
Specific toilet difficulties (if any exist, excluding those which might be due to retarded development):
Date   Difficulty

Does the child cry or scream a great deal? Where? When?

Physiotherapy sessions (comments)

Known conditions   Date   Remarks
earache
enlarged tonsils
adenoids
bronchitis
persistent colds
persistent running nose
anaemia
heart conditions
general fatigue
obesity
extreme thinness
malnutrition
enuresis
boils, skin defects
unclean head, body
inflammation of eyes
postural defects
squint
thumbsucking
nailbiting
bedwetting
severe headaches
vomiting
chilblains
allergies
asthma
diabetes
coeliac
fallen arches

144 Cumulative record cards

Further information on general health of child
Dated items:

Fears (of parents, child):

Traumatic experiences (e.g. death of parent, serious accident, divorce):

Child sent home/to clinic
Date   Due to

Absence record (term by term)

Year						
Number of absences						
Reasons						
Number of absences						
Reasons						

Cumulative record cards 145

Section 4: Psychological Report

(This section will be completed by the educational psychologist, the teacher, or a speech therapist.)

Date   Tests used

Score at the time of testing . . . .   Grade of defect . . . .

Mental level at the time of testing . . . .

Observational techniques used (e.g. in child's home/class)

Summary of findings

Recommendations to the teacher

Review (date)

   Summary of findings

   Recommendations to the teacher

   Language skills

   Recommendation

   Developmental profile (bi-annual)

146 *Cumulative record cards*

Section 5: School Experience Record
(To be based on recorded observation by the teacher.)

Moves purposefully: Date   Reason   Date   Reason   Date   Reason
    in class
    in school
    in precincts
    of school

Spontaneous use of Basic Materials (water, paint, sand, paste, clay, dough, wood, cardboard, bricks, toys, pushing toys, pulling toys, jigsaws, dressing-up materials, musical instruments, puzzles, construction toys, etc.):
(All items to be dated. How material is used should be indicated. Some indication of how long a child works at a particular activity should be entered from time to time.)

Spontaneous use of Tools (paintbrush, scissors, needle, crayons, saw, hammer, drill, screwdriver, etc.):

Spontaneous use of Apparatus (climbing frames, climbing trees, slides, seesaws, balls, bicycles, scooters, skipping ropes, skates, swings, etc.):

Response to Stories:
Date   Date   Date   Date

Response to Singing:
Date   Date   Date   Date

Response to other Musical Activities (e.g. free experimentation with sound, listening to sounds, to records, to radio, to tape recorder):

Response to directed Physical Activities [e.g. dancing, swimming, skating, walking, apparatus work, creative dance, other kinds of dancing (folk, etc.), cycling, pony riding]:
Teacher   Date   Difficulties/Achievements noted   Remarks

Cumulative record cards 147

Response to Other Directed Activities (e.g. woodwork, weaving, sewing, basketry, ironing, painting, washing, simple cooking and baking, gardening, looking after pets):

Teacher   Date   Activity   Remarks

Special difficulties noted by:
Teacher   Date   Difficulty   Special help   Result
                                           given:
                                           Referred to:

Experiential deprivation noted by:
Teacher   Date   Deprivation   Action taken   Result

[Should include references to lack of appropriate play material in the home, lack of space, lack of attention from adults, lack of language stimuli (parents/teachers not talking or singing especially for the child), lack of out-of-home trips to the shops, holidays, too-frequent change of teachers, etc.]

Response to 'Reading' Activities. Degree of understanding described.
Teacher   Date   Activity   Methods used   Remarks

Response to 'Mathematical' Activities. Degree of understanding described.
Teacher   Date   Activity   Methods used   Remarks

148   *Cumulative record cards*

Section 6: Language Development
(This section should give dated samples of the exact gestures, sounds, words and sentences used by the child as he proceeds through school. Only dated precise words, etc., are of value. It should also record dated samples of instructions understood by the child at different times during his attendance in school.)

Section 7: Expeditions from School
(This should include all the weekly expeditions from school.)

Section 8: Other Relevant Comments

Home and school (Sections one and two)

Each of these sections will now be examined in turn so that broadly speaking my reasons for including certain items can be fully explained.

In all fields of education the influence of the home upon the achievement and attitudes of the child is steadily being recognized.* It is reasonable to think that the same might be true with mentally handicapped children; perhaps future research workers will become interested in this hypothesis.† It may be tested experimentally and provide precise details about the nature and the effect of encouragement from the home upon the development of these children. Also considered might be the effect of encouragement and supportive attitudes from teachers upon the attitudes of the parents.

If we believe that teachers need to help the parents to encourage their children, it follows that the teachers of mentally handicapped children need to come to know the parents in almost as many different ways as they know the children. Some teachers will be more successful than others in this. It might, however, be valuable for all teachers to cultivate positive attitudes towards making closer home contacts. They might also begin to see their role in a wider sense: a role which embraces not only their work in the classroom but also the many ways in which they could support, encourage, and communicate with the family of a child who is handicapped. Many will consider that this is not their responsibility. No doubt there are still some authorities who look most unfavourably on teachers visiting the homes of the children from their own classes, however informally. Parents will give nothing but an appreciative welcome to a visitor with time to listen to and share a problem. There will always be an invitation to 'come again'. A student carrying out a simple investigation as part of her training on the special-care child at home had initial difficulty, some years ago now, from the authority concerned in obtaining permission to do the work. When permission was finally granted she found that the parents were very willing indeed to co-operate. They talked freely to her about their handicapped child and several of them expressed pleasure that someone was interested enough to do this sort of study.‡

The teacher's part in visiting a home from time to time is not to supplant the services of other specialists, but is intended to be of a supporting, encouraging, and informing nature. The kind of encouragement that she will give will not include counselling. It will be encouragement that only a teacher can give because of her special relationship with the child in the learning situation and because she knows very often what the child can do and what he needs to learn. Since 1971 there are no official visits being made by social workers on any regular basis to the homes of mentally handicapped children. This being so the family often feels isolated and without adequate support for obtaining the many services they need additionally to those already provided in school. It seems to me to be an

---

* Douglas, J. W. B. (1967) *The Home and the School*, Panther Books, London.
† Put forward in 1968 edition in order to stimulate known research workers to work with parents. We still have no results in terms of parents having support.
‡ Christine Bailey (NAMH, 1965–7).

150 Cumulative record cards

essential part of the teacher's work to be in close contact with the parents. There is no place at all for the attitude, often heard even among students, that the parents are not interested in their child's progress in school. Teachers must keep on reminding themselves that all families with a mentally handicapped child have a potential life-long disappointment to cope with. Not all parents can be outgoing in these circumstances, so they need someone else to make direct contact with them.

The following examples will illustrate the kinds of encouraging attitudes I am thinking about:

A little girl of five and a half with a social age of nine months was said by her parents to be making no sounds. During the interview one of them gave her a piece of paper to play with. She strummed on it with her fingers and licked it. She made a crying sound. We suggested that mother and father should imitate the crying sound and thus respond to their child, for as Professor M. M. Lewis says, 'for a child's speech sounds to become a means of communication there must be plentiful and frequent opportunities of communication. The transformation of a child's primary utterances into communication depends to an enormous degree upon the response of others to his speech sounds.'

'Mary *will* take out the toys from the box.' An understanding teacher will explain to mother that this is a part of the play development of all children and that, therefore, her child now needs someone to fill up the box or basket over and over again for her. She will add that this will be a stage in her play development until she is ready to empty and fill up the box for herself. Perhaps she might also explain that because Mary is handicapped this stage might not occur for many, many months. She will tell mother that she, too, will play with Mary in this particular way in school. In doing so, she will encourage the mother to be more enthusiastic about helping her child and to see that in playing with her thus she is, indeed, helping her to learn.

When mother pulled the child's nose and spoke in a forceful tone of voice there was a very positive response from Joyce. She showed some interest and, with her expression, indicated she wanted more. Mother was encouraged to play in this 'rough' manner each day. She was also helped to understand that if loud sounds accompanied this activity, her rather sheltered child might begin to respond more readily to her parents' efforts. They often felt they were 'getting nowhere with their child'.

Encouraging parents by thanking them, appreciating them, and praising them for the information they offer *us* about their child's development is another way that the teacher can help and be supportive in the home. The discussion following as a result of this interest will surely be beneficial to all concerned. 'I have noticed that R can pick things up.' 'She used to put things on the fire. She used to smash things. She's like a child growing up and getting out of her baby ways.' 'There are others who have one worse than we have.' 'When someone calls her she comes.'

Mother was told by the teacher that her child was now at the stage of understanding some language but was not yet at the stage of using it. She was pleased and grateful. She was reassured that the child would develop some language as the years went by.

Whilst talking with parents about their handicapped children, I have often found that they hold certain attitudes needing explanation and further discussion. As the teacher becomes the welcome and trusted friend of the family, she might very well hear about attitudes which may have

Cumulative record cards 151

harmful effects, not only on the handicapped child but on the other children in the family. Wherever this is the case, she needs to accept responsibility for gaining help for the family from other specialists. Some typical examples of attitudes met whilst visiting parents will enable the reader to judge where such help ought to be obtained.

'That's why we had another one (*a child*) so that she can look after her when she is old enough to understand.' 'He scratches his mother. She lets him, without punishment of any kind.' (*Father reporting about mother.*) C, aged eleven years, was made responsible for his mentally handicapped sister, aged nine years, during her visits to the toilet. This was quite obviously distasteful to him. He had begun to worry about his part in this as his sister grew older. 'If she grows up, Mummy, she can be with you. You can take her to the toilet—it's all right for girls to be together.' J was in the park. A child came up to him and said, 'You have a sister who is daft.' J hit her. 'I don't want J to be left with her [*a mentally handicapped child*] because he's clever, our J. It's a shame.'

Wherever a family with a mentally handicapped child has these attitudes they surely need support, interest, explanation, and encouragement from the teacher. The modifying of such attitudes might be something which demands a great deal of worthwhile co-operation between a doctor, the psychologist, the social worker, and the teacher, working as a team. The teacher's part, therefore, in these circumstances, seems to be that of informing those present at case conferences about the difficulties—in other words providing a key link between the various specialists and the parents.

If we think about any individual child it is always helpful to see him against the background of the people he comes into daily contact with, i.e. his immediate family as well as his more remote relatives. Having normal brothers and sisters gives him the benefit of play experiences and opportunities for language development, probably greater than if he is an only child. James (a boy of 12 and one of six children) used to play cricket and football in the park with his brothers and sisters. 'It's the younger ones who've brought him on,' his mother reported, 'he plays with our little girl of 7. They play very well together at painting, school, house, doctors. He plays snakes and ladders with her too. She helps him.' Two and a half years later his mother reported, 'He plays snap with the others. They let him win sometimes. He plays hide and seek with the others. His independence has increased. The other children have helped him a great deal.'

If mother goes out to work it is possible that she is happier in many ways than if she stays at home and broods over her problem. A knowledge of the number of adults living in close proximity to the child might give us some idea of the amount of attention or spoiling the child receives. Factors contributing to family strain, or to family advantage if a grandmother is part of the household, might also be discovered.

Knowledge about the conditions and attitudes of the home will give the teacher some idea of the experiences of the child within the family circle. She will also discover the experiences he lacks and be better able to assess what she must provide as part of the day-to-day work in school

152   *Cumulative record cards*

in order to compensate for his lack of experience or to supplement the experience he has.

The following examples will illustrate more clearly the kind of general experience mentally handicapped children are so often denied. Sometimes this is because of understandable fear or sometimes because of ignorance on the part of those having close contact with them. Many of the examples chosen concern the lack of opportunity for the child to become independent. Others describe ways in which children were often denied opportunities for playing with other children. Space is a necessity for all children and many of the children visited were deprived of space. In an overcrowded home, it is difficult for any child to develop. Mothers and fathers with handicapped children often forget (or give up) talking and singing to them because no response in terms of what, to them, is recognizable language is forthcoming. Wherever these circumstances exist, the teacher must examine them closely and consider how best to compensate the child for these very necessary and vital experiences during the child's time in school.

'We never give her scissors.'
'We don't know if she can spread anything on her bread. We always prepare everything for her.'
'She likes to have a go [*combing her hair*] but mother does it for her. She has long hair and it saves time.'
'If I undo his blouse he can get it off—but I usually do it for him, it is quicker.'
'Tries to clear table for me but not usually.' (*This is about a boy of 14 years with four sisters.*)
'Father baths him. Father puts him to bed every night.' (*14 years.*)
'Mother cuts up meat for him.' (*14 years.*)
'She dusts. She will take a cup to the table when asked but we don't ask very often.'
'She usually just uses a spoon. We are afraid she will hurt herself. She can stick a fork into her meat.' (*8 years.*)
'Is always carried downstairs or given donkey rides by her father.' (*8 years.*)
'I haven't ever tried him with that.' (*Using a crayon or a pencil.*)
'She tries but of course I usually dress her.'

There seem to be countless ways—simple everyday actions relating to a child helping himself—where the mentally handicapped child is denied opportunities to become independent. Teachers have not only to provide these opportunities in school and ensure that their classroom assistants do but they need to encourage the parents to do so too.

Perhaps too little is still known at the present moment about the social development of the handicapped child. This is particularly so in his relationships with normal children. One thing is quite certain, however, and that is he will not learn to mix with other children by being prevented from doing so, either in school or at home.

'She will go to other children but we are afraid to let her.'
'The type of children we would like her to play with have left the district. Children can be very vicious, you know, and we've sheltered her.'
'Children come to the door to talk to her but we don't let her out.'
'I cannot bear the children [*in the street*] to ask her questions, so I bring her in.'
'The children on the bus [*training school bus*] were rough—we didn't like her to go on the bus so we took her ourselves.'

Cumulative record cards 153

Perhaps some teachers of mentally handicapped children are limited in providing opportunities for the children to mix with children of more normal intelligence. There seems to be no justifiable reason, however, why she should not plan the programme in such a way that her own group of children are afforded maximum opportunity to mix and interact with each other and other adults during the better part of every day, in the school itself. The imaginative teacher will, no doubt, think of ways and means of bringing her children into stimulating social contact with children from other kinds of schools during sports days, singing, dancing, and drama events, afternoon outings, puppet shows, etc.

When the group is quietly seated and busily occupied with a variety of interesting tasks, the teacher may well think about the actual amount of space her children have at home in which to move freely, to practise large movements, to explore, and to grow in. So many children, both normal and subnormal alike, and from all classes of parents, live in cramped conditions, or in conditions where mother becomes troubled about 'a mess' and a noise. They are, indeed, deprived of an important experience and a basic need—the need for space in which to move around and do things in, the need to make a 'mess'. By keeping them sitting too long at tables, teachers too are often depriving them of using the space around them. Added to this is the fact that many mentally handicapped children cannot explore even their immediate neighbourhood alone until they are teenagers, and some of them not even then. It should be clearly seen, therefore, that another feature of our role is to provide these children with as much opportunity as possible to use the space within and immediately around the school environment.

The information gained from an item concerning itself with the eating arrangements in one home led to some actual counselling being given in the following case.

It involved a family with a little girl of 8. 'We eat our meals in silence,' her mother said, 'because she tells us to "be quiet" repeatedly at dinner time.' The child was merely imitating what she had heard in school. When the situation was explained to the mother she was able to handle her child in a much more sensible way at meal-times.

A great many items concerning the sleep of the child have been included because in gaining information of this kind the teacher will have more insight into the many and varied difficulties of a family with a handicapped child.* From this the teacher will be able to appreciate more readily the problems of a mother with the kind of hyperactive child whose restlessness continues well into the early hours of the morning. She will be able, perhaps, to decide whether the headteacher might talk to such a mother, suggesting that the family doctor may be able to help. The teacher will learn whether the child rules the family situation in that she will not retire until mother 'goes too'. It is known that quite a few mothers are thus forced

---

* I am surprised at the paucity of research being carried out on the sleep problems experienced by families having a mentally handicapped child. I wonder how many schools have this information available.

154   *Cumulative record cards*

by young children to go to bed unduly early. In one case, a 10-year-old enuretic girl was in the habit of creeping into her parents' bed in the early hours of each morning. She disturbed their sleep every night. Their way of solving this particular problem was to take it in turns to leave their own bed and sleep in the child's!

Information concerning the amount and quality of sleep might indicate to the teacher that a child needs a short period of planned rest during the day. On the other hand, the teacher might conclude that the parents should be encouraged to decide on the management of their child with regard to sleeping arrangements.

Most mothers and fathers enjoy a night out together without the need to worry about their children. The parents of mentally handicapped children are no exception to this rule. One feature of the teacher's role might be to encourage the community to undertake some responsibility for a 'baby-sitting' service to these parents.* Teachers will see from the record cards whether or not the parents have been successful in finding their own regular 'baby sitters'. A useful line of action might be to enlist the help of members of Youth Clubs, the Guide and Scout movements. Boys and girls in the top forms of grammar and technical schools could also be approached to become involved with the families of handicapped children. By making such arrangements the teacher is perhaps being supportive in yet another way to the family concerned.

Another item in Section 2 of the record cards needing a little more explanation is the one referring to 'peculiar' habits. Examples taken from the records of some very disturbed children will clarify the meaning. Examples from the teacher's own experience will no doubt come to her mind as she reads them.

'Lifts carpet up and sometimes rolls himself in it.'
'She has a rocking horse—it must lie on its side.'
'We have a fireguard but she would take it off if she could. She stands near the fire till it almost burns her.'
'When mother prevented him from drawing he put his fingers right up his nose and went on doing this to seek attention. When ignored he stopped.'
'Likes to pick paint of doors and will scratch it off.'
'If he sees a wool end on sock or pullover he will pick at it until it unravels.'

Health and psychological assessment (Sections three and four)

Sections 3 and 4 of these record cards need less explanation than the two previous ones. Most of the items will be completed by and will be the major concern of the relevant specialist, i.e. the doctor, the psychologist, the speech therapist, the physiotherapist, and the audiologist. Many of the items have been included because they may be useful to the teacher.

---

* This is a feature of the life situation for families of mentally handicapped children that does not seem to have had a solution in the past 20 years. Everyone knows there should be a baby-sitting service but it is a debatable point whether parents would use it. Perhaps what we need are some formalized Baby-Sitting Courses with adequate selection procedures organized by the NSMHC and the Spastic Society with Diplomas awarded.

Cumulative record cards   155

Through them she will gain a more complete picture of each individual child from more standardized procedures. If the teacher is given an opportunity to share and discuss the particular findings recorded in terms she can easily understand, the idea of a team approach to the problem will perhaps be reinforced. Perhaps the time is not too far distant when the records are discussed with those parents wishing to have such information as they contain.

An observant visitor to a school for the mentally handicapped in the early and mid-'sixties would have been tempted to ask, 'why are so few children seen to be wearing hearing aids?' It was an interesting question then. Perhaps in some areas or places it still is, particularly as research workers in the 1950s found that 44 per cent of hospital residents in the 10–19-year age range with mental levels of 5 or more had some hearing loss in one or both ears. One in twenty of those tested had a serious hearing loss, and more than a quarter had losses sufficiently great to handicap them in ordinary life activities. These results were later confirmed by other research workers. By reason of these findings, teachers needed to ensure that the children periodically had their hearing carefully checked. Young mentally handicapped children with a tendency to catarrh and colds need to be carefully observed with reference to the possibility of intermittent deafness.

Professor Tizard drew our attention to ways in which this problem could be solved. 'Since hearing aids able to be worn by babies as young as 6 months are available, remedial measures to correct deficiencies in hearing, which is probably a more important sense than sight in fostering mental development in man, can now be undertaken from the earliest age.'

Bearing in mind this knowledge, it is feasible to suggest that no handicapped child who is mentally handicapped should have his intellectual deficiency made worse by an extra defect, and the effects of deafness can be greatly minimized if the appropriate specialized aid is worn. Periodical references to the Health Card should keep this very important aspect of a child's health at the front of the teacher's mind. The entry 'Date by which habit of using hearing aid established' is there to remind the teacher that her job is not finished when the child receives his hearing aid. Jackson* reminds us, in writing about deaf children, that 'when a hearing aid has been supplied without adequate tuition in its adjustment and use, the effect has so distressed the child that he has refused to wear it and only the most tactful and painstaking reintroduction of the aid has persuaded him to wear it again.'

It will be obvious that it is much more difficult for a mentally handicapped child to learn to use an aid effectively without special help from the adults as well as from a visiting specialist. Now that the children are within the normal educational system there should be few difficulties. The peripatetic teachers will be available in each area for the teacher to call upon. My one concern is that children living in some of the voluntary

---

*Jackson, S. (1966) *Special Education*, Oxford University Press, London.

156   *Cumulative record cards*

societies' homes may not be attending a school and will consequently be missed.

No less important than the attention which should be given to hearing disorders is that which should be given to the possibility of defective vision. An item recording the results of eye tests is, therefore, necessary to keep the teacher informed. She should not hesitate to refer a child for a sight test if she notices unusual features about the child's eyes or his use of them. She should always remember that it does not matter if her suspicions prove to be unfounded. What does matter is that the child should receive the best attention obtainable for him at all times, and the professionals need to support the parents in obtaining all the benefits they can. An example comes to mind where the child of one of my mums had a very specific eye defect. Her first consultation with a specialist took place early in the year with promises of further ones in the near future. By November, several months later, she had still not had the help she needed for her handicapped child. We suggested she marched up to the consultant's door and forced her attention on him. She did ultimately. Two or three weeks later she had obtained treatment. Looking at objects too closely, refusal to move around in the environment, obvious squint, and sometimes even 'naughty' or withdrawal behaviour may be the warning signals. Waving fingers in front of the eyes may even suggest an eye defect, too. Such behaviour could be telling her that here is a child needing treatment. Jackson gives an excellent list of professional organizations in his book* dealing with specific defects. Teachers would be well advised to consult this book. They would gain useful information from it about defects (deafness, partial sightedness, physical handicap) which if untreated or undiagnosed further prevent the mentally handicapped child from developing all his abilities satisfactorily.

Two more items need a comment or two to remind the teacher that she can perhaps be instrumental in promoting better health in the children she teaches. The first concerns dental treatment.† A student compiling a questionnaire about the physical care of children attending Special Care Units wrote: 'I thought of points that I had observed about the children having decayed or decaying teeth, long finger nails, wearing ill-fitting clothes and shoes.' A good amount of subjectivity is obviously entering into this student's judgement. Her view is only based upon a small number of children. However, any attitude among those working with the mentally handicapped may be more common than we can say, and is, therefore, worthy of our attention. 'These children have enough to put up with without going to the dentist's. He never complains.' This indicates another

---

*Segal, S. (1967) *No Child is Ineducable*, Pergamon Guides, Oxford.
McKay, R. (1976) *Mental Handicap in Child Health Care*, Butterworths, London.
   These also contain lists of useful information regarding organizations concerned with specific handicaps.
   † Even now in 1977, knowing that mobile dental units visit schools, I still think it important to draw your attention to the need for dental care on a very regular basis. A child banging his chin or grinding his teeth repeatedly may be communicating 'My teeth *hurt*'.

Cumulative record cards   157

point—care of the teeth. Regular examination and treatment of the teeth is not only important in the physical health of the child; it is also important in considering those particular speech problems which are undoubtedly due to the malformation of the teeth.

Whilst discussing the medical treatment by doctors of their mentally handicapped children, several mothers reported to research workers that these children were treated differently from their normal brothers and sisters even when they had the same complaint. The mothers also mentioned the difficulty they had in obtaining local clinic treatment for minor dental troubles and as a result were often forced to take their child to an out-patient's department of a hospital, with all the difficulties which this involved. Although 75 per cent of the families in this particular study were satisfied with the general medical treatment they were receiving for their child, there was a minority who were not. It is this minority group (and it is probably larger than we think) that teachers must be especially on the lookout for when considering those problems which affect the health of the children; for such problems, if left unattended, will ultimately affect the all-round development of the children.

The second item in Section 2, which demands some attention, is that which concerns itself with the weight chart. So often it is said by those who do not work among the handicapped, 'Is it necessary for mentally handicapped children to become so ungainly, so fat?' The majority of them, perhaps, do not become so; but there are others who perhaps need more help than we can give them as teachers. There will be a minority who need very special help. An eye on the weight chart might at least suggest to the teacher that she ought to be discussing its entries with other specialists.

The points covered in the previous paragraphs are those which it is considered should be looked at most carefully. Lack of attention to the possibility of such serious defects existing will certainly prevent the progress we hope will occur.

The remarks which have been made about particular aspects and the rest of the items which are listed are only intended to act as reminders to the teachers, for they need to become aware of such conditions in considering the health of the children they are teaching. By including such a section, it is not suggested that teachers should diagnose and treat the various conditions, but that teachers need a very practical working knowledge of those general factors concerning the child's health so that they can co-operate more intelligently with the experts whenever the need arises.

Psychological assessment

This section is included to emphasize how important it is for the teacher to feel part of a team by receiving information from other specialists and having the feeling that she too has an important contribution to make. In particular, she needs to have opportunities for co-operating personally

158 Cumulative record cards

with those whose training is highly specialized and who, because of this, often consider that their findings will perhaps not be understood by those not so trained. The information gained by a qualified educational psychologist (because of the procedures he uses) can be of the utmost value to the teacher. It would be perfect if the results could be discussed with her individually or at progress review meetings, as circumstances permit. In view of the relatively small number of children in each authority tested and finally admitted to schools for the mentally handicapped it should be possible for the examiner to have time for such discussion.

There are many educational psychologists and doctors who undoubtedly feel that the testing situation, especially that in which mental abilities are being examined, is their domain and theirs alone. This attitude is justified in view of the dangers of putting the actual test items into the hands of those not trained to give standardized tests. Some teachers exist who will try to give practice to the child on the test items, if they get to know them. One can fully appreciate the assessors' predicament, particularly when they must transmit their findings to those with such attitudes. With the growth of better understanding about such matters this situation will slowly change and, if the results of these tests are well interpreted, the sharing of them with the teachers will undoubtedly be for the ultimate benefit of the child concerned.

The knowledge of the score is not so important to the teacher as a simple explanation of the successful and failed items which go to make up the score. It is not intended to discuss here the actual tests which are in current use at the moment, or of the meanings of the terms which psychologists use, e.g. mental age, performance test, verbal ability. Books dealing most adequately with these will be found in most libraries or may be obtained on request. Nevertheless, it is important that the teacher has certain facts from the psychological findings conveyed to her.

The psychological record card is one way in which the busy psychologist or doctor can give the information the teacher needs in order to understand the child, i.e. his general intellectual level at the time of testing; any degree of maladjustment or neuroticism; his behaviour during the test; some examples of his language; and any particular abilities or difficulties.

The record card contains some rather general headings; they do not list the tests to be used and do not suggest precisely the information which the examiner might give. The form the card takes leaves the tester rather free to use his own judgement and words, bearing in mind the particular staff he is conveying his findings to. This, of course, presumes that he will get to know the teachers as well as the children he has tested.

One of the popular current trends in schools for mentally handicapped children is that of teaching useful words to the top classes. This is often carried out by the teacher without any information or recommendation to the effect that a child is ready for this particular activity. In including an item headed 'Recommendations to the Teacher', it is hoped that the expert examiner may one day be instrumental in helping the teacher to judge better whether a particular child is ready for more academic learn-

Cumulative record cards 159

ing. He might even be able to suggest the best methods she should use with an individual child and what his special difficulties and abilities are likely to be in this kind of learning.* Many handicapped children are being forced to attempt such learning in groups without due regard to individual differences and difficulties. In the beginning, all such learning needs to be through experience of the words in the *real situation* and as often as possible. Any learning of an academic nature needs to be in an individual situation with the teacher—at least in the early stages. The item 'Recommendations to the Teacher' might also include suggestions about how to handle the child and even how to communicate with him.

In the past, it has not been customary for a child who is found to be mentally handicapped to be retested, unless the parents or headteacher has especially requested it. Retesting may at some future date be carried out periodically on all handicapped children. This would not be solely for ascertainment purposes but in order also that their growth could be reviewed and further recommendations for their education made. Hence the 'Retest' item on the card.

By including the item 'Other Tests' in Section 4, it is suggested to the teacher that she too has a part to play in completing the record card, relating to the psychological aspects of the child's development, i.e. in giving her own tests to the children and in using school achievement tests of reading and number where these apply. She could also include here dated results of the tests she might use to estimate the social sight-words the child has learnt, i.e. a record of actual words known, as well as some form of identification of the method she has used in teaching a particular child, for these will often differ from child to child. To illustrate this point, if the teacher chooses a simple picture book and takes each child in her class in turn and asks about the picture, 'It is a ——?' 'Who is this?', and records the responses, she will discover interesting differences between the children. If exactly the same procedure takes place at the end of each term or year, she will not only see differences but changes in the children's responses. Some of these changes will show that learning has taken place; some will show development. There is another useful and simple test which will show differences and changes after retest between children in one class: it can be called the 'Mother-goes-Shopping Test'. A basket full of the real items mother would buy from the grocer's is presented to the child. He is asked to take one at a time from the table and put it back in the basket, telling his teacher what it is. He has freedom of choice in returning the items. Once more the recorded responses will tell his teacher many interesting facts about each child's knowledge of everyday things and his observation.†

---

* An article in the July (1966) edition of the *United Kingdom Reading Association Bulletin* indicates that, in three training schools, 10 out of 250 children were considered as being able to benefit from reading instruction. On the Daniels–Diack Standard Reading Test they had reading ages well above their mental levels.

† I have written elsewhere a whole chapter on the question of possible 'tests' that can be given by the teacher to explore the varying abilities/disabilities of the children in her class.

160   *Cumulative record cards*

Records which suggest a programme of activities (Sections five, six and seven)

The items in this section are intended to give the teacher a very general picture of the kind of programme of activities which, perhaps, she needs to be providing for the children and keeping records about, though to some extent these will also appear in a longer form in the teaching notebook. The chronological age that a particular activity should commence or cease has not been mentioned. In no other field of education is there such a case for the teacher to follow the level and the interests of the individual child and to provide for this level with a very wide range of well-thought out, meaningful experiences and purposeful activities throughout his school life.

The teacher in this field of work cannot be told exactly what to do with each child or with each group of children. In view of our present knowledge about the learning abilities of handicapped children, she still cannot be told the exact stages which she should present to help them to learn. Her own initiative and imagination will always be her main resources. She will also need to refer to books from the normal field of primary education from time to time. Perhaps teachers will see from this section that the children need to be 'doing'. They need to be 'exploring, experiencing' new materials and new circumstances, all the time. The times at which the teacher introduces the various activities and enables the child to remain interested in them will naturally depend upon her skill and sensitivity at assessing the 'moment' and upon her preparation and provision.

You will notice the occurrence of the word 'spontaneous' in some of the items. Experienced teachers have always found it useful to observe the ways in which children use basic materials, apparatus, and tools without prior suggestion or help from them. They can then see where the children need the most help, where they need encouragement to try out their own ideas with new activities and where further experiences and materials must be provided to help the children to learn.

The idea that the children should be able to choose their own activities for a good part of every day has been stressed and commented upon over and over again in these pages. It is important too that one or two short periods during each day might be planned so that the children can come together as a group with the teacher for varying amounts of time. Throughout these group sessions the teacher still needs to observe the response that is made by each child. There always seem to be one or two children, even in the top classes, who remain on the outside of their group. Whilst the teacher should encourage the children as they grow older to participate with the group in music, movement, cookery, story-time, and other creative work, she should, nevertheless, respect the child's need sometimes to continue his activity on his own. Of course, she should make sure there is something in the classroom to attract his attention and keep him purposefully busy and active. Future participation with the group,

Cumulative record cards   161

of his own free will, will then be a sign of co-operation, interest, and growth.

Need to record difficulties
Mentally handicapped children have such a variety of difficulties that it would be impossible to list them. Therefore, the teacher needs to be constantly on the look-out for any sign which tells her that the child is experiencing difficulty over and above that which she feels is caused by his general intellectual level and stage of development. If she cannot sort out the difficulty herself, she should adopt the attitude of finding the appropriate specialist to help her. This might be a more experienced teacher, the headteacher of the school or, of course, the visiting doctor, or psychologist. The time may come when teachers of mentally handicapped children will be able to call upon the local education remedial service to help them sort out some of their children's learning difficulties. When it does we must be sure that the remedial teachers concerned have a wide understanding of the problems of this particular group of children lest they adopt inappropriate methods and introduce inappropriate teaching materials into the schools.

Lack of experiences, particularly in the home
I have already dealt at some length with the idea that parents often deny their children important experiences in their own homes. From time to time the teacher perhaps needs to record such instances, hence the section on what I have termed 'experiential deprivation'.

The section dealing with school experience perhaps needs little further explanation than that already given. The remaining sections, i.e. language development, expeditions from school and other relevant comments, complete the suggestions I have to make regarding Cumulative Record Cards. A few words about each will remind you of their purpose.

Language
To develop all aspects of language is surely one of the main aims of the teacher in schools for the mentally handicapped. The word 'junior' has been purposely omitted to underline the idea that language development as an aim does not cease at the junior level, for it will need concentrated attention from teachers throughout their lives. One of the ways in which the teachers might become vitally interested in the language development of their children is if they are expected to record samples of the ways in which the children in their classes communicate throughout their school lives. The importance of encouraging language might also be understood in a practical way if some form of continuous record is kept.

Perhaps the best way we learn about the world in which we live is by personal experience of it. For the mentally handicapped, movement around his immediate environment from a very early age, as well as around a wider one, is an essential part of the school programme. If he is not afforded opportunities to move around he will, indeed, be severely

162 *Cumulative record cards*

deprived of the conditions known to be necessary for satisfactory learning. Therefore it is considered important for the children to spend a great deal of their programme time outside school and for a short record to be kept of such expeditions. This record could also include information about the one-day-a-year school outings we know are usefully and happily part of the school provision as well as about school holidays and camps. They will include a brief mention of the visits made to see the trains go by, to see the postman collecting the letters, the farmer haymaking, the boats in the harbour, the fish in the canal, and the concrete mixer, etc. Reading such records, teachers in receiving classes will be able to see the kind of experiences the child has had, the kind that he will need repeating again and again and the kind he still needs to have.

However detailed record cards are in their suggestions, there is always something a teacher wishes to record that does not seem to 'fit in'. I have added the 'other relevant remarks' section to fill this gap for the zealous teacher.

12 Observations on some historical aspects

Myths abound in all spheres of life until the facts are reported by those actually concerned. One of these myths repeatedly heard amongst students on present courses for teachers of the mentally handicapped is that education for these children only began in 1971 when the Education Act (Handicapped Children) 1970 was implemented. Only the other day a new student, describing her experience before coming to college, told me that her headteacher had had some kind of training in —— but that it was not to be a teacher. The place she named was indeed one of the colleges where teachers of the mentally handicapped were trained from 1960 onwards until radical changes taking place in 1971 phased out something valuable that had been developing in the hands of imaginative committed professionals over a decade.

One of my aims in writing this chapter will be to continue to illuminate the kind of specialized courses teachers followed prior to 1970 before they were considered to be sufficiently competent and caring to teach this very special group of children coming from families also having special needs.* Another of my aims is to draw your attention to the informed people and to the unpublished documents existing that will throw light upon what really happened in the 'sixties to ensure that mentally handicapped children were seen to be educable and therefore accepted in the normal stream of educational administration. Perhaps one of the results of my chapter is that academics will be interested to discover the facts from the material available. Perhaps some of this material will be useful to those needing a historical bias in the new B.Ed. courses in the colleges of education.

Another reason for this chapter is to encourage students to persuade their colleges that their training is to some extent inadequate and that much of their course is irrelevant and does not allow enough time for them to examine relevant aspects in sufficient depth and to work with the children and their families. I am certain that with the present cut-backs in education, in-service training will not be available in the quantity needed unless teachers are prepared to pay for extra courses themselves.† Many

---

* I have written 'continue to illuminate' because I have already outlined in some detail the special kind of training needed by teachers of these children in my other book. I also wrote an article for the *Times Educational Supplement* in 1974 entitled 'A time to compromise'. In this article I tried (but obviously failed) to argue the case for changes in the way teachers were currently (and still are) trained to teach the mentally handicapped. Many of the students become disillusioned with their courses for no one listens to their complaints.

† Principal Tutors and their staff were invited to attend a week's refresher course organized annually by the National Association for Mental Health up to 1970. Not only did they participate in these courses by lecturing and by seminar work but THEIR knowledge was

164   *Observations on some historical aspects*

students talk about their feelings relating to an inadequate course. Usually it is without knowing what might be considered more adequate. Clearly, if they have nothing to compare their own course with they cannot demand changes in what I often describe as an 'enlightened ignorance' climate of opinion.

As I write I am reminded of an interesting report. It was written by Winifred Curzon, an Inspector of the Board of Control (later an HMI), and published in the 1958 Autumn edition of *Forward Trends** In the article she states that 'there was a need for increased co-operation and close integration between school and occupation centre, and between staffs of both.' There are 329 occupational centres of various sizes, the largest having more than 230 pupils of all grades and ages including adults; the smallest about 12 in attendance. In order to show the present lack of school interest, Mrs Curzon asked how many teachers had any knowledge of the local occupation centre; how many had visited and had invited return visits; how many sending children to the centre from the school had sent on some kind of progress report to the staff concerned; and how many realized that the children on occasion found their way back into the school. In future it was hoped that the two-way traffic would be more early recognized and considerably eased for the benefit of the children. In this event understanding between teachers (note the word) would be essential.

Teachers in the centres felt the need for a greater understanding of what their aims were and how they were trying to achieve results. Mrs Curzon continues to say that 'the centre routine is that of the ESN school but as yet they are not satisfied that the subjects included in the curriculum and the methods of presentation are right for the child who at best will only fit into a sheltered unskilled employment. Building personalities is our joint job and only closer co-operation and team-work will provide the solution we are seeking.'

The article followed on from an interesting account† the previous year in the same journal of an experiment in co-operation between an occupa-

---

constantly updated because of the other specialists they met, listened to, and talked with during the week. To my knowledge there is now no such course for Tutors to the MENCAP courses in colleges. High academic qualifications (often in psychology) plus some experience in special education seem to be the recognized qualifications for becoming responsible for a course where training of these teachers takes place (in-service training for them seems to have lost ground). Perhaps this is an improvement on the early 'sixties. At that time not one of the teacher trainers appointed had had much to do with severely subnormal children. Some of us did have high academic qualifications though. However, perhaps this meant that we looked with new eyes at what was happening to these children. We certainly looked at the needs of children and not the demands of a college syllabus. We also looked most carefully at the growing needs of a new group of teachers and changed our courses accordingly over the years to meet *their* needs in the schools.

* Curzon, W. (1958) *Report on Occupation Centres, Forward Trends*, Guild of Teachers of Backward Children, Autumn Edition.

† Mrs Sally Halsall and Mr W. Murray. Mrs Halsall for many years has been the Principal Tutor to a course (a two-year one, then a three-year one within a college of education) for teachers of the mentally handicapped at Chiswick Polytechnic, London.

Observations on some historical aspects 165

tion centre and a school for ESN(M) in Cheltenham. Referring back to the article by Mrs Curzon I should point out to you that she in fact uses the word 'teacher' throughout her talk. Even before the Mental Health Act of 1959 the National Association for Mental Health was training teachers in London and Manchester.* I was interested to note that the timetable in 1958 was the timetable for the ESN(M) child. It is my personal impression that this is still the practice in many schools for the mentally handicapped. Teachers are not really considering the needs of the child with due reference either to his present or future life. The increase in money for the schools seems to mean that a substantial amount has been spent on static table apparatus for academic learning—a great deal of it seems to me to be irrelevant to the needs of the child. A great deal of this table apparatus ensures that the children sit once more for long periods of time†—the teaching method is not very special. It is made easier for the teacher because classroom assistants often sit with the children too. For this the teacher is paid a substantial amount of extra salary. I wonder if I have the right impression? Perhaps I am wrong. I hope so.

I should like to clarify the situation and say that in the main the reason for the lack of teacher interest was indeed for financial reasons. The salaries of those dedicated women in the 'fifties amounted to less than $\frac{1}{5}$ or $\frac{1}{6}$ of what qualified teachers were receiving in normal education. Inevitably they were receiving very much less than colleagues in special education. This state of affairs existed in spite of the fact that they often coped most successfully with children in the centres that could not indeed be catered for and coped with in the schools for the ESN(M), even where there were qualified special education teachers. Disturbed ESN(M) children were admitted to the centres where often they were happy with the so-called unqualified members of an unrecognized and badly paid profession. There has been no lack of career interest in these schools from the traditionally trained section of the teaching profession since the salaries 'were right' for the job. Indeed, many teachers without special training in mental handicap have gained professional promotion in this field of work.

Kathleen Jones in her extensive and excellent historical study of the Mental Health Services‡ outlines the developments leading to community care in the 'sixties. Her study begins with a description of eighteenth-century attitudes towards the mentally disordered. She mentions the growth of provision in local health authorities for mentally handicapped children. She touches on the training of their teachers. However, she does not examine in any detail the implications of the Scott Report, the setting up

---

* Hargrove, A. (1967) *Serving the Mentally Handicapped.* Published by MIND, 22 Harley Street, London W1.

† Some of us spent a very long time in the 'sixties encouraging teachers to provide children with more opportunities for moving away from table activities and interacting with their peers.

‡ Jones, K. (1972) *A History of the Mental Health Services*, Routledge and Kegan Paul, London.

166   *Observations on some historical aspects*

of the Central Training Council for teachers of the mentally handicapped, or the events leading up to the Education Act 1970.

The unnamed DHSS author of *A Decade of Progress** reports upon the growth of the responsibilities of the Central Training Council in accepting new courses, in examining all aspects of these courses, in awarding the only recognized diplomas in this field of special education. She does not mention the names of those who were actually involved in the training of these teachers and clearly the main promoters (in partnership with the schools) of the changes that came about in the schools. The report gives the names of those who served on the council, those involved in assessment. It does not reveal the names of the external examiners involved in the examining of the practical teaching—and these were probably more important than those assessing academic standards in written examination questions for they saw and approved of standards in teaching skills *and* the current teaching methods. I wonder if this omission was because these external examiners were in fact chosen by the tutors to courses and not the council itself. The report does not really stress the point that the pilot courses of the National Association for Mental Health under the tutorships of educators were in fact the basis of the curricula for all subsequent courses; that some of the tutors indeed acted initially as consultants to members of staff to the newly established council courses.

Whilst the report records the 6-month course offered to three potential tutors to courses it makes no reference to the annual refresher courses that were held by the NAMH for its tutors and staffs in the training centres right up to the 'seventies. Its report on the DES course organized for tutors in the late 'sixties does not reflect the amount of knowledge that was gained by those DES officials attending the courses they arranged, from tutors experienced in this special field over a decade. Its claim to bringing the tutors together three times a year hides the fact that the DHSS acted as host to a tutor group already organized for several years and indeed welcomed us and provided us with an admirable lunch. It did not initially bring the Association of Tutors into being. This happened in 1965 because of the efforts of four tutors—Mr J. MacMasters (now in Newcastle University), Mr R. Fechnie (Preston Polytechnic), Mr B. Flanders (Principal Tutor, Leeds), and myself. We compiled the first constitution of a professional body of tutors following on from the positive model of the NAMH where tutors met together at 3-monthly intervals in London to present reports on the progress of their courses to the committee concerned with the training of teachers. The newly formed body of tutors decided that they should meet at regular intervals and that the group should consist of those training teachers of the children as well as those concerned with the adults. In the early years tutors met in different parts of the country.†

**A Decade of Progress*. History of the Training Council for Teachers of the Mentally Handicapped. DHSS publication, HMSO. Written by a person officially unknown, as is the fashion with government bodies.

† The first meeting was held in a hotel in Preston, Lancashire. We were the guests of the

Observations on some historical aspects 167

Owing to the geographical convenience of London we began to use the premises in Alexandra Fleming House (DHSS). Our presence there was conditional on having a lecture from someone in the field of subnormality for at least part of the day. The rest of the day was spent discussing the various courses. At no time were tutors persuaded to present written reports to colleagues about the methods used in their courses to train teachers. To my thinking this was a loss for we had no way of knowing what students were being taught or what ideas were being introduced into the schools in different parts of the country.

I have mentioned this last document* for I wish to remind you that writing history seems to be a personal affair and that though documents are often based upon facts that can be checked, the personal involvement of the persons concerned will naturally influence the conclusions that are drawn.† It will be a long time before a comprehensive history of the development of educational approaches to the mentally handicapped is written by an interested outsider. Perhaps the snippets I am introducing, even though these are from a personal point of view, will contribute a little. Perhaps they will encourage my colleagues from the past to do the same.

Most of this chapter will give you information about a course as I knew it between 1961 and 1971. As far as my memory serves me I shall be factual.

---

newly appointed Tutor to the Preston course, Mr Alf Boome (now at Bulmershe College). I should like to say that from 1964 onwards all teachers employed by the Lancashire Health Authority had to attend this course if Lancashire seconded them.

* I have already referred to *Forward Trends*, Journal of the Guild of Teachers of Backward Children. This journal is now discontinued and has become incorporated in the Journal of the National Council for Special Education, *Special Education*. Libraries in colleges/universities should be able to obtain back copies for interested readers. Mr Stanley Segal, a founder member of the Guild of Teachers of Backward Children in the early 'fifties, has a complete set of these journals presented to him in Bradford in 1975 by grateful colleagues. The *Journal of Mental Subnormality* (Ed. H. C. Gunzburg, Monyhull Hospital, Birmingham), *Teaching and Training*, and *Parent's Voice* if examined critically will also provide the history student with useful historical evidence.

† One of the highlights of this document is the description it makes of the way in which the training council fought for proper recognition by the teaching profession of the professional standing of Diploma holders. Whilst they lost the 'battle' in terms of immediate recognition by teachers' unions for all teachers of the mentally handicapped, their struggle enabled these teachers to have the recognition that was their right after an agreed number (5) of years of post diploma experience.

As far as one can ascertain the Council never concerned themselves with the 'fate' of those who had trained the teachers over a decade. Nor did they seem concerned with the watered-down versions of these courses (whatever the academic quality of them) that were to be introduced into the colleges in the 'seventies. The amount of time I was allotted in one college of education to train teachers of the mentally handicapped amounted to $4\frac{1}{2}$ hours a week for the first 2 years of their course in an otherwise normal teacher training programme. A main subject was only gained for the subject 'Mental Handicap' after many struggles with a hierarchy of committees who did not know the kind of children we were thinking about or the problems inherent in training their teachers. It was accepted by the academic board concerned by a majority of one or two votes only!

It was interesting to note that no official appointments were made from the body of existing tutors to the committee of the Training Council until the very late 'sixties. This happened in spite of the fact that a very wide variety of professionals and non-professionals were selected to represent different interests.

168   *Observations on some historical aspects*

However, I should like to think that students studying the modern history of these children and their education will also refer in part at least to the following books and documents additionally to those mentioned elsewhere.

(1) *Serving the Mentally Handicapped* by Aphra Hargrove (1967) published by the National Association for Mental Health (MIND). This small, useful book contains a description of the early beginnings of occupation centres, then training centres, and training schools, then schools. It also contains descriptions of the very early recognized courses for teachers of the mentally handicapped pioneered by the National Association for Mental Health. It is essential reading for it enables the reader to understand the 'sitting down at table' methods of education deemed relevant for the mentally handicapped prior to 1960 (and to some extent these methods have now returned in some areas of Britain since 1971 under the guise of 'normalization' of schooling and under the misconception the 'new' people have that these children cannot organize their own behaviour in a way that will bring learning about). I might add that such methods are easier for the teacher but they do not seem to need teachers who are paid special education salaries to carry out such formal group methods with these children. Initiative is not observed and interests are not followed up. Aphra Hargrove's booklet is also essential reading to gain a picture of the ways in which caring authorities developed positive attitudes towards these children by having them educated in the community—a direct contrast to the caring 'out of the community' advocated by early 'reformers' in the first 20 years of this century though.*

(2) *Scott Report of the Training of Staff of Training Centres for the Mentally Subnormal* (1962) HMSO. This 51-page report reviews the work that was carried out by a body of fourteen people during 1960 on the problems inherent in training staff to work with the severely subnormal child. The report superseded the experimental initial 1-year courses of teacher training organized by the NAMH in 1960 with qualified teachers in charge (Mrs Maureen Forrest, Bristol, 1959; Mrs Mildred Stevens, Manchester, 1961; Miss Wynne Willis, London, 1960; Mrs Marjorie Lettice, Sheffield, 1961) and the Training Council for teachers of the mentally handicapped in 1964. It recommended 2-year courses as soon as these were feasible. The course in Bristol was the first to become a 2-year course under the NAMH. Their college was named after Mary Lindsay, i.e. Lindsay House, Apsley Road, Bristol. The Manchester course followed in 1965 and of this I will write later. The Scott Report not only contains detailed information about the staff employed in centres for the mentally handicapped in terms of their qualifications, age, marital status, etc.

---

* Pritchard, D. G. (1970) *Education and the Handicapped 1760–1960*, Third impression, Routledge and Kegan Paul, London.

Observations on some historical aspects 169

(and this might very well be a useful exercise to repeat nearly 20 years later in order to see what changes in personnel have occurred), but it made twenty recommendations for the future all of which have now been implemented. The recommendation that 'a period of ten years from the date of the first course should be a period within which all staff employed at that date eligible for training should have received it' should have been a warning to those becoming tutors that after that date (i.e. 1970) we could expect a different form of training from the one we were currently involved in. In rereading the Scott Report I certainly understood more clearly the reason for the NAMH advertising in the *Times Educational Supplement* (*TES*) for a retired College of Education Lecturer to become tutor to their course in Manchester in 1960. That body being closely involved in the training of teachers of the mentally handicapped were certainly not seeing their training courses as ones developing into 3-year training courses within colleges. It had a job to do and it certainly did it. I was the head of a remedial department in a secondary school in 1960. I needed a new teaching experience and I thought the word 'retired' in the advertisement was a misprint! The following 10 years were among the most exciting of my professional life.

The Scott Report contains the syllabus that was used by the NAMH and later by the Training Council Courses to guide its tutors in the work they had to do. It made no suggestion about the methods that were to be used in this task. These were largely developed by individual tutors using the resources of the particular area of the course as they became experienced and knowledgeable about the students and the children with whom they were involved. I have described the methods I and my colleagues used in Manchester in some detail in my other book.

(3) *Simple Beginnings in the Training of Mentally Defective Children* by Margaret MacDowell. This little book was written as a memorial to Margaret (died 1930), a pioneer in teaching mentally handicapped children. After being a pupil of Dr Shuttleworth, Superintendent of the Royal Albert Hospital, Lancaster, himself a pupil of Edouard Seguin, she opened a school herself at Avonhurst, Burgess Hill, Sussex. Her attitudes about the necessity for looking at each child as an individual, her ideas for making individual teaching aids and about the necessity for the teacher to have maximum support in her task, are as fresh and as relevant today as they were almost a half century ago. As a teacher of these children she seems to have been forgotten and her messages ignored until the late 'fifties and early 'sixties. Mention of her might encourage others to study her work. She certainly never doubted the value of TEACHING these children.

(4) *Are We Good Enough* by P. F. Simpson, Special Adviser for Special Education in Leeds; editor to the National Council for Special Education (Conference Report 1975, Bradford). This paper read at the above conference contains a reasoned discussion regarding

170 *Observations on some historical aspects*

integration and segregation in the field of handicap. It also examines the DES circular 2/75 *The Discovery of Children Requiring Special Education in England and Wales and the Relevant Points for Teachers*, viz. 'the present ascertainment procedures under section 44 of the Education Act 1944 will be phased out except where the parents object to their child's attendance at a special school. This will certainly mean that teachers and possibly parents will be much more closely involved in assessment than hitherto.'* The paper continues with a discussion on the qualities needed by teachers in special education generally and ends with the suggestion that a variety of compulsory in-service training courses shall be available for teachers wishing to enter special education and that all teachers shall be expected to take one or other of them within a specified time of their appointment unless they have initial training in special education.

(5) *The Quarterly Reports of the NAMH Tutors* to the four courses organized by that body during 1960–71. They, perhaps more than other documents in that decade, trace the history of the changes and development of an educational approach to mentally handicapped children and the training methods that were used to create a competent, professional, caring body of teachers. Present members of staff in the Head Office, 22 Harley Street, London should be able to direct you to these records.

(6) *The Minutes of the Training and Education (Sub-committee) National Association for Mental Health* from 1960. I do not know if such a committee met before that date.

(7) *The Annual Reports* submitted by Principal Tutors to the Central Training Council, Alexander Fleming House, Elephant and Castle, London. These reports were very detailed. They described in very clear terms what each tutor was doing on his course and the aims of the course; these reports contained the expertise of tutors and a very wide body of multidisciplinary professionals all over the country, many of them unknown to these same tutors for they never met and never corresponded directly.

(8) *Introductory Handbook on the Severely Subnormal* by T. W. Pascoe; obtainable from the College of Special Education, Pembridge Hall, Pembridge Square, London W2. This third guide-line for teachers was written to provide 'those interested in becoming teachers of the mentally handicapped with information regarding training, and as a contribution to the task of arousing the general public to a greater appreciation of their responsibilities for the education of the mentally handicapped'. It will repay a brief study for it fills in some of the historical gaps in the 'sixties.

(9) *Teaching the Mentally Handicapped* (November 1968). This small pamphlet obtainable from Alexander Fleming House (cf. above) was

---

* Simpson, P. F. (1975) 'Are we good enough' Conference Proceedings, National Council for Special Education, Bradford.

Observations on some historical aspects 171

compiled by the Training Council. It was one of the first official documents to have photographs of the work that was going on in the centres—the loveliness rather than the horror of mentally handicapped children was publicized. It followed on from the films made by Veronica Sherborne in Bristol on the play of these children (1963) on the movement films* and of the observation film made by me† in Manchester with the help of the Technical Aids Department of Manchester University (by permission of Professor R. A. C. Oliver), and a small sum of money from my employing body. The document is useful because it describes the salaries and conditions of service of the teachers almost at the end of the decade in question. The word teacher is used throughout the document for there was never any doubt in the minds of those who were informed that the staff of the centres were teachers—a large percentage of them had indeed been trained by teachers too as I have emphasized in this chapter.

(10) *Transfer or Transformation* (1969). This seventh guide-line of the College of Special Education contains the papers of a number of well-known specialists in the field of the education of the mentally handicapped. The booklet indicated the expectations of some of the speakers concerned in the 'seventies when the responsibility for this education was transferred from the local health authorities to the local education authorities.

(11) *Organization and Content of Courses leading to a Diploma in the Teaching of the Mentally Handicapped Children.* This was a document representing the fruits of some very hard work carried out by tutors and some DES officials at a meeting of both (designated a course) in Bristol in 1968 (cf. p. 166). This document enabled tutors to examine the current thinking of the Training Council about future training. It enabled them to see that some of the thinking had been based upon past experiences gathered from the Teacher Training Course by themselves and described in tutors' reports; had been based upon the experiences gained from observing the educational work taking place in the centres as a result of these courses. It heralded the advent of 3-year courses in Colleges of Education and Polytechnics and supported the first 3-year initial course for teachers of the mentally handicapped in this country. This was to be held in the Northern Counties College, Newcastle upon Tyne. Its Principal Tutor was Bertie Brown, one of the three teachers taking the Training Council's short 6-month course in Institute of Education, London in 1966 (cf. *A Decade of Progress*, p. 166).

(12) *A Survey of Services for the Mentally Handicapped in the North West*

---

*In Touch, Concord Films, Ipswich.

† College staff wishing to see this observation film (old, silent and unedited) should contact me at my home.

You only need to order the documents mentioned at 16–19 (overleaf) in the Records Office in your area and they will be made available for your perusal by the archivists. They will usually arrange to have the Acts of Parliament photocopied.

172   *Observations on some historical aspects*

1959–64. Hertzog, D., unpublished M.Ed. Thesis, Department of Education, University of Manchester.

(13) *DES Circular 15/70* to local education authorities and other bodies. This was a document explaining to local education authorities the implications of the Education (Handicapped Children) Act 1970.

(14) *The New Pupils.* A South West National Society for Mentally Handicapped Children Conference Report. The Conference was held in Bristol and it was opened by Margaret Thatcher. In her paper she surveys a hundred years of progress from the Education Act of 1870 to the Education (Handicapped Children) Act 1970. It was the first time that these children were officially recognized and talked about as 'pupils'.

(15) *The Education of Children in Hospital Schools* by Gordon Bland. A College of Special Education, Special. This small booklet outlines the nature of the children, the staff, and the methods current in a number of hospital schools in England during the mid-'sixties.

(16) *The personal diaries* of the physician superintendents of asylums in the late nineteenth century, often obtainable in the archives of the area in which you happen to live, or in the hospital records themselves.

(17) *The reports of the visiting justices* to the hospitals, houses of correction, workhouses.

(18) *The Board of Guardians Minute Books* for a particular town or area.

(19) The following Acts of Parliament:
Amendment to the Poor Law Act 1834;
Idiots Act 1886, Elementary Education (Defective and Epileptic Children) Act 1899, Mental Deficiency Act 1913, Elementary (Defective and Epileptic) Act 1914, Mental Deficiency Act 1927, Mental Treatment Act 1930, National Health Service Act 1946, Mental Health Act 1959;
Education Act (Handicapped Children) 1970.

(20) *The Overseer's Returns* for pauper lunatics in various institutions in a given area and his returns also on lunatics and idiots in a stated area.

I have included points 16–20 because in reading these fascinating documents you cannot fail to become aware of some of the reasons, at any rate, for the very slow changes in the attitudes of the general public and even some professionals today towards the mentally handicapped child; of the reasons for the kinds of restraint that were still being used in the late 'fifties and early 'sixties in dealing with the children; of the reasons for present-day restraints on the part of those who should know better.*

---

* In the past 4 years I have been in areas of England where I have been told that mentally handicapped children are smacked if they wet their pants/knickers; or if they move away from the table as little children, for 'they are practising to sit still for the next class' or to be 'normal' for mother at home. I have even heard recently of a child who was put in a 'cupboard' because he would not eat his dinner. It was also reported to me that in another part of the UK such a method was used as part of a 'time out' activity. What always bothers

Observations on some historical aspects   173

And now I must come to the main theme of this chapter, the development of the Manchester course to which I became tutor in May 1961. My predecessor had been a social worker of high standing—Miss Ross Hogg. She had organized courses in Manchester under the aegis of the NAMH for 8 years. The place in which the course had been held was the Quaker Friends Meeting House in the centre of the city. For the most part the four NAMH courses were held in Church Premises until the mid-'sixties.

My first encounter with my students, most of them mature older ladies, was in one of the small prayer rooms of the Friends Meeting House. High-backed, hard-seated wooden benches were the order of the day. The course consisted mainly of lectures given by interested people some of them professionally qualified in medicine, teaching, social work, and administration. 'Cuppas' were obtainable in a wee kitchen off the main lecture room, and a very large congregation room served as the movement hall one day a week for which I believe there was an extra payment by the Association. My office was away from the students but I had to lock up everything each night in a cupboard specially set aside for my use. It was startling to think that courses had been held there for 8 years from 10 a.m. in the morning till 3.30 p.m. over 36 weeks of the year. The times were arranged to cater for married women travelling to the course from a wide area. Several students from Northern Ireland also attended the course each year until this country had a course of its own in 1964/5.

Alterations to the building forced the NAMH to look for new premises. It fell to the lot of an administrator* in the Manchester Welfare Department to help us find other accommodation.† The first two 1-year courses (1961/2 and 1962/3) were housed in Manchester's old workhouse in the city slums of Ancoats—I knew the district well for my own research in the late 'forties had been triggered off in Every Street County Primary School and this was just round the corner from the workhouse. Of course it was not called the workhouse in the 'sixties, but if I use that name the reader will perhaps get a more appropriate picture of the kind of place we had for a 'college'. It was an old institution. It is now demolished. We had a complete wing to ourselves (and this was more in terms of space than some of the courses for teachers of the mentally handicapped have in the colleges of education even at the present time),‡ warmth, hot water,

---

me when I hear these stories is that these children cannot tell anyone what happens to them. The adults concerned with them therefore need to be extra special in order not to contravene the responsibility of completely ethical conduct towards them.

    * Mr Simpson.

    † I can remember one of the best training centres in the North West being held in a church hall where each night the staff under the guidance of their imaginative headteacher, Mrs Edith Lord (now headteacher Robert Clive School, Shrewsbury), had to lock everything away each evening and to reassemble the following day all the things they knew would stimulate the children in their care. The whole operation became an educational device in the socialization of the children. It certainly afforded the children plenty of opportunities for natural movement.

    ‡ To my knowledge only one college has a purpose-built wing. This was paid for by the National Society for Mentally Handicapped Children and the Lord Mayor's Fund. This is the College of Westhill, Birmingham.

174   *Observations on some historical aspects*

and SPACE in which to do things. We also had freedom. The dirt and the grime and the pitiable sight of my native city's aged and destitute did not deter us in our enthusiasm. Nor did the gobfuls of yellow spit seen along the footpaths we had to tread each day to reach our rooms. We used the space to best advantage for the serious task we had to do to train those attending to become teachers of the mentally handicapped.*

The old 'rooms' (more like cells), only large enough to contain a bed and a locker and with high windows, became our stores for creative materials. We had a room for a library and, albeit the 'tatty' state of the furniture, it was there for our use. We also had a very large room for lectures and movement. We had space to display the art of the mentally handicapped as well as that of the student group. I had a large room of my own for tutorials and general office work. It was several years later before I had a secretary and full-time colleagues. That room also saw the visits of a number of interesting people—amongst them Stanley Segal, M. M. Lewis, Dr Gunzburg, Edna Mellor (of Infant School fame), and Lady Norman NAMH. They were all a part of the experience of these students. I forgot to tell you that I removed the few belongings of the course from the Friends Meeting House to this institution on the back of an open lorry.

After 2 interesting years in which three important aspects of the curriculum started to develop in the training centres, i.e. play, movement and creative dance, and art, we were forced once more to find another 'college'. Whilst a dignified and rather beautiful place had been found in Bristol for that particular course nothing of this kind was available in Manchester, although our welfare friend had done his best. Voluntary bodies have little to spend on lavish premises, so once more we found ourselves in the slums of Manchester in a building that had served as a Town Hall. We occupied the top floor of a three-storey building, the Youth Employment Bureau and a library being the other two. Both were useful to us. We were in these rooms for $3\frac{1}{2}$ years. One large room decorated with brown and cream paint served as our main lecture/activity room/observation laboratory,† the other served as kitchen and home economics room for students and mentally handicapped children, woodwork shop (each student spent about eight sessions on this; Dorothy Jeffree, HARC now was invited to be our first woodwork teacher in order that she might discuss mentally

---

* In reading an NAMH document the other day I came across the following information: 'In 1954 the Association for Teachers of the Mentally Handicapped asked that the word "teacher" should be incorporated in the course title. This request was forwarded to the Ministry of Education who, much to everyone's surprise, raised no objection. From 1955 onwards the course became known as The Diploma Course for teachers of the mentally handicapped (in Occupation Centres, Mental Deficiency Hospitals, and their own homes). At this point the Ministry of Health stated that staff would *not* be called teachers.' [Review of the Training (Centre Staffs) Subcommittee 1954–70.] Presented by Frances M. Dean to this NAMH committee meeting in the Queen Anne Street premises in 1970–1.

† An experimental approach to training teachers of the mentally handicapped in direct observation methods in Chapter 8 of *The Educational and Social Needs of Children with Severe Handicap*.

Observations on some historical aspects 175

handicapped children with the students and help them to make some teaching aids), dining room, and Tutor's Office. When the NAMH decided to extend its lecturing staff on the courses I was able to persuade the local adult training centre to make another 'room' with a temporary wooden wall within this multipurpose room. Two years later I once more had my own large room on the ground floor with a telephone! This was such a change from my first experiences in the building. I can remember on one occasion before a new course was due to begin (and an industrial firm of cleaners had let me down) that I got down on my knees and scrubbed out the dining room, and washed down all the chairs on which the students were to sit. I knew that some of them at least would be turning up in their 'best' light-coloured clothes! It was hard work being a tutor for a voluntary body single-handed in the early 'sixties, but it was exciting, challenging, and allowed one to use one's own initiative and imagination without fetters.

Perhaps one of the main advantages to students was that many of them were introduced for the first time in their lives to an understanding of 'how the others live'. They met the visible dirt and grime of other people's lives too. I had *always* known it. New fire regulations forced us once again to move. A large new school for the mentally handicapped had been opened—their old 'school' was empty so I managed to persuade our friend in the Welfare Department to make some enquiries regarding rental by the NAMH. It was a large mansion in its own grounds with an outside building as well. It was at the bus stop where the trees began after terraces and terraces of dilapidated houses and shops. When giving people instructions about how to find us I always used to say 'look out for the trees'. At that time the trees started about 2 miles from the centre of the city. At last we had a place with lots of activity rooms, outside space, and not only tutorial rooms for each member of staff but a junior common room with easy chairs for the students. We were *really* progressing. By this time too (1965/6), there was the promise of sixty students on two 2-year courses. The first one in Manchester started in 1965. At last the course had more appropriate premises for the first time in its 14 years of existence. When Didsbury College agreed to take over the course from the NAMH in 1970, its academic board agreed to let us name the house Frances Dean House* so that another woman who had spent her life working for the mentally handicapped should always be remembered. The course moved completely into the college in 1973 and the house was empty for a period. However, 1976 saw the launching of the Hester Adrian's Toddler Project there. This means that once more this much used house will be improved for the purpose of educating little handicapped children. It is called Anson House once more. Perhaps one day someone will write *its* long story. Mr Frank Davis, Tutor to the Bolton Course for Teachers of the Adult Men-

---

* Frances Dean was the Organizer of NAMH courses and is currently Editor of the journal of the Association for Teachers of the Mentally Handicapped, *Teaching and Training*. She was awarded the MBE for her services to the mentally handicapped in the late 'sixties. She lives in Harrow.

176   *Observations on some historical aspects*

tally Handicapped, will certainly have early facts about this house at his finger tips for I know he spent several years there in the workshop with mentally handicapped adults.

I want to write briefly about the staff in this short history of an era not because I wish to be parochial but because it was their work, their efforts, their influence, and their knowledge of children in educational settings that counted most and brought the changes about in the schools. Change is much more difficult to bring about in the normal system of training teachers. There is a sort of emotional 'blackmail' at work. If the schools don't like what students or staff from colleges do they can close their doors. The colleges must have schools in which to train their students so they adopt an attitude that the student and the supervisor are visitors in a school. A visitor is expected to 'behave' himself. Students are caught between the desire to get good marks from the schools yet wish to implement ideas they are learning in college in order to receive high marks from college also. The children do not seem to enter into these transactions—transactions which indeed can, and I am sure *have*, militated against the good of normal children in schools all over the country for years. Fortunately, in the kind of training we gave our students in those early years our aim was to seek the best for children and not to 'dodge' our responsibility in this by condoning what we saw if we considered what we saw worth fighting about. We worked 'through' relationships. We did not prevent them. We were obviously encouraged by the lovely purpose-built buildings that progressive health authorities produced after the Mental Health Act of 1959. Equally were we encouraged by the changes we saw brought about yearly by our work and that of the teachers we trained. I want also to encourage others to write similar histories of this period. A curriculum for the mentally handicapped had been developed in the schools by 1968 and many of the schools because of my particular emphasis on teaching the individual child in a one-to-one situation had begun to carry this out.* Many schools now have individual teaching rooms, but the concepts for this kind of teaching were in fact encouraged by the particular ways in which we trained our students from 1964 onwards.

I was the sole tutor to this course from 1961 to 1963. I had to give lectures, organize visiting lecturers from a very wide variety of disciplines (medicine, education, research, social work, and administration. I had to introduce, through a body of competent, enthusiastic teacher specialists, a wide variety of professional study activities. I also had to organize and

---

* I also gave all the students on the 1964/71 courses opportunities for practising working with individual children for I knew from experience as a teacher that it was not an approach every teacher would enjoy. It certainly seemed a vital one when one was teaching the mentally handicapped. More schools have now appointed extra teachers to work almost entirely with individual children. One disadvantage I can see about this 'withdrawal' practice is that consideration might not always be given by that particular teacher to what the child might be doing and he or she might be absorbed in the group at the time she wants him for individual work. Another is that the children might in fact miss out on outings.

Observations on some historical aspects   177

supervise teaching practice for thirty students (there were two teaching practice periods of 6 weeks each on the 1-year course in centres in a widely spread area, e.g. from Birmingham, Wolverhampton, and Newcastle under Lyme in the south to Kendal and Colne, Blackpool, and Lancaster in the north). The amount of time I spent in travelling was enormous, as were the distances. I also had to carry out administrative duties without a secretary and encourage the visiting members of staff to learn about mental handicap. Most of us were all new to the field at that time, and no one was thinking he knew what it was all about.

Two physical education lecturers, one an adviser from Oldham and the other, Miss Heron from the Manchester University Department of Physical Education, each gave their services for a year. Then, because of Mrs Barnes, PE Organizer for the Manchester LEA, I discovered Pat Thorley. She was a fully qualified teacher of physical education and under my guidance and encouragement (for I too had specialized in creative movement as a young teacher) she changed 'the face' of physical education in the centres in the north-west over a decade. She was the first person in this large area to persuade the teachers to get the children out of boots and shoes and into bare feet or plimsolls. The picture I must remember to give you is that there was no small or large apparatus in the centres at this time. We considered that modern educational dance (creative movement), therefore, was something that would not only develop the students' sensitivity to awareness of their own movement but additionally it would give them a useful creative activity for the children. The students did in fact observe that these children could be spontaneous and creative with sensitive and imaginative stimulation. Current methods in vogue consisted of formal drill-like exercises where the children stood on a mark on the ground and copied the teacher.

We found time for the students to have this very important part of their programme every week for the *whole* of their course both on 1- and later 2-year courses.* As the apparatus in the schools began to appear so all aspects of a physical education curriculum were covered with the students, including swimming. Students were supervised and assessed in this special subject during teaching practice periods by Pat Thorley. It was a subject of great importance in our minds for the children had spent so many

---

* One of my genuine concerns in the present form of teacher training is that students wishing to teach these children are not being given time to develop adequate knowledge of this subject or skill in teaching it. Too much responsibility is being left to the teachers in the schools to 'train' the teachers when they qualify—a questionable practice because some of these teachers have in fact had no special training and Local Authority/DES in-service courses are not compulsory. Creative movement is almost non-existent in some schools, though of course a wider range of apparatus and outdoor activities (pony riding, and swimming) is being presented. It was heartening to see that the British Association of Lecturers and Advisers in Physical Education have recently published a booklet on PE called *Physical Education and the Severely Subnormal Child*—the first book since the one by Robinson C. M., Harrison J., and Gridley J. (1970) Edward Arnold, London. They were tutors on the Lancashire Course 1964 onwards and did a great deal to support and extend Pat Thorley's work in some of the Lancashire schools for the mentally handicapped. C. M. Robinson is now an HMI.

178 *Observations on some historical aspects*

hours huddled over tables at sedentary occupations of doubtful value. No wonder their language was undeveloped and their concepts stunted; no wonder their noses were dirty. They were not being encouraged to use their lungs in a way natural to children.

A creative approach to these children seemed a possibility in order to give them some quality of life instead of, as I used to express it, a 'living death'. Local health authorities in the main were not allowing centres enough money for creative materials and the money allowed by the NAMH for the teacher training courses was minimal. It had to be, it was a voluntary body. What we needed was someone who could show students how to make the best use of all the waste materials that could be collected from the environment. This concept was not really a new one for 'good' infant schools had been applying this theory for a very long time. We were fortunate indeed in Manchester for one of the headteachers, Mrs Dorothy Burrows (now retired) from the Laurels Centre in Oldham, introduced us to Pat Simpson,* and Don Gittins the North West Regional Secretary for the National Society for Mentally Handicapped Children supported her claim that in Pat we would have someone who could help the most uncreative of teachers to be creative and as a result help children to create. We thought that this was another important feature of the curriculum. Once more students were afforded the opportunity to work with Pat for 2 hours a week over the period of their course whether this was on the 1- or 2-year courses. It would seem to me that the more academic the students are coming to present courses to do B.Ed. degrees, the more they need this creative possibility, and yet time for it is minimal in most colleges unless students are taking Art as a main subject and Mental Handicap as an option. Some schools have appointed a specialist in Art to take the children in small groups; the results are outstanding but it seems to me that all the teachers of the mentally handicapped must have an element of creativity and spontaneity in their teaching technique, and certainly from our experience such qualities can be fostered if the students are given opportunities to develop their own innate creative abilities and skills— sometimes even in individual sessions. Not only did Pat Simpson develop the skills of the students over the years 1962–71 in this direction, but she played an important part in the teachers workshops organized by Manchester's first 'curriculum development leader 1971', Mr Gore, now the headteacher of the newest school for the mentally handicapped in Manchester.

In addition to examining the many possibilities for creative work with mentally handicapped children (and I carried the results of this work all over England to refresher courses and to Denmark in the early 'sixties and have many many slides in my possession of the creative work of these children), we felt that the students themselves would benefit from art sessions at their own level. Accordingly, John Attwood, Lecturer in Special

---

*Pauline Tilley, author of *Art in the Education of Subnormal Children* (1973; Pitman, London), played a similar role at Lindsay House in Bristol.

Observations on some historical aspects   179

Education at the time at Long Millgate College, Manchester,* and later on Mr J. Whittaker from the Royal Manchester College of Art, came to encourage students to paint and do sculpture work for themselves and their own development. The many students passing through the hands of these people owe a great deal to them for their quality was shown in their enthusiasm and dedication to their subject.

When one visited the centres in the very early 'sixties the doors were locked. In fact there were one or two authorities in the north-west where one had to write to the Medical Officer of Health to inform him that one was making a visit in order to 'get in'.† Locked doors meant in fact that children never went outside of them into the community (and remember we are only talking of 15 years ago when there was a boom in Primary School visits). Encouraging students, therefore, to see the necessity for giving these deprived mentally handicapped children an opportunity also to be a part of the community, to let the community see *them*, and for them to have the many rich experiences that the community afforded them was another part of their programme. Encouraging them to give the children experiences of all forms of living creatures was another aspect of the outdoor studies programme. It could only be achieved by enthusiasts and educators who knew its value for children. Accordingly, I contacted two retired headteachers from the Manchester area, both known for their keen interest in outdoor life and their long experience with socially deprived children. They had both been heads in educational priority areas (Ancoats) in the 'forties.‡ They had also supervised teaching practice in the centres and the mental subnormality hospitals before my arrival as tutor. Their names were Miss Taylor Jones and Miss M. Alcock. Together they built up the students' knowledge and interest in outdoor life and as most of the students came from cities we arranged some 3-day residential field study courses in nearby Derbyshire. During these, great emphasis was placed on the systematic observation of natural things. They in fact laid the foundations (which Joan Fitch, my first part-time tutor colleague, extended) for all the outdoor experiences later given to mentally handicapped children in the north-west. It might not seem important now to mention these facts because we take all of these aspects of the curriculum for granted. I must hasten to assure my readers that all these innovated aspects of a developing curriculum had to be struggled for and 'battled' for before they became accepted practice in the schools. As a primary teacher myself in the 'forties I had had a weekend rambling club for the juniors I taught. When I first became a tutor to the Manchester course

---

* From 1976 tutor to the course for teachers of the mentally handicapped, Matlock College of Education.

† Liverpool, one of the most forward of authorities where special education is concerned perhaps to some degree leading the country, kept this rule almost to the passing of the Education (Handicapped Children) Act 1970. I did not break it for after a year or two I stopped using the centres for the practice of my students—in spite of the fact that some of the very best teachers of the mentally handicapped did in fact come from that important town.

‡ One of them had been my headteacher in the second teaching appointment I had.

180   *Observations on some historical aspects*

I wished to see if mentally handicapped children enjoyed the same kind of experience. Two months after my appointment I managed to persuade the Head of the Salford Longworthy Road Centre and the parents of the children attending it that the children would enjoy a ramble. The day arrived and I took them, with two or three students to help me and members of staff, to a youth hostel in Whalley Bridge, Derbyshire. After a train journey, we had to climb a mountain to get there. It took us three times as long to walk there as it had taken normal 10- and 11-year-olds, but we succeeded. I needed no more convincing that this was indeed a must for all mentally handicapped children, i.e. experience of outdoor life. My slides still remind me of their enjoyment—and ours.

The medical aspects of mental subnormality were an important ingredient of the old courses together with a certain background knowledge of genetics and physiology. We were fortunate in attracting a number of experienced psychiatrists to our course, the first one being the medical superintendent of the Royal Albert Hospital, Lancaster, Dr Cunningham. The hospital's chief male nurse lectured to us on genetics and physiology. Dr Cunningham's knowledge and experience of his subject was profound and far-sighted and we learnt much at his hands. In later years Dr R. I. MacKay, now consultant pediatrician at the Manchester Royal Children's Hospital Assessment Unit, became the doctor to our course supported by Dr Inceman, Consultant Psychiatrist to the Swinton Hospital, Lancashire. I am reporting this information in order to give present-day teachers of the mentally handicapped the picture of the breadth of the training that was given in terms of the personalities students came into contact with. Too often do we hear of the 'narrowness' of outlook on these courses from those who have had no experience of them. Meeting people from a wide variety of disciplines is a form of adult education which our colleagues in the Education Departments of Colleges of Education might emulate on more occasions.

It was with these specially chosen and devoted colleagues that the Manchester course got on its way in the early 'sixties. Joan Fitch came along as a part-time tutor when a 2-year course was imminent, but several months indeed before it began. She had been a part-time lecturer in child development at the Charlotte Mason College of Education in Ambleside and a keen advocate of the methods of the PNEU. She was a mother of six children, a JP, and Chairman of the Friends Meeting House in her home town—Ambleside—and also a governor of the College of Education there. Her passions were outdoor studies, children, and literature. All her enthusiasms were ultimately used in developing the students' appreciation of these in relation to mentally handicapped children. She had the added advantage of some short teaching experience on a part-time basis with the mentally handicapped in a centre in Kendal. It was what students respected. They were always quick to note the practical inexperience of mentally handicapped children of some of the visiting lecturers, even though some of these had senior positions in other educational establishments. What is more they were very quick to challenge them.

Observations on some historical aspects   181

Developing the curriculum in the centres was something we did as we became increasingly aware of the children's interests and their deprivations of normal experiences. I have intimated at the beginning of my discussion on the staff lecturing on this course that outdoor life was an aspect we had to work hard to persuade the centre staffs to accept for these children. There was so much prejudice against introducing the children to life in the form of plant or animal study. For many years we got the cry 'they will eat them' (both plants and animals). Of course it took us quite a considerable amount of effort and reasoned discussion to show that 'eating' things was indeed a part of normal development and that all young children under 2 years would eat all kinds of things if they were not watched or prevented. We knew that not all the children's mental ages were below 2. I can well remember Dr Winifred Langan, an early visiting lecturer to the course on child development, saying to a student in exasperation when she rigidly upheld her argument that the children (in hospital) would eat the worms, 'Well, if the child wants to eat the worms let him. They will only come out at the other end!'

Joan Fitch put Nature Study as yet another interest for these children firmly into the curriculum content during the 'sixties. It was not easy for there were entrenched prejudices on the part of the staff and also a lack of knowledge and feeling for the subject on the part of the students. Stimulating their initial interest through (twenty) lectures, bringing an awareness of plant and animal life into their experience, and residential weeks in the Lake District and Derbyshire laid the foundation not only for helping the teachers to enjoy giving the children experiences of animals and plants, but also for going away together with the children camping, hostelling, and caravaning. Only an enthusiast for natural things could have gained the results Joan achieved. It is most noticeable that this subject either has not taken a hold in many schools today or it has indeed suffered a serious set-back. I do not see the same interest as I visit these schools—a pity, for the children certainly enjoyed this learning experience, and if the work was structured, learned about living things too. Joan wrote a useful pamphlet on the subject but did not get it published. What a loss!

Joan became responsible too for encouraging students to think about the role of story telling in the lives of these children. She enabled students to gain and give pleasures in the story telling sessions. She also emphasized the fact that these should not be 'filling in' sessions whilst the children were waiting for the bus (a common occurrence) or for the helper to take each child to the cloakroom. The story session with a willing group of children had to have a beginning and an end. It had to be a session where the teacher would be thinking about her own language structures and the link up between this creative activity and cognitive development through real, 3-D story-aids or clearly outlined pictures. Again one rarely sees the kind of story time approach that was suggested in the 'normal' environments of present-day schools for the mentally handicapped. I wish my readers would deny my impression—for the attention and the fun the children had cannot be denied. The exercise of finding suitable stories was

182 *Observations on some historical aspects*

indeed a 'stretching' exercise for their teachers. Joan's pamphlet on story telling, published by the College of Special Education and entitled *Story Telling for Slow Learners*, is as valid today as when she first published it in 1969. Her interest in literature at an adult level caused her to find examples of mental handicap in the stories of Charles Dickens. An interesting article on this subject was published by the Association of Teachers of the Mentally Handicapped in their Journal *Teaching and Training* in 1969. It suggests another source of information for students wanting an historical approach to these children.

Helping students to ensure that they make children happy is a task that not all lecturers in colleges of teacher training succeed in. Whilst a sound knowledge of the cognitive development* of young children is essential to the teacher of the mentally handicapped, as indeed for all children, an equal amount of time was spent by Joan Fitch on emotional and social development. Perhaps these lectures, along with the very small group and the individual tutorial sessions we all held with our students, were responsible in no small way for the caring attitudes that were encouraged—positive, searching attitudes where children were always safe. Positive attitudes were encouraged that enabled teachers to ensure that children's rights were studied as well as their needs.

Present teachers in schools for the mentally handicapped child will hardly believe that the first activity of the day as the children entered the centres was assembly and registration with the whole school present including the young children (whose mental levels would be anything from $2\frac{1}{2}$ downwards) and those with additional handicaps. These children (sometimes as many as eighty) sang hymns, said prayers, and then listened to their names and those of their peers. The whole affair lasted for nearly 40 to 50 minutes—and then it was time for mid-morning lunch. The waste of time, the lack of understanding on the part of the children to anything as abstract as prayers, was much felt by those of us who were trying to understand the needs of these children. One could only conclude that it was the adults with the needs. Joan Fitch in her lectures on moral and spiritual development brought into focus the necessity for change in this aspect. Now it is very rare indeed to see children in assemblies lasting for more than 5 minutes—their rights and needs in this respect are being met at last.

It was not until 1967 that the National Association saw its way to appointing other full-time tutors and this when there were sixty students on two 2-year courses. One of my serious hopes was that I would find someone particularly knowledgeable about the physically handicapped child so that more training could be given to students regarding profoundly physically handicapped children. Few of the courses in the

---

* Stephen Jackson, author of *Special Education* and *A Teacher's Guide to Tests* and at the time at Long Millgate College, Manchester, was our visiting lecturer for 5 years and also Dr E. Lunzer now Professor of Education, University of Manchester. Joan lives a busy retired life in her home in Ambleside attending to the responsibilities she has taken on in that area.

Observations on some historical aspects 183

country provided time for the students to examine the needs of these children *under skilled guidance*. My personal interest had been captured in 1961 when I saw a Piagetian approach being applied in a Special Care Unit in Salford under the guidance of Eric Lunzer, alongside a multidisciplinary team approach to the problems of the parents. In fact the team concerned ultimately became the nucleus of an assessment unit staff.

We were fortunate to get Bryan Narey,* a teacher of physically handicapped children. Not only was he able to guide the students in lectures about these children, but as he became interested in the profoundly handicapped child who was also physically handicapped he worked with several groups of students and the children over a number of years in Leacroft School, Manchester, and to some extent extended the foundations for an educational approach to these children in many Special Care Units in the north-west. Students on those courses received several lectures from him about the implications of physical handicap; visited on four or five separate occasions the Spastic Society Units in the area; and worked in Special Care Units under the guidance of tutors for at least 8–10 mornings in their second year. Our aim was to bring them into contact academically as well as practically at least with these children in a way that was not threatening. This was considered a fundamental part of their training even though we knew that most of them were not likely to teach the profoundly handicapped when they qualified.†

In addition to all his other duties as a tutor, Bryan Narey ran woodwork sessions with small groups of students and helped them (mostly women) to make the necessary teaching aids that were not being provided in the centres. I might add here that in spite of these children coming under

---

* Now headteacher of Oaklands P. H. School, Salford.

† It was not really until the 1970s that more people became visibly involved with the profoundly handicapped child in the community and literature regarding a variety of approaches to them was published. Dr J. Hogg from the Hester Adrian Research Centre, University of Manchester and his colleagues found by a survey of over two thousand children in all the schools for the mentally handicapped in the north-west that 24 per cent of the children (621) were in fact of the 'special care type of child'. This number perhaps suggests that more in-service courses need to be organized to cater for the staff of these units. One can be sure that not all of them will have qualified teachers in charge of them. Indeed, a useful DES survey might be to publish these figures for parents and professionals to see. Parents could make their own surveys. Dr Chris Kiernan at the Thomas Coram Research Centre, Institute of Education, London began his researches by observation of free activity and a structured assessment/teaching programme using behaviour modification methods. Castle Priory College has been filling the teaching gap by organizing several courses each year for the wide variety of professionals and para-professionals involved with these children. In 1976 Bertie Brown and John Presland from the Northern Counties College, Newcastle on Tyne organized a 4-day course to deal exclusively with the educational problems of the profoundly handicapped child and his family. Of course we must not be deceived into thinking that because there has been a move forward in academic interest that this inevitably means a better quality of life for the child. Those on the ground floor are often not consulting in any practical way with those on the 'top', and those on the 'top' often have difficulty communicating their findings effectively and immediately to those who need the knowledge first—the families, the teachers, and all the other specialists coming into direct contact with these children.

184   *Observations on some historical aspects*

education some schools still do not seem to have the appropriate aids for the children, particularly in terms of their play needs, neither are teachers using their time to obtain or make them. Each student had 6–8 sessions (a session being an afternoon). He would also spend time after the sessions were over advising and helping students with their teaching aid designs.

Olwen Gregory* came to us in 1967 also. I had met her during her Advanced Diploma year in the University whilst supervising her work with mentally handicapped children in the centres. It was apparent she had a flair for working with them. In addition to lecturing in child development and extending the exercise of observing babies in their own homes, carried out in the first instance by my colleague Joan Fitch, she *also* became fascinated in the problems of special care unit children and spent the allotted 8–10 sessions for students supervising their work in the Piper Hill School, Special Care Unit of Manchester. Those acquainted with my other books will know that she became also the first person in this country under the tutorship of Professor Mittler to describe her assessment work with profoundly handicapped children in Glasgow Day Centres. She also worked with little babies in front of their mothers and students as part of another form of skilled observation training. She used her own deepening knowledge of the sensori stage of development, and an extension of my structured list of play activities compiled for staff and students in 1967. She worked alongisde Monica De Paulo,† a very experienced teacher of the mentally handicapped and one who was particularly interested in play in early development. Both of them contributed later to the First Hester Adrian Workshop (1970) for parents with an emphasis on the use of particular toys in structured play activities.

Monica De Paulo joined the NAMH course as a tutor in 1969. She remained with us for 2 years. Her responsibility for lecturing on the education of young children to students enabled her to give students the benefit of her very long experience with the mentally handicapped. She was the first teacher in England with a diploma in the teaching of the mentally handicapped to become a tutor to a 2-year course. Her supervision of teaching practice was valuable because students knew that she had 'done the job' too. Following on from Joan Fitch she continued to stimulate the students' thinking about the importance of outdoor life in the lives of these children. The realization that she would not be as involved with the children themselves when we went into a college of education to run a course there forced her to seek another headship for it was the children

---

* Now one of the first full-time tutors to a 1-year course for instructresses in day centres and occupation centres in Western Scotland. The other 1-year course is in Fife. These courses came about as a result of a Royal Commission on the training of staffs in occupation centres to which I gave evidence on teacher training in 1970.

† Headteacher in Ashton's Green Training Centre until 1969 when she became one of the tutors to our course. She had been one of my students trained in the 'workhouse' days (p. 173). Later she became headteacher to the school in Weston-super-Mare. Presently the headteacher of the New Fosseway School (the old Bush Training Centre, Bristol), the largest school for the mentally handicapped in the country, and a co-opted member of the Warnock Committee.

Observations on some historical aspects 185

she cared for more than anything else. Her influence will continue to be made in the field of handicap for anyone meeting her will not fail to take something of value from her caring personality.

There remain only two other visiting lecturers I would like to write about in this synopsis of educationists concerned with developing an appropriate curriculum for teachers of the mentally handicapped in the north-west during the 'sixties. In describing my own work with a mentally handicapped man in my other book I have written about the cooking sessions I gave him in my own home—the preparation of very simple meals and the pictorial sequencing of graded steps in the process for him gave me ideas for the children visiting us in the Newton Town Hall. From an early introduction to the idea that mentally handicapped children would enjoy cooking, staff and students helped the children make their own lunches after buying the ingredients from nearby shops. Home economics in the training centres was born. The opportunities for learning through this subject were before us.*

We were fortunate in that the wife of the doctor (Dr R. I. Mackay) to our later courses was a fully qualified domestic science teacher. She also knew the 'feel' of the mentally handicapped through her husband's long association with them. Like the rest of us she had a great deal of adapting to do when she first joined us in the late 'sixties at Anson Road but I had written some guide-lines for students† when first introducing 'cookery' in the schools. It took her no time at all to work happily and efficiently and creatively in this subject with both students and children in small groups. Sometimes she did this in College and sometimes in the schools. The subject became her complete responsibility. She was so enthusiastic, conscientious and able that she became a highly valued member of our teaching practice team. I should like to take the opportunity of saying here that all final-year students in these 2-year courses were seen by the specialist subject people as well as by their own supervising tutors and the Principal Tutor. This meant a great deal of hard work on everyone's part but we knew we were training special school teachers and therefore promoted very positive attitudes in our students regarding our visits. They knew we had to get to know the children as well as them before we could evaluate their practice with any meaning. The team supervising approach was therefore developed over the years. I think it has possibly disappeared now on present courses of training. Mrs Mackay's standards were high. Few students failed to live up to them.

I first remember Philip Bailey with a heavy holdall full of tools and materials to make musical instruments—coming to our college in the

---

* Many teachers now favour teaching the children the attributes of a square by making a jam sandwich. If the teacher seizes the opportunities, the children are learning in real-life situations—big, small, thick, thin, red, white, sticky, sweet, bitter, yellow (lemon curd), orange (marmalade).

† I lent this guide, 26 pages in length, to someone either in England or Northern Ireland and never got it back. Please return it if you have it. It took many hours to write and I know it was useful.

186 *Observations on some historical aspects*

workhouse in 1962. He must have been a retired teacher even then. He had white hair, was small in stature, with a high-pitched voice. He also had twinkling eyes. He was responsible, and remained so throughout the 'sixties, for music and the handicapped child in Liverpool.* We had met at an NSMHC meeting in Manchester. As soon as I talked with him I knew he had much to give to my students. I wanted his enthusiasm for music for the handicapped. I wanted his skills. Our meeting started off a fairly long relationship with the Manchester course. It was only when he became a Carnegie Research Fellow in Liverpool University in music for the handicapped that we somehow lost touch with him. His work left its mark for students, in all the years that followed (irrespective of whether they were musicians or not), gave the children a great many musical experiences using some of the ideas he had initially promoted particularly in the making of home-made instruments. Some of these instruments were especially adapted for physically handicapped children.

Music of all the curriculum subjects we introduced was perhaps (and still is) the most difficult one to interest students in, in spite of all the developments that have taken place over the last 20 years in Primary and Secondary School music. Never did students feel that they knew enough about music to enable them to let children enjoy it. Over the years we tried to dispel these ideas by giving them all plenty of ideas that could be tried out with some chance of success. We did music with them and the mentally handicapped together.†

The multidisciplinary nature of training teachers of the mentally handicapped means that ideally they should 'rub shoulders' with members of all the professions concerned with these children. Accordingly over the years a great many professionals from medicine, psychiatry, language disorder, social work, administration, and all the special aspects of special education, e.g. epilepsy, and maladjustment were involved on our courses. The list of their names would probably fill many pages. However, they are all listed in the documents I have mentioned kept by the National Association for Mental Health. They are all in my mind for their contribution can never be forgotten.

You will have noticed that the words 'enthusiast' and 'enthusiasm' have recurred in this brief description of those members of staff working with me in the 'sixties in Manchester. It was a quality they all had. Students were on the receiving end of it throughout their course. I believed they all gained something valuable from the experience not only for their work with children, but for life itself.

---

* His ideas are now available in his book *Let Them Make Music*, published in 1973. OUP.

† I have written about music and the very young mentally handicapped child in my other book, and also in an article for the non-specialist musician in Laing, A. (1973) *Education and the Mentally Handicapped*, University of Swansea. Another useful pamphlet on music for the handicapped is that by John Colson. It is called *Getting into Rhythm*, and is obtainable from Fieldhead Hospital, Wakefield.

13 Observing the special needs of mothers of mentally handicapped children

During 1972–5 I became involved in a very practical way with several families having a mentally handicapped child. This was on a voluntary basis. I was not attached to any official group. One of my life practices has been to do voluntary service on at least one evening a week in an area of interest and need. This particular community service to some extent answered my own need and practice at this time to 'keep my feet on the floor' so that any academic lecturing I did on mental handicap would always be against a background of continued 'informed' experience.

One of these families had two children with Down's syndrome, another had a dying child, another a child with Down's syndrome who was blind and had a congenital heart defect. Yet another of these families had a beautifully normal-looking child who was like a baby of 9 months intellectually when he was physically $2\frac{1}{2}$-years old. Another of the families I helped had a perfectly normal child with a very serious speech defect. They all needed help and support from someone for none of them was getting it officially to the extent that they needed it. I worked with these families for between 6 months and nearly 3 years. Some of the material for the chapter on the pre-school mentally handicapped child in my other book was taken directly from some of the experiences during these years. I had had no intention of collecting material for a book when I was introduced to the families. As my experience grew, however, I felt it would be wasted if I did not share it with others. The families did not mind, indeed they welcomed it.

I enjoyed this work with the little mentally handicapped children and their mothers* so much and to such an extent that when I failed to obtain a grant to set up a Family Teach-In Centre I decided to find another avenue to continue something I considered would be worthwhile for such families. Full-time lecturing prevented me from doing a daytime activity with them so I considered an evening commitment. Initially this was to be for 2 years. I offered a 2-year course to mothers of handicapped children. The editor of the *Manchester Evening News* inserted a notice free of charge to this effect in his newspaper. The date, the times, the place of contacting me were described and a telephone number was given. I 'advertised' as an author and previous trainer of teachers in the north-west. You will no doubt be surprised at the response, particularly in view of the

---

*I am at the grandmother stage of my life with no sons or daughters. Perhaps my work with these little children and their mothers satisfied a deep natural urge.

188   *Observing needs of mothers of mentally handicapped children*

expressed needs of parents of mentally handicapped children for a wide variety of support systems and a readership of the paper of almost a million. I had three telephone calls during the whole of the day. As I was getting ready to go home I received a call from an individual phoning on behalf of a group of mothers already functioning as a group but obviously open to further group experiences. They invited me to tell them about my 'dream'. My plans for a family teach-in centre were unfolded at a branch of the NSMHC. We then discussed what we might do on a 2-year course. The ideas were not entirely clear then. There was no goal except to get together and in some way or another help each other. I had been a lecturer on several parent/teacher programmes in Manchester and in Liverpool and I knew about the Hester Adrian Workshop programmes even though I had not been a part of them. Perhaps the long-practised technique I had of following up a child's interests from observing him could be employed in this situation as well, while at the same time giving the group lectures and organizing lectures I thought they needed.

The mothers decided to give it a try. Over a period of 2 years then, we met in one of the mother's homes* on one evening a week with about six evenings away from each other during major holiday times, i.e. about one week at Christmas, one at Easter, and several during July and August. A group of about ten mothers, with almost a hundred per cent attendance on the part of six mothers, have attended this two-year course. It is with their permission that I am writing this chapter for once more it was not my intention to write about the experience when I started exploring the possibilities of a 2-year course for mothers of the mentally handicapped. In the first instance I did not know that they would attend for that length of time. Furthermore I did not anticipate the response and the development that has occurred. We are now perhaps in a stronger position to state goals for such a group through the action research that has taken place without financial support of any kind.

Whilst we had no specific goals initially, nevertheless, I decided that a minimum of time would be spent upon child management, i.e. how to manage each child in the group better at home. Helping parents to manage a child depends on so many other factors that this did not seem to be a realistic goal. I was not going to be able to meet the children except on very rare occasions. I certainly was not going to be able to observe the child and his parents in the home without a full-time commitment and involvement. I consider such a contact with the home an essential element in such a role for me, at least, if advice on management problems are to be valid and satisfying for both parents and child alike. However, this policy does not mean that we have in fact not discussed the children and the day-to-day problems that have cropped up over the 2 years. A regular feature of the course has been for each mother in turn to review the progress of her own child. This was always done spontaneously and with no warning beforehand that this was going to happen at the next

---

* My plan for the future is a small house of my own in which to run such courses.

Observing needs of mothers of mentally handicapped children   189

meeting. I should say that these reviewing exercises have taken place about every 6 months. Some mothers have brought photographs to show the physical growth they have seen in their children after such sessions.

We could perhaps spend a little time now looking at the composition of the group. Its members are originally from working-class backgrounds, except one. Four members of the group are Roman Catholics. Some of them are one-parent families. One is a widow in her early fifties. It cannot be said to be a middle-class orientated group. I have stated this fact because one of the criticisms levelled at so many projects in this field is that they are middle class biased. The handicaps of the children vary very much indeed and this means that the mothers are indeed learning about the problems of mothers with a different kind of handicapped child.

During the early part of the course I invited members of staff from the school to which most of the children go to become members of the group. One teacher in fact attended for a whole year but left to go abroad with her husband. A health visitor has also been a constant attender during the 2-year period only having occasional absences.

Seven mothers had mongol children between the ages of 3 and 14 years. With the exception of three of these the others had conditions extra to the chromosomal abnormality. One child was born with an open bowel; two have congenital heart defects, and one of these is blind as well, while the other child has a dietary disorder and has a coeliac condition. The heart condition of one of the children is such that he can only walk a few yards without becoming tired and overcome. He has to be pushed around in the streets in a wheelchair by an ageing mother. When he reaches 16 and is ready to leave school there is the likelihood of there being nowhere for him to go during the day.* Two of these children with Down's syndrome are girls. Two young mothers under 30 also had mongol children. They left the group in the first year quite informally—they did not write to me to tell me. Family problems over removal and possibly the absence of feeling a real need to be a member of this particular group were responsible for one withdrawal from the group. The other mum remained with the group until the genetic counselling I advised her to have (in view of my experience with the mother with two mongol children) was satisfactorily completed and she was assured by the doctor that she could have another child and it would be 'normal'. One of the present mothers is in constant touch with this young mum and acts as her support to some extent. In any case she knows where we meet if she needs us.

Of the other three families one has a boy now of 16 who is vaccine damaged. He is so hyperactive that he lives during the week in a hostel

---

* Perhaps some unemployed teachers could perform a useful service to these homebound mentally handicapped adults—possibly somewhere between 30 and 50 per cent of all mentally handicapped children when they become adult! Job creation programmes might certainly be an answer in terms of real 'care in the community'. Those who are interested should contact their nearest special school for the mentally handicapped [ESN(S)] and find out which children leaving school already have a place in the adult training centre run by the Social Service Departments of our cities.

190   *Observing needs of mothers of mentally handicapped children*

alongside the school he attends. He comes home to the family at week-ends. Of the two remaining mothers, one has a child with mild hydrocephaly with associated eye defects and some spasticity; the other has a seriously brain-damaged child with a congenital heart defect. You might be surprised to hear that one of the mothers in the group with a mongol child of her own is fostering a child of the same age with spina bifida. With the exception of two mothers, the handicapped child is a member of a family where there are other children. The age range of the mothers attending is between 30 and over 50. I wish I had taken photographs of the group when we first met and also tape recordings of their ideas. I am almost sure that their faces have become more relaxed. They all seem to have become more aware of their dress. They have certainly become beautifully vocal. Perhaps it is on account of their increased knowledge and confidence in themselves. They know they are supported.

Without my having kept a tape recording of each session over the 2 years it is not possible for me to give you an accurate picture of my methods of working—how much listening I have done, how much talking, when the group started to talk more themselves both to me and within the group itself with me there but listening. I should have had an independent observer to keep records. The experiences we have shared together have nearly always been arranged as a result of my 'picking up' something from *their* conversation or as a result of opportunities that I had of giving them a particular experience. Thus a doctor friend of mine rang me and asked me if I would like to meet a social worker from Iceland to tell her about my 'mothers' group'. 'She had better come along and meet them,' was my response. Perhaps the experience of meeting people from other lands is a widening experience for all of us. Professionals very often get this opportunity in their jobs, but not so hard-working mums with a mentally handicapped child. We had a lovely evening together with this worker from another land and of course together we learnt something of the provision for the mentally handicapped in Iceland.

When I was invited to lecture about this action research I was motivated to order my thoughts. The task enabled me to review what we had been doing. I had to reflect also upon its value. Discussions with the group and reference to my own notes revealed the following.

We started the course in January 1975 with a supposed conclusion date of 31st January, 1977! The experiences we have had together have included lectures, visits, discussions about the visits, discussions about a wide variety of subjects, events, films, reading, projects, research, child reviews and an evaluation session for each individual mum conducted by an 'external' assessor. Let me elaborate the model of this particular course.

One of the needs of parents is to know how our own society functions particularly in the realms of medicine, education, and the social services. These needs appeared as we got to know each other. Accordingly, lectures were arranged on the following:

the training and work of the health visitor;

Observing needs of mothers of mentally handicapped children   191

the role of the advisers for special education in a local education authority;
the training of doctors;
the training of teachers of the mentally handicapped both past and
present;
the training and work of a qualified social worker for the blind;
the training of physiotherapists;
the training of a social worker and the specific task of a new social worker
in a nearby mental subnormality hospital.

All the lecturers concerned came from the immediate vicinity or from just outside the Greater Manchester area. They gave their services free. As I have explained no finance was available. They were all receiving adequate salaries anyway and did not seem to mind an opportunity for this particular experience. Other lecturers included the social worker from Iceland; a headteacher of a school for the mentally handicapped from Australia; a Manchester headteacher describing her scheme for holiday play arrangements; the Development Officer describing the work of the Rossendale Unit, Macclesfield, Cheshire; and the Chairman of the Michaelmas Trust, Vale Royal Hall, Whitegates, Cheshire, describing its aims and training courses.

Amongst the needs of parents of mentally handicapped children is the one to know something about the possible provision for their child in the future. They also want to know what exists at the present time if there is a family crisis and they need emergency short-term care for their child. I have no specific record of how or when this topic arose in the group, but to meet this need I arranged some visits for the group. Three of these were to hostels—two to hostels for children, one to an adult hostel. One of the hostels I had already decided was not a very good one. The other was more homelike. Discussion about other hostels I had seen, and about the kind of place the mothers wanted for their child, took place before the visits and some kind of planned questionnaire was compiled. You can imagine that the impressions they gained from the actual visits took two or three sessions to report back upon and discuss. The mothers introduced the question of training for the staff of such places and I emphasized the need for adequate inspection by those knowing the mentally handi-capped—perhaps even paid teams of parents from each local authority not having a child living in them (by a team I mean two). Unfortunately not all the mothers visited the two children's hostels. The vivid descriptions of both by the mothers to me and to each other gave a clear picture of what went on/or did not go on in them. During the early summer of the first year we all had a day out to a Church of England Hostel in Derbyshire. A coach was hired and mothers and children together did the long but beautiful journey to the home. It was a picnic day. Students helped the children while the mothers listened to a short lecture about the home and looked around it.

An interesting full programme of activities is carried out in the Parkwood Adult Training Centre in Alfreton, Derbyshire. Additionally

192   Observing needs of mothers of mentally handicapped children

they have a purpose-built Special Care Unit for those adults with multiple handicaps. Another full day's outing was arranged and the Manager* and his deputy made arrangements for the children to be 'looked after' whilst the mums toured the centre. So much interest was generated by this particular experience that the mothers organized a visit themselves to the adult training centre in their own area. Comparison stimulates thinking. This experience certainly did. Not many mothers after full-time education is over have the opportunity at the moment to set foot in a University. However, this experience came about for this particular group when a film I wanted them to see (and an Open University film from the course *The Handicapped in the Community*) needed a qualified projectionist and a special projector to show it. It was a warm summer evening and they had a night out going to a University. How lovely they all looked. What an educational experience for all of us.

One of the visits I had planned in MY mind at least was a visit to a large mental subnormality hospital. However, somehow this visit has never been arranged for the group. One mother actually told me on one occasion that she thought she was brave enough at last to face the experience of visiting a large subnormality hospital. A small subnormality hospital nearby afforded the mothers a chance to make their own arrangements to make a visit to an institution. Some of them visited and commented upon the visit to the other mothers and me. They were clearly not entirely satisfied with what they observed but they found some new attitudes emerging and were pleased. I wonder how many mothers of mentally handicapped children can ever be emotionally satisfied with the residential arrangements society makes for their children—perhaps the dissatisfaction lies within themselves. We know, however, that present residential care for the mentally handicapped does in fact still leave a great deal to be desired whether this is provided by voluntary or statutory bodies.

Perhaps more time has been devoted to discussion on this course than to any other aspect. There has been no thought of a therapeutic approach in my technique. As I have seen it, it has become a meeting of minds with differing needs—perhaps a developing structure for coping.† After every visit there have been several weeks of discussions. These on occasions have been introduced by a mother describing her personal impressions from a short written paper. On occasions discussions have followed the visits of the various lecturers. These discussion sessions have acted as a kind of reconstruction of the experience in adult terms. I might add here that all lecturers had been 'warned' that by and large they would be interrupted throughout their talk for it had been my intention to stimulate spontaneous thinking and the expression of it in these mothers. Most lecturers found this comforting for it meant that they did not have complete responsibility for the success of the evening. On occasions when I had

---
* Mr Marron.

† Bayley, M. (1973) *The Mentally Handicapped in the Community. A Study in Sheffield*, Routledge and Kegan Paul, London.

Observing needs of mothers of mentally handicapped children 193

prepared something specific there were periods within the session when something I said or read to them triggered off discussion amongst and between members of the group that did not involve me. It was a salutary experience for a teacher and it taught me the methods to use to encourage larger groups in increased audience participation in lectures and workshops.

Other discussions centred around the following:

(1) language and the mentally handicapped child;
(2) home school diaries and the different techniques teachers use in order to get them out each week;*
(3) sex and the mentally handicapped;
(4) holiday schemes;
(5) hostility towards professional workers;
(6) despair in getting services quickly enough to meet theirs or their child's need;
(7) sleep problems (many weeks on these);
(8) intelligence testing and intelligence tests;
(9) development through drawings;
(10) the syllabus for the course each term;
(11) a review and general evaluation with suggestions for the following term;
(12) PAC forms;
(13) record cards,† should parents see them or not;
(14) death (several weeks);‡
(15) baby-sitting services.§

You will have noticed that one of my categories of experiences was called 'events'. I felt it an unreal experience to work with such a group without meeting their children at least once. Accordingly, in the first 10 weeks or so of the course each mother, wherever this was possible, brought her child to the meeting. I played with the child or gave him the new

---

* They listened to a tape recording of a young teacher from the Robert Clive School in Shrewsbury making up her home diary with one of the children in her class. She does this with each child individually on Friday mornings. She helps her classroom assistant organize the group in the classroom.

† At least one LEA in 1977 is thinking of allowing parents of normal children to see the School Record Cards. There is much consternation on the part of the teachers. However, we can be sure of one thing if parents *do* claim their right to consult their own child's record card, teachers will become much more objective in reporting the child's progress and his behaviour—a very positive step for children's welfare. *Times Educational Supplement* news flash 22nd April, 'Record Cards raise libel fears'.

‡ These probably helped a widow through her bereavement period. They were also useful in view of the questions about her child relating to his dad; and also because of the fears at least three mothers have relating to the possibility of early deaths of their particular children.

§ It strikes me that not a great deal of research has been carried out on this aspect of the life of a family with a mentally handicapped child, yet open discussion with parents will reveal that they do exist in no small measure in some parts of the country.

194   *Observing needs of mothers of mentally handicapped children*

Imitation Test of Language described for you in Chapter 8. This was a lovely experience for all of us and I do not think I need to emphasize the interest that was aroused because of how I handled each child in front of the mothers. It also gave them a chance to observe several different kinds of mentally handicapped children in a new setting.*

Arising from this experience someone suggested that we might have an evening with one or two of the brothers and sisters of the handicapped children. Two girls, one of 14 and one of 12, attended this event and also a boy of 17. The event was taped for further discussion at another meeting. The form of the evening was that of an interview. The mothers interviewed the children for about an hour. At one point the response from the children was so interesting that the group forgot both me and the children. We just sat and waited for the mothers to return to the topic in hand—how did it feel to have a handicapped brother or sister? One child knowing that her sister might die early denied thinking about the matter and said she thought her mother was wonderful, another pronounced his mother a saint, and the other child with a whimsical smile said that 'her mother managed very well in the circumstances'.

We did not repeat this experience during the first year. Somehow the experience and the topic has arisen again quite spontaneously in the third year. This I will describe in another paragraph.

Two parties or picnics with the mothers and the children have been held in my home and two parties for the mothers (and where possible their husbands) were amongst some of the experiences considered to be events. Perhaps one of the most interesting events was one where seven young medical students spent an evening with us. There were enough 'doctors' for 'one between two' mothers, as it were. I was rather superfluous on this occasion for the mothers and doctors were interviewing each other and there seemed no place for someone who was neither a doctor nor a mother of a mentally handicapped child. The impact of such an event on either party cannot be evaluated. I know it was highly enjoyable from the 'feel' of the social climate existing. As I had said to the mothers beforehand in arranging the event for them, if we cannot influence the older and experienced members of the medical profession perhaps we need to think about the future and start with the young students in training. The mothers certainly did their best. Unfortunately I did not follow up on this vital and interesting experience. It might be something for me to think about in the future. A result of this meeting was that the group wished to gain more knowledge about the training of doctors. This was arranged for them in the second year of the course.

Whilst films are a valuable source of information we had no official money and no 16 mm projector or projectionist. However, several films

---

* Most of the mothers had met all the children before. They organize their own Saturday playclub once a month/fortnightly. Some of my lectures and workshops were undoubtedly about the importance of play. Some of these stimulated the mums to think more carefully about the play materials they were buying. I know that they now have their own developing Toy Library.

Observing needs of mothers of mentally handicapped children 195

were seen by the group and discussed either during or after the showing. The films shown included:

*Stimulating Self Feeding in the Profoundly Handicapped Child;**
The Wessex Experiment. An Open University film, very worthwhile seeing;
The Stevenage Opportunity Class;
They Can be Helped. A National Children's Home production on special care children;
The Coeliac Condition. Obtainable from Concord Films, Ipswich.

I have a variety of old 8 mm films of my own on play and the mentally handicapped child, and also a very large collection of slides. These were shown to the group as was a film on development in play activities throughout a school. This was shown by the headteacher of the Robert Clive School, Shrewsbury. I have a humorous recollection of taking my slides on the art of mentally handicapped children to one of the meetings. The group had said they would like to see them. I took them on three occasions, set up the projector and then began the session. On two occasions projector and slides were waiting but the spontaneous discussion of the group drew our attention away from the goal of the evening.†
Another of my techniques, indeed, was to have several things up my sleeve to do with the group but to let them take over as and when they wished. This technique seemed highly relevant in a group of this kind. We did finally look at the slides in a very short space of time at the end of the third evening I had taken them.

Modelling language for children is a method used now by most experienced teachers of young normal and mentally handicapped children. I thought that a useful technique of stimulating discussion, particularly at the beginning of our relationship together, might be read to the group from selected books. Several simply written books on mental handicap have been available in the last 5 years. Accordingly, I started to read *Bernard,*‡ and passages from *Parents and Mentally Handicapped Children,*§ my own books, and recently from Dr Robert MacKay's book,¶ for they all know him. It certainly was a useful technique. I was never reading long before discussion took over. Sometimes I lent the book to a mother requesting it. One very nice result of this technique used with a mother on her own was the production of an article. Whilst this mother is now

---

* An old film on this subject made in Holland in 1965/7 and given to me through the Dutch Embassy by the psychologist responsible for making it (Dr Vosvinkel). It is now housed in the Castle Priory College on Extended Loan. They have the special magnetic projector needed to project it.

† Being a Lancashire lass of the Gracie Fields success era I was nostalgically reminded of the old Gracie Fields song *I took my harp to a party but nobody asked me to play!*

‡ Wilks, J. and Wilks, Eileen (1974) *Bringing Up your Mongol Son, Bernard,* Routledge and Kegan Paul, London.

§ Hannam, C. (1975) *Parents and Mentally Handicapped Children,* Penguin Mind Special, Harmondsworth, Middlesex.

¶ McKay, R. I. (1976) *Mental Handicap in Child Health Practice,* Butterworths, London.

196   *Observing needs of mothers of mentally handicapped children*

part of the group I first met her whilst waiting for telephone calls from mothers wishing to take my course. She lives in a different district to the rest of the group. I take her each week to join them. However, to return to the 'reading to mothers' technique, it was intended to be a relaxing situation too—more soothing perhaps than listening to a lecture. After listening to the chapter on 'Life with a mongol brother' in the Wilks' book *Bernard* she proceeded to tell me about the questions her child of 5 asked about his little mongol baby brother. 'Mammy', he said one day, 'Why has Callum got slanting eyes?' These words were spoken beautifully in terms of inflexion of voice and intonation. I immediately 'saw' a title for an article. I suggested that she started to write an article about the questions her little normal boy had asked and HOW she had answered them. I encouraged her over a period of 10 or 12 weeks—she wrote a few lines each week before I arrived. It was probably the first bit of 'academic' thinking she had done for a long time but she was capable of such an exercise. Finally the article was complete. It was about 1500 words in length. I typed it for her and sent it to *Parents Voice*. They published the article a year later. I also sent it to the Social Services free weekly magazine. They published it very quickly and paid her a fee. The popular woman's magazine to which I sent it, returned it!

One of the results of my reading books to the mothers was that I began a kind of book loan scheme. This was always on the basis of interest and a request from a particular mother or on my assessment of her specific need. The Barnaby books* were lent to several of the mothers, as were *The Man with the Shattered World, Care of a Child Facing Death, Bernard*, my books, *The Slow Learning Child in the Classroom, Bereavement*, etc. Sometimes, I asked a mother to tell the group about the book she had read. This activity was a rare one but useful on some occasions. It certainly gave mothers a great deal of confidence in their ability to address a group.

My full-time work takes place 60 miles away from the Family Teach-In Centre. Inevitably there were occasions when I was prevented from being present. However, whenever I knew this was about to happen I reminded the group that they were taking a course and that I would give them a task to carry out in my absence. One such project involved thinking about and discussing the needs of families having a mentally handicapped child. The thoughts were to be theirs in the main. Each mother was expected to contribute at least one thought that was feasible. The aim when the task was finished was to distribute the leaflets to libraries in the area; to all the hospitals concerned with children; to the GPs of the group members; to the Area Health and Social Services Department; and to the consultants known to be interested in mentally handicapped children. It was an interesting assignment and one that enabled mothers to work out for themselves what they felt they needed. I present it here in full for your reflection.

---

*Jeffree, D. and Cunningham, C. (1976). *First Pictures* 2; *Learn to Look* 2; *Help Yourself Stories* 1, 2, 3, 4. Published by LDA Park Works, Wisbech, Cambs, PE13 2AX.

Observing needs of mothers of mentally handicapped children 197

Project 1. Action research

Family Teach-In Centre. Director: Mildred Stevens, M.Ed.
Mothers with a mentally handicapped child are attending a 2-year course
at the above address on Tuesdays at 7.30 p.m. If you know a mother needing such a group please inform her.

One aim of the course is to encourage the group to (think out) for themselves methods by which efficient services for them, and new families with
the same problem, become a reality.

Project 1 aims to draw the attention of the public as well as the professionals to their specific needs and to devise methods by which these
needs can be more easily satisfied. The following suggestions for immediate Action are thus recommended:

(1) if a mentally handicapped baby is born in hospital the parents *together*
should be informed before discharge, if born at home as soon as the
mother is physically well;
(2) trained mother/contacts should be available *in the hospital* to give support to the newly informed parents, these would be parents with a
handicapped child;
(3) on leaving hospital (or within 6 months at least) each family should
be put in touch with a family with the same experience [names and
addresses of parents from the above Centre supplied on request (sae
please)];
(4) that the most recent information regarding the services should be
made available *as a right* once handicap is suspected/confirmed;
(5) that the following extra information is available
   (a) the names of all the voluntary organizations in the area concerned
   with handicapped children
   (b) the names and addresses of the Pre-School play groups in the area
   (c) the names, addresses, and telephone numbers of the Special
   Schools in the area
   (d) the name and address of the nearest assessment centre and genetic
   counselling clinic
   (e) the names of some publications on the handicapped baby.

Several hundred of these leaflets have now been given out all over the
country at lectures. I have also given them to students training to be
teachers of the mentally handicapped. There has been little actual feed-
back from anyone receiving the leaflet. We shall never know the results
of the leaflet in any direct fashion. My own experience of the field of Mental Handicap, however, reminds me that ideas are always welcome to those
involved. They are continually being implemented to benefit those they
are meant for.

When the pamphlet was complete and distributed we had many discussions on its contents. One of the points made concerned publications on
the handicapped baby. 'Where were they?' we were forced to ask. Rex

198 *Observing needs of mothers of mentally handicapped children*

Brinkworth* perhaps was alone in writing about the problems in the first year of life for a family with a mentally handicapped child. Our second task was to think about the possibility for every mother to write her own experience about the first year of life. This was to be in terms of herself, her feelings, and the practical problems surrounding a handicapped baby. It was several weeks before a mother felt secure enough to read her effort— probably the first piece of continuous writing she had done since schooldays—and also to reveal her real feelings to the group. I should say that we were just about ready as a group in the latter part of the second year to listen to these 'stories' in an informed way. Grief was expressed, grief was felt, not only by the mother reading her story, but by the whole group. Perhaps the real value of this experience was that the grief was shared by all of us without fear and without embarrassment. It was a safe group. A factual account of a mentally handicapped child's life within a particular family was listened to and accepted. A description of the real feelings that were felt was also accepted by an empathic group.

Three mothers have not yet written about their experience but as I still have contact with them all, no doubt this will be done as they feel the need to complete the task. Another task we hope to complete is that of compiling a list of all the services available for mentally handicapped children in the area in which most mothers live. Whilst the Social Services Department of this area have published a useful document, it is far from complete in any sense that the mothers would like.

One of the mothers in the group needs a short-term-stay place for a child with very special physical needs. Both he and she need a holiday apart. The cost of such a holiday, even for a fortnight, is expensive for a one-parent family, even with help from the Social Services Department. The mother wanted to feel free to choose what she considered to be a suitable place for her child. Accordingly we have set up as our fourth project a Short-Term Self-Help Fund. A few pence contributed by every member each week and the fund is growing—a practical solution it seems to many a parent's real worry.

The last project of the first 2-year course was to discuss the future of the group, for it had almost terminated its sessions in January 1977. It seemed that there was a need now for clearly defined goals. The response was exciting indeed:

(1) three new mothers were found to attend a *new* 2-year course;
(2) a dozen or more young people from the fifth and sixth forms of two local grammar schools were wanting to 'take over' the Saturday Play Club as a school project. Could we therefore provide them with a course on mental handicap?

The form the course has therefore taken in its third year is as follows:

(1) I meet the new mothers on alternate weeks. The course will be de-

---

* Brinkworth, R. (1973) The Unfinished Child. Effects of early home training on the mongol infant. In *Mental Retardation and Behavioural Research*, eds. Clarke, A. D. B. and Clarke, A. M. Churchill Livingstone, Edinburgh and London.

Observing needs of mothers of mentally handicapped children   199

veloped as the previous one on *their* needs, *their* suggestions. I am sure that in another 2 years quite a different syllabus will have evolved.

(2) The 'old' mothers, the new mothers, and I* all meet the dozen or so young people on the other week and discuss mental handicap with them—sometimes in small groups, for there are enough mothers to be the 'teachers' now AND they are informed, sometimes in a large group altogether doing art, music, or drama or having films on play and play workshops.

(3) The old mothers are now taking an 'advanced' course based upon their own suggestions during the half-hour evaluation periods they spent with the external assessors. This is on the evening I spend with the new mums. At the moment we meet on that night in two houses. My dream is to have all groups under one roof, so that although we are doing different activities the feeling of 'group' continues to be engendered.

One of the suggestions made by a mother during her evaluation of her experience was that she would like to have her child's teacher to give a talk about her work. Accordingly, I am arranging that the teacher of each child in the group shall give some kind of talk to these mothers. Another suggestion was that the group might like to know what the various methods used to teach mentally handicapped children were all about. Accordingly, a series of lectures has been arranged so that these mothers will become acquainted with some of the theories underlying what goes on in the schools for the mentally handicapped today.

Mothers having a mentally handicapped child will have heard the term 'research' mentioned in connection with their problems. Few of them, relatively speaking, have had the opportunity to meet real research workers or those students carrying out research topics for a higher degree or indeed their first degree. Following on from the visit of the student doctors, two of them from the Medical Faculty of Manchester University came to talk to the mothers about their particular undergraduate work and to show them slides. Their research involved examining the perceived needs of parents with cerebral palsy. David Wilkins, a DHSS funded research worker in the department of Preventive Medicine at Manchester, talked to them about support systems for families with mentally handicapped children in Salford and other areas of the north-west. He had the needs of this particular group in mind when he talked to them, and he interpreted his research findings and methodology at a level they could understand without 'talking down' to them. Jean Dean, a mother of four children and now the deputy headteacher of a school for the mentally handicapped in the Greater Manchester area, told the group about her research with parents of profoundly handicapped children. This concerned their perceived educational goals for their children in the Special Care Units they attended in school.

---

*And a new colleague who has become interested in this course as a voluntary member, Mrs Sheila Beardmore of Poynton, Cheshire.

200 *Observing needs of mothers of mentally handicapped children*

Such experiences gave the mothers a great deal of confidence not only to listen to academics but also to question them carefully with their own background of knowledge about mental handicap and society's attitudes towards it.

There is little left for me to describe of the actual programme now. I have already mentioned the child review sessions which took place quite regularly. Mothers were asked to report on anything they considered of value to the group whenever it occurred and to comment upon it. Thus one of the mothers is an elected member to a Community Health committee representing three districts. She reports to the group, whenever she attends, what she feels is relevant. This mother has also met the National Development Team* on their way round their appointed regions.

One could not be a directing member of such a group without at some time or another being consulted on specific aspects of their problems. I should say that 50 per cent of the members at least have had specific phone call consultations, but as one mother said, 'We know we can phone Mrs Stevens; we don't trouble her very much but she always has time for us if we need her.' The others have not availed themselves of my professional expertise. They have consulted the other mothers in the group. Perhaps this is the greatest strength of the course membership—there is always someone there to talk with.

It would have been a wasted opportunity had I not planned some kind of evaluation experience for my first group of mothers to attend a 2-year course in Mental Handicap. Accordingly, I invited (on two separate evenings) two headteachers from schools for the mentally handicapped. One a head who has worked through the parents and the community for many years now to gain every conceivable benefit for the children as well as their families—Mrs Joyce Cathcart from Leacroft School, Miles Platting, Manchester. The other, Mrs Edith Lord from the Robert Clive School, Shrewsbury—not only a headteacher of many years' experience, with a thriving parent group, but also once a mother of a mentally handicapped child herself.

I explained to them that I would like them to interview each mother individually for about 20 minutes and tape the conversation. They were given four specific questions for each mother to discuss. This did not preclude them from using their own ideas in the interview if they wished. To some extent I wanted to 'standardize' each interview. The questions were:

(1) What do you think you have gained from the course?
(2) What have you liked about the course?
(3) If another course is started for new mothers what should be changed?
(4) If the present course could be extended what would you like it to contain?

---

* A government body set up by Mrs Barbara Castle to solve some of the problems inherent in the field of mental subnormality. Professor P. Mittler was invited to be the Chairman.

Observing needs of mothers of mentally handicapped children 201

Whilst it would be interesting to present a detailed analysis of the talks I do not intend doing this because I did not state my intention to do this to the mothers before their evaluation sessions took place. However, I can describe a number of points that might give you an indication of their thinking. Most of them referred to the support they felt such a group gave to them and the friendship that existed between members of the group. Many had lost their feelings of 'isolation'. Some of them had obviously gained much more confidence to get what they needed for their child from the various services involved—as one mother put it 'it gave me the confidence to battle and fight for what was needed'. For one or two it was a much needed and enjoyed evening out.

With reference to an extended course most of them had ideas relating to what they would like. One stated that the course needed now to have some clearly defined and well-stated aims and that she would like to have lectures like student teachers on various aspects of child development and development in play. I remember starting off the course in a 'formal' lecture fashion but it soon became apparent to me that this was not what the group wanted at that time. This was one of the reasons I have developed the 'following up of *their* communication' technique. Another mother suggested lectures on the hierarchical structures of Local and Central Government in order to know one's way around the services. Whilst all these have been mentioned during the course in passing nothing has been presented to them in 'lecture form' on this particular topic. Most of the mothers emphasized, particularly in regard to continuing in the holiday what was done in the schools, more contact with the teachers—this indeed was a constant cry throughout the course itself. Another mother suggested a series of lectures on further education programmes for the mentally handicapped; yet another a course to train them in assessment and evaluation in order to offer their skills to other mothers. The general impression one gained was that they now seemed much more able to take a formal lecture and did not feel the necessity to talk about their own problems at every opportunity. The problem in arranging such a programme would only be a financial one for most lecturers require a fee. With reference to this desire to talk about their children I found that on occasions during the course many weeks would pass without reference being made to specific individual children in the group.

Other aspects of the course brought out during these evaluation sessions were that some mothers had started to read more about mental handicap. They had begun to realize the problems of the other children and to see the wide variety of problems existing; they had begun to see other people's points of view. One or two mums expressed the view that all the children interested them now and not only their own. They enjoyed the detail of some of the things we went into and the opportunity to discuss these— 'It wasn't just being lectured to', 'We could have different opinions', 'We have a whole wider outlook on mental handicap'. There appeared to be a certain pride in having attended a course 2 years in length.

One of the experiences that I have nearly forgotten to mention was in

202 *Observing needs of mothers of mentally handicapped children*

the nature of a task to be carried out on an evening when I could not be present. The task was to discuss what they thought should be the personal qualities of a 'mother/contact' (mother adviser). What an interesting evening it was. They certainly showed their ability to evaluate each other's potential in the group (the reporting of the evening was taped), to see each other's strengths and weaknesses, as well as to describe those features they thought to be most desirable in a person who was going to be a source of help to them when help was most needed.

My work with these mothers has been on a voluntary basis and only on one evening a week. The problems that have arisen—needing telephone calls to the various services, the way in which mothers wanted to see a place for their child to stay before they let him stay there, the additional personal problems of the families where an extra hand could have been useful, or when the services of someone with a car would have been highly desirable—all made me realize that one full-time worker 'permanently' attached to such a small group of families would be a useful concept for providing all forms of the services. Such a worker would need to have some kind of training to know his way around all the services, to educate both mothers and children for more appropriate management in the home, to give specific support by real practical help in times of need. I should like to think that some authorities at least might consider such an appointment in the future for a paid advocate would certainly enable the system to work more efficiently for the benefit of the families concerned.

The impression I have of the whole experience has been that these mothers have enjoyed absorbing knowledge. Many of them have become able speakers and more organized as thinkers.* The course has given these mothers a chance to continue helping themselves, the opportunity of thinking that they might still have to be doing this more frequently in the future. They have also been able to share every problem, to share their grief, to come just that little bit nearer to a fuller understanding of themselves and their families. It has certainly made me feel that any family having a mentally handicapped child, who is able to cope without breaking down, is not a handicapped family, but is indeed a family with much to share with the rest of us in terms of how to cope with life's problems—in other words a supernormal family.

---

* During February 1978 there was a Conference of Community Physicians in Manchester. Four of my 'mums' were invited to participate in one of the sessions by David Wilkins. He later reported that the doctors thought that this practical session was one of the most valuable of the conference and desired a full day working with the mothers. (Cf. Stevens, 1976, Chapter 11, p. 185.)

14 Concluding remarks

There may be some who are overwhelmed with the amount of observing and recording they think is expected of them after reading this book. The reason I wrote this book has been merely to suggest ways and means that we can adopt in looking with some purpose at mentally handicapped children. If we are able to do this it will become obvious to us how we can best help the children to learn and what, in fact, they need to learn.

All those in schools for other kinds of children have to plan out their work (i.e. lessons) carefully and in some detail. These plans are very often written out and presented at regular intervals to the headteachers. Most of us keep some kind of record about those we teach.

The major concern of those teaching children who are mentally handicapped is the individual child. In view of this, the emphasis on the keeping of notes about the children and their development does not seem out of place. An examination of such notes by the headteacher will, incidentally, reveal the teacher's plans for helping the child to learn. They will therefore also serve as a 'Preparation of Work' record. This is the way for teachers to regard the need for observation and the detailed recording of such observations in the rather special ways that I have described. In view of the intensely individual nature of the work, the teacher cannot present 'lesson notes' to show the thought that goes into her work. These are not relevant. She can, however, show her understanding of the child and his needs through the preparation she makes for his learning in her records about HIM.

The ultimate aim in presenting these rather simple yet basic ideas again in 1977 in a somewhat lengthy form has been to try to interest new teachers in the kind of qualities these children have in common with all children. By observation of detail and accurate records she will begin to discover what these are. The descriptions in this book of real mentally handicapped children and the activities their teachers carried out with them will enable others to see the kind of stimulating, permissive, and well-planned conditions which are considered necessary if these qualities are to emerge.

Appendix 1 Early notes on observation taken from my lecture notes (1961)

It also seems important to consider some aspects of a child's behaviour and activities which might be observed and which may not have been made apparent in the foregoing paragraphs. Whilst developmental scales and achievement charts aim to give the teacher a formalized and standard pattern of qualities to observe, they do not, perhaps, always give a complete picture of the child as a living and vitally interesting being.

The following list of suggestions may be found useful by those working with handicapped children. As they become skilled and their skill is supported by reading, other interesting features will, no doubt, be included:

(1) Small and large movements of all kinds, e.g. of the eyes, head, face, fingers, legs, whole body.

(2) Degree to which the child can help himself in eating, dressing, toileting—stages of these developmental aspects are described more thoroughly in standardized scales and in achievement charts.

(3) The exact kind of instruction the child can understand and respond to by appropriate action. Examples of language responses (and sometimes the words used and the situations in which they were used to gain the response), recorded occasionally over each year, would give the teacher some idea of the kind of progress that was made by the child in understanding instructions of all kinds, as well as indicating difficulties and how they were overcome.

(4) The sounds, words, sentences used at varying stages in the child's life. It is important for the exact words used to be recorded (if possible they should be recorded on a scrap of paper immediately they are heard). These would then be a useful guide to the teacher in considering the language levels of each child and the language needs of the children. Not sufficient use of the tape recorder is yet being made to help the teacher in this most important aspect of her work. It is hoped that more use of the tape recorder is seized upon by the teachers, not only to motivate the children to communicate their ideas and needs, but to give the teacher a more scientific record of severely subnormal children talking. It is also important to remind teachers that, with non-speaking children, descriptions of the exact gestures used to communicate need to be included.

(5) The readiness with which the child co-operates with the teacher in an individual teaching situation. Does the child attend to the teacher, given that the work is attractive, interesting, and appropriate? How long does this co-operation last if the teacher allows for the spontaneous reaction of the child? Can the child work at something specific alone or does the work stop immediately the teacher's full attention is withdrawn?

(6) The child's ability to make contact with the teacher, with the children in the group, with other children, and with adults in and out of the immediate family circle. Ability to play alone without help; to play at the side of but not with the other children; to play with one other child; to play with a group of children, leading it or just being part of the group.

Appendix 1   205

(7) Activities when the child is allowed to choose. Behaviour when the child is given opportunities to become self-activated.

(8) Objects brought to school such as pictures, drawings, nature specimens, books, pets, toys, etc.

(9) Play behaviour. How and when the child plays with materials such as water, sand, dough, clay, wood, sewing materials, musical instruments, etc?

(10) The length of time taken to set to work or to play. Length of concentration on some self-chosen activities.

(11) Behaviour when the child is expected to work or attend for short periods in small groups (music, cookery, movement, storytelling).

(12) Displays of initiative, curiosity, aggression, withdrawal, lack of interest, length of enthusiasm, lack of energy, special interests, and gifts.

(13) The slightest change in the child's behaviour.

(14) Drawings and spontaneous creative efforts.

In connection with looking at the children's drawings and paintings, samples of these (and any other graphic work) should be kept throughout the child's attendance at school in specially provided folders.*

No doubt there are a great many more qualities to which the teacher should give her attention. Those described, however, are felt to be useful pointers for those who are beginning to think about the necessity and importance of observing in detail the developing personality of a child who has learning difficulties.

---

* A collection of the drawings and models over a period of 6 years of a man in his early thirties drew my attention to the possible value of such a procedure in tracing the path of a child's development. The drawings in this particular case not only revealed measurable mental development but also an increased ability to note details, and an increased knowledge and interest in a wider environment, particularly that outside his home. They also indicated an increasing awareness of his relationship with his father and of the many activities he could successfully and happily carry out in his company.

Appendix 2 Interviewing mentally handicapped adults

One of my aims in training teachers of the mentally handicapped has always been to show them that in a relatively short time a teacher can learn a great deal about the pupils she has to teach. If she presents each one of them (cf. 'Planning for the individual child' in *The Educational and Social Needs of Children with Severe Handicap*) with the same activities she will see how they compare with each other, she will find a starting point for teaching, she will learn about their lives and interests and knowledge in specific areas of their lives.

It was with this concept in mind that I compiled the following two interview sheets for a group of students to use in their experience with adult sub-normals. Each interview lasted about 20 minutes to a half-hour. Two separate occasions were used to gain the information asked for. Both students and the young people in the adult training centres enjoyed the experience. In compiling the questions my thinking was stimulated by the *Manchester Scales of Social Adaptation* by Eric Lunzer, published by the National Foundation for Educational Research.

Interview Sheet 1

Time started: *Time finished:*
Name of interviewer:

  (1) Tell me your name:
  (2) How old are you?
  (3) When is your birthday?
  (4) Can you write your name?
     Put it here . . . .
  (5) Copy your name (have a copy ready).
  (6) Tell me your mother's/mum's name:
  (7) Tell me your father's/dad's name:
  (8) Have you a brother?
     What is his name?
  (9) Have you a sister?
     What is her name?
(10) Where do you live?
     Where do you work?
(11) Tell me the address of your house:
(12) What is the number on your door?
(13) Can you write your address?
     Write it here.
(14) Have you a garden at your house?
     What do you grow in it?
(15) Have you a telly in your house?
(16) What do you like watching?
(17) Have you any pets in your house? Tell me about them.
(18) Do you go out at night? Where to?

Appendix 2   207

(19) Do you go out on Sunday? Where to?
(20) Where do you go on your holidays?
(21) What do you like to eat for your:
   breakfast:
   dinner:
   tea:
(22) What do you like to drink?
   Anything else?
(23) Can you draw something for me? Go on, do it then. Do it here (please have your two sheets of paper ready + ball pen, pencil and some felt-tips). Sheet 1. Name it.
(24) Draw a man. Draw me a man. Do it here (Sheet 2 named).
(25) Colour this for me (we shall have a picture of a car ready).
(26) Can you use scissors? Cut along this line, now this one, now this. Cut this (point to shape) out for me. Cut string, cotton.

Standardized procedure in the interview.

Please follow the instructions in the order they appear and use the words I have written for you.

Interview Sheet 2

Time started: *Time finished:*
Name of interviewer:

Time
   (1) What day is it today?
   (2) Is it morning or afternoon?
   (3) What day is it tomorrow?
   (4) What day was it yesterday?
   (5) Tell me all the days. (To student, write down the days as they are said.)
   (6) Do you know any months?
       Tell me the months.
   (7) What time do you have your dinner?
       What time do you have your tea?
   (8) When do you go to bed?
   (9) Can you read the time? (Using a watch show him 10 o'clock, quarter past 7, half past 2.)
Number
(10) Can you count for me? Start: one, two—go on now. Record.
(11) Count these pennies for me.
       (Put thirteen in a line and add more if necessary. Note the one to one pointing relationship/or not.)
(12) Show the number ...
       (Refer to special number sheet.)
(13) What size shoes do you take?
(14) How many spoonfuls of sugar do you put in your tea?
(15) Tell me the name of this money. (Point to each one in turn. Present one at a time only.)
       50p, 10p, 2p, 5p, 1p, $\frac{1}{2}$p, £1.
(16) Do you go to the shops with your mum or dad?
       Tell me which shops you go to.

208   *Appendix 2*

(17) Do you buy sweets for yourself?
      How much money do you pay for them?
(18) If you bought some soap how much would you pay?
(19) How much is a Coke, a cup of tea, fish and chips, a big record (LP)?
(20) Do you go and watch any games?
      Which ones?
(21) Do you play any games with your mum and dad, brothers or sisters, friends?
(22) Do you go out to tea sometimes?
      Where do you go?
(23) Have you been to the theatre or a concert?
      Where?
(24) Have you been on a bus (where to)? a train (where to)? a boat (where to)?
      an aeroplane (where to)? a motor car (where to)?

9	7	5	13	10	18
20	99	11	4	15	2
100	43	12	1	86	6
49	68	3	50	153	75
27	149	8	3	201	210

Find me (Point to chart above) (tick in box provided):

5 ☐   10 ☐   8 ☐   3 ☐   9 ☐

4 ☐   7 ☐   2 ☐   1 ☐   6 ☐

What is this number? Point to the number in chart above (tick in box):

13 ☐   18 ☐   99 ☐   43 ☐   86 ☐   29 ☐

100 ☐   201 ☐   50 ☐

What do these words say? Point from top one down (tick if correct):

on	entrance	ladies
off	private	gentlemen
press	toilet	Mr
ring	keep out	Mrs
push	keep off	Miss
pull	exit	man
stop	danger	woman
walk	vacant	
cross here	engaged	
cross now		

Now read across (tick):

tree   little   milk   egg   book   school   sit   frog
playing   bun   flower   road   clock   train   light
picture   think   summer   people   something

On the basis of the results of these interviews further attainment probes can then be made.

Appendix 3 Musical games to stimulate fun and language

(1) Modification of 'How green you are'
Child goes out of the room whilst an object is hidden. At a signal he enters room. Children clap loudly if he gets near the item. Children clap softly if he gets far away from it.

Variation. Stamping feet loudly/softly. Use instruments in the same way.

(2) Walking over the water   Marching/Running music

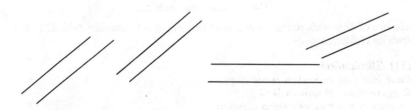

No jumping over the lines. If you walk *in* the lines when the music stops you are out. Consider age of child here. A good game for adolescents.

(3) One in the middle
Thread a small bell on to a piece of string. The string must be long enough for a group of children standing in a circle to hold the string which has been tied with a small knot. As the music is playing the children pass the bell round the string *under* the hands of each player. When the music stops the child with the bell has to hide it in his hand without making a noise. The one in the middle has to find it. He can have one/two/three tries before the music begins again. When he finds the bell he exchanges places with the child holding it.

(4) Passing shapes
Wrap up 6–8 items, e.g. bells, pipes, wooden pipe, moo sound, monkey sound, kazoo. Pass *one* at a time round. When the music stops the child who has the parcel opens it plays the instrument and keeps it.

(5) Put the ball into the bucket/the box/the paper bag
Six balls of different sizes, shapes, textures. As the music plays, ONE of the balls is passed round. The child who has it when the music stops puts it in the bucket/box/paper bag. Important that child sees a variety of balls, forks (plastic, small steel, wooden handled) in order to conceptualize.

(6) Passing the parcel
Each parcel has a sweet in it. Child holding parcel when music stops eats sweet.

210   *Appendix 3*

(7) What is in the box/the bowl/the basket/the bag?
Lots of variations. Pass a box round to the music; this can be a round box, a square box, a tin box, etc. (Variety of experiences in holding.) Child takes out one item and names it. All answers accepted but child told name.

(8) Variation on the game London Bridge
Child chooses from two kinds of hats 'on my fair lady'. Two different coloured paper/cloth hats.

(9) What is in the handbag? What is in the box?
Pass the handbag round. When the music stops open it and take out an item. Use the item in the appropriate manner, e.g. if it is a comb, comb hair. If in a box and an instrument, play it; if a glove put it on.

(10) Singing game (Joan Fitch)
Teacher goes up to a child and sings to any tune she likes

> 'I'm going to a party
> Oh will you come with me'.

The two of them walk round singing and then each goes to another child. Continue until all children are up.

(11) Elimination
Jump into *your ring* when music stops.
Rings on floor. Hoops/chalked.
As each turn is had, one hoop removed.

Additional. Square, box, cube, line. (Quick marching.)

(12) Group Elimination
When music stops all those with red dresses, black dresses, jumpers, black socks, etc. sit down.

(13) Walking with an instrument or something that makes a sound
When music stops, last one to control sound OUT.

(14) The big ship sails through the Alley Alley O (cf. Opie)

(15) Sing on two notes G/E (child's name)
When he hears it he puts:

(1) hands on knees;
(2) one hand on knee;
(3) one hand on head, etc.;
(4) Does any pre-arranged action you tell him.

Children must listen for their name.

(16) Hiding an object
When child is near to it sing his name very loudly. When far away sing very softly.

Appendix 3 211

(17) Guessing game
(1) Going towards the source of the sound. Blindfold.
(2) Items in a basket. People in the audience with the different (same as in the basket) sounds. Imitate when teacher makes them.

| Pipes | Kazoos | Bell | | |

| Eggwhisk | Spoon in cup | Lid on pan | Paper | Lid on jar |

Child turns his back and then points to the picture after he has heard the sound.

(18) When the music stops find
(1) Something red like this.
(2) A named object.
(3) Your name.

The teacher has placed the items about the room.

(19) The Miming Musicians
To a record 'play' any instrument you want. When music stops, last to stop is out.

(20) Ron Heavey's game
Stand anywhere you like. When I touch you on the shoulder: shout your name, or whisper your name.

(21) Elimination
Musical Chairs. Statues. Bumps.

(22) Passing the object
Nail brush. Toothbrush. Hair brush. Shoe brush.
When music stops do the appropriate action.

(23) Variations
(a) passing the pictures of the objects above;
(b) pretending to have the object.
Mime the action.

(24) Anticipation
Spin the bottle in a circle. When the bottle stops spinning: clap, stamp, sing a song, etc.

(25) Put five interesting items in the middle of a circle of children (sitting)
The items can be varied to suit the aims of the teacher for a particular child/group. Suitable for all groups who are able to work as a group for short periods of time. Pass round a torch to the music. When the music stops the child shines the torch on an item. He is either asked to:

(a) Show the ——
(b) Name the ——
According to level (a before b).

212   *Appendix 3*

(26) Spread a very colourful patterned cloth, carpet, etc. out on the floor
Throw a handful of objects on to this background. Children walk to the music with a bag on their arms. When the music stops, children pick up anything they can find/ see on the cloth. Start music up again after a very short time. After several turns let children show what they have found. See what has been missed.

(27) Hats
The children sit in a ring. In the middle of the ring there is a selection of hats (these could be of the same or different colour, texture, shape; they could be role-playing hats, e.g. policeman, cowboy, nurse). When the music begins, the children pass round an object. The one to have the object when the music stops chooses a hat to put on. Make sure that each child has a hat by the end of the game. Then make up to a simple tune (e.g. 'Here we go round the Mulberry Bush') a song about each hat: Jimmy's got a fur hat on, a fur hat on, a fur hat on, etc.

(28/29) Variation on hats
Gloves, shoes.

(30) Make tunnels with the tables and paper/blanket
Children crawl through the tunnels. All those not in a tunnel when music stops are out of the game. Lots of fun for the under 11s.

Useful reading

Brennan, W. (1975) *Some Educational Needs of Severely Subnormal Children*, National Council for Special Education (NCSE). Bradford Conference Proceedings.

Carroll, H. M. C. (1972) The assessment of severely subnormal children; a psychological view point. In *Educating the Mentally Handicapped*, A. Laing (Ed.), Swansea University Publications.

Connolly, K. (1973) Ethogical Techniques. In *Assessment for Learning in the Mentally Handicapped*, Mittler, P. (Ed.), J. A. Churchill, London.

Cortazzi, D. (1969) The bottom of the barrei, *Journal of Mental Subnormality*, **XV**, Part 1, No. 28.

Cummings, P. (1973) *Subnormality in the seventies*, No. 6, National Society for Mentally Handicapped Children, London.

Dziduszko, N., Stomma, D. and Wald, I. (1970) Medical needs of institutionalized children with low grade mental retardation, *Proceedings IASSMD*, Warsaw.

Gregory, O. (1972) The Characteristics of Handicapped Children attending day care centres in Glasgow. *Unpublished M.Ed. Thesis*, Manchester.

Gregory, O. (1973) Film *Piagetian Assessment of Profoundly Retarded Children*.

Gregory, O. (1973) *The Use of Piagetian Assessment Techniques in the Assessment of Profoundly Retarded Children*.

Grodzicka, I. (1970) Schools for the Blind Mentally Handicapped in Poland, *Proceedings IASSMD*, Warsaw.

Haskins, M. (1971) *Survey of 13 units*, Department of Health and Social Security, London.

Hewett, S. (1970) *The Family and the Handicapped Child*. Allen and Unwin, London.

Hogg, J. F. T. (1972) *Application of Behaviour Modification Techniques to the Development of Profoundly Handicapped Children*, Hester Adrian Research Centre, Manchester.

Jordan, J. E. (1970) Attitudes towards mental retardation in five nations. A. Cuttman facet analysis, *Proceedings IASSMD*, Warsaw.

McKay, R. I. (1976) *Mental Handicap in Child Health Practice*, Butterworths, London.

Mein, R. (1967) Changes in intelligence test scores in CP patients under treatment, *Proceedings IASSMD*, Montpelier.

Penfold, J. (Ed.) (1977) The Education of the Child in Special Care. Northern Counties College, Coach Lane, Newcastle-upon-Tyne. Conference Report 1976.

Stephens, Elspeth (1967) Psychological assessment of severely subnormal children in hospital with associated physical handicap, *Proceedings IASSMD*, Montpelier.

Stevens, H. A. (1966) *Care and Management of the Multiple Handicapped Mentally Retarded*, Central Wisconsin Colony, Madison, Wisconsin, USA.

214 Useful reading

Stevens, M. (1964) Training observation in teachers of the severely subnormal, *Proceedings IASSMD*, Copenhagen.

Stevens, M. (1965) *Breakthrough to Kenneth*, National Society for Mentally Handicapped Children, Manchester.

Stevens, M. (1968) *Observing Children who are Severely Subnormal*, Edward Arnold, London. (Out of print)

Stevens, M. (1971) *The Educational Needs of Severely Subnormal Children*, Edward Arnold, London. (Out of print) Dutch Translation 1973.

Stevens, M. (1971) *Ibid.* Cf. Ref. Chapter 9. *Planned Systematic Individual Teaching.*

Stevens, M. (1971) *Ibid.* Cf. Ref. Chapter 7. *The Same Teacher and a Special Kind of Teacher.*

Stevens, M. (1976) *The Educational and Social Needs of Children with Severe Handicap*, Chapter 4, Edward Arnold, London.

Stone, I. R. (1970) The changing institution for the mentally retarded, *Proceedings IASSMD*, Warsaw.

Uzgiriz, I. C. and Hunt, J. McV. (1966) *An Instrument for Assessing Infant Psychological Development*, University of Illinois, USA.

Vosvinkel, A. (1967) *The Stimulation of Self Feeding in Profoundly Mentally Deficient Children*, Pedagogisch Instituut aan de Fijdsuniversiteit, Utrecht.

Wiseman, A. G. M. (1963) A Special Care Unit service and experiment, *Teaching and Training*, NATME, London.

Woodward, M. (1959) The behaviour of idiots interpreted by Piaget's theory of sensori-motor development, *British Journal of Educational Psychology*, **29**, 60–71.

Woodward, M. (1960) The application of Piaget's concepts to mental deficiency. *Proceedings London Conference in the SSMD*, May and Baker.

Woods, Grace E. (1970) The blind mentally retarded child, *Proceedings IASSMD*, Warsaw.